Coping and the Challenge of Resilience

Erica Frydenberg

Coping and the Challenge of Resilience

Erica Frydenberg
Graduate School of Education
University of Melbourne
Melbourne, Victoria, Australia

ISBN 978-1-137-56923-3   ISBN 978-1-137-56924-0   (eBook)
DOI 10.1057/978-1-137-56924-0

Library of Congress Control Number: 2017931837

Cover image: © Maciej Bledowski / Alamy Stock Photo

Printed on acid-free paper

This Palgrave Macmillan imprint is published by Springer Nature
The registered company is Macmillan Publishers Ltd.
The registered company address is: The Campus, 4 Crinan Street, London, N1 9XW, United Kingdom

Preface

We live in an era in which there is an ever-increasing emphasis by psychologists on ways in which we can cope successfully with the problems and setbacks that are inevitably part of the human condition. For example, there has been a dramatic increase in the number of articles focusing on mindfulness, positive psychology, hardiness, and the like. These topics are obviously of vital importance, but the insights produced by psychologists have often been lost from sight in popular self-help books that emphasise the obvious or are simply wrong.

Erica Frydenberg has decided (absolutely rightly in my opinion) to focus her book on two topics of special importance: coping and resilience. As she points out at the very start of her excellent book, the huge number of articles on coping has recently been overtaken by an even greater number of articles on resilience. It would take an exceptional individual to provide a coherent and balanced account that integrates these two literatures, and Erica is that individual. Her expertise is unusually extensive (covering educational, clinical, and organisational psychology) and all of this expertise is brought to bear on indicating the ways in which coping as a process can produce resilience as an outcome.

In essence, Erica includes within the first part of her book a masterly exposition of what psychologists have discovered about the optimal coping strategies when dealing with different highly stressful situations and events. She also greatly clarifies the meaning and significance of 'resilience', a term that is far too often used very vaguely. Erica identifies a number of aspects of resilience including recovery, sustainability, and growth.

In the latter part of the book, the emphasis switches more to an expert analysis of ways in which individuals' resilience can be enhanced. More specifically, Chap. 7 considers resilient approaches to stress among older individuals. The focus in Chaps. 8 and 9 is on increasing resilience during the early years of life and the notion of family resilience. The discussion broadens to encompass spiritual approaches to resilience in Chap. 10. Finally, in Chap. 11, there is a positive focus on successful resilient copers including examples of inspirational individuals have proved to be exceptionally resilient in very difficult and stressful circumstances.

In sum, this is a book that very successfully makes use of all of Erica's very extensive and deep knowledge and expertise. This knowledge and expertise (and her personally sympathetic nature) are all manifest on every page of this outstanding book. I would strongly advise anyone who remains sceptical of the contribution that psychology has made to enhancing the lives of individuals and society at large to read this book and take heed of what it says. Of course, psychology remains 'a work in progress'. However, Erica has shown us just how far we have already travelled and points the way to an even more successful future.

Michael W. Eysenck

Introduction

Resilience is the magic bullet that everyone wants to acquire—our teachers want to put it into the curriculum, our legislators want it to transform the country, our corporates want it for their staff to be the best they can be against all odds. Parents want their children to be resilient as much as they themselves want to be resilient against the challenges of twenty-first-century parenting. Additionally, our insurers want us to be resilient against disasters and natural hazards of our environment.

This book addresses how best to meet those challenges. It is focused on how to think and act differently about what we do every day as our world throws up challenges; how to assess each situation as one of challenge rather than threat or harm because we believe that we have the strategies to cope. And just in case we don't we have the strategies or the resources, we need to know how to augment our strategy pool.

My search over the past three decades has focused on the best way to provide the core skills for life to children, adolescents, and adults, and how that is best achieved through the contemporary theories of coping. Coping has the potential of explaining a process that leads to an outcome of resilience. It has the ability to integrate a range of theories and methodologies that have the capacity to explicate how development is shaped by individuals' capacities to deal with the stresses, adversities, and hassles of daily life in ways that contribute to resilience.

Psychologists are telling us to be hardy, have grit, be emotionally intelligent, have social-emotional skills, adopt the principles of positive psychology, and grow our well-being. For me it all adds up to one thing: understand how we cope, build up our coping resources, and keep growing them as a fertile crop from which to benefit. As we breathe we cope, but theoretically we can always cope better. It is about our performance in life. The theory is easy, the lessons can be learned, and practice leads to improvement.

The good news is that everybody is talking resilience: the bad news is that resilience is an ill-defined construct and therefore does not readily lead to prevention, intervention, and post intervention. However, coping in its broadest form does all that. Additionally, we know a great deal about how it is defined, developed, and evaluated.

The introductory chapter explores the contemporary concept of resilience and Chap. 2 demonstrates how resilience is underpinned by principles of positive psychology along with socio-ecological perspectives of human endeavour. Additionally current constructs of grit, hardiness, emotional intelligence, mindset, and mindfulness each contributes in some way to resilience and augments coping theory. Chapter 3 presents the key contemporary theories of coping and in subsequent chapters variations of the transactional and resource theories of coping are presented in the form of proactive coping, dyadic coping, and communal coping.

Throughout the volume, whilst the emphasis is on coping and coping theory and practice, there will be links to complementary constructs where appropriate connections can be made. Coping is considered to be the most helpful approach to building resilience.

Finally case studies are presented which illustrate how the heuristics are enacted in the lives of individuals and what we can learn about resilience through their stories.

This volume builds on the research and publications that I, along with colleagues, have produced over the past three decades. Whilst it is not exactly a compendium of published work, some of the research and writings may be familiar. The intention is not to be repetitious but to bring together much of the research published to date in the volume so as to make explicit the close links between coping and resilience.

In the month prior to finalising writing this volume, I opened my daily newspaper (*The Australian* May 5, 2016, p. 3 the Nation) to read that scientists have found that long-term perspectives give people an evolutionary leg-up. Using applied twenty-first-century computing, it has been determined that those who attached more weight to long-term happiness than momentary bliss and also remember past happiness far longer were the survivors. That is, steadfast optimists were the better survivors. The study was reported by Cornell University's Professor Shiman Edelman in the journal *Plus One* using algorithms which were applied to computer characters. I hope that we all become long-term optimists in the active pursuit of resilience and that we can lead rich and fulfilling lives.

Acknowledgements

The acknowledgements for a book like this are so vast. Much of the coping research reported in this volume has been a result of long standing collaborations. Most particularly Ramon Lewis, and his contribution to the *Adolescent Coping Scale* and the *Coping Scale for Adults* in both editions, is a valued colleague without whom much of the coping research would not have happened. Ramon has been involved in many of the research collaborations using the two scales. My colleagues at the University of Melbourne, Jan Deans and Rachel Liang, have been actively involved in the 'early years' research programme over the last seven years. Their collaboration has made the early years research programme possible. Rachel has also been a most valued research and editorial assistant for this volume. Her contribution has been invaluable in bringing the volume to completion. My colleague and friend Carmella Prideaux provided her most astute editorial assistance to the manuscript.

Along the way there have been too many postgraduate psychology researchers to mention individually. They have contributed to the field over the last 25 years in all facets of the coping research programme and thus appear in the reference list which cites their work. It is a unique volume of refereed published work from a small research community. But most importantly their research has provided insights that have propelled my work and that of others to reach this point.

The amazing professionals who have provided interviews that appear in Chap. 11 and which in reality tell much of the resiliency story gave their contribution so generously. I am indebted to them for the insights and lived experiences that they shared.

My family has been the joy of my life. Harry, Joshua, and Lexi have been on this coping journey with me since the mid-1980s. They have amazing achievements and contributions to the well-being of patients, community, and scholarship, both national and international, in their own right. For that I salute and admire them. In recent years my family has grown with another set of wonderful people, Adam, Oscar, Claudia, and Luca, bringing joy to our lives in countless ways in all that they do. Amie, Gemma and Blake are the gems that have become part of our family. I love you all and appreciate all that you do in your professional and scholastic lives. We become resilient as a collective as we journey through the years dealing with our varied life challenges as we travel joyfully through the years.

Contents

List of Figures

List of Tables

1

Capturing the Resiliency Construct

Resilience appears to have surpassed coping as one of the most highly researched areas in the field of psychology. Using search terms such as resilience, resiliency, or resilient from 2010 onwards, there were approximately 96,442 peer-reviewed academic journal articles, complemented by 1357 reviews at the time of writing. In contrast, the highly researched field of coping produced only 95,858 peer-reviewed articles with 406 reviews.

Resilience has become a part of our everyday vernacular. It is an extension of the research in the field of stress and coping and a good fit with the positive psychology framework that has become a major focus of psychology in the twenty-first century. Nevertheless resilience remains elusive. The literature abounds with studies that demonstrate the predictive power of resilience for health and well-being. Measurement tools are increasingly becoming available but generally are limited in their utility, and operate as screening tools rather than as predictors. In contrast, coping can be used as an index of resilience and has utility in practice.

---

*My mother gave me belief in myself, by treating me as **special** every day of my life. I got from her a real belief in myself.* (Martin, property developer)

© The Author(s) 2017   **1**
E. Frydenberg, *Coping and the Challenge of Resilience*,
DOI 10.1057/978-1-137-56924-0_1

Resilience and coping are linked with resilience considered as the ability to 'bounce back' despite adversity or setbacks and it is generally achieved by having good coping resources. Coping is a key means of contributing to personal or collective resilience. It is an asset that can be acquired. Coping can be construed as the process and resilience as the outcome.

Resilience

Like most concepts and constructs in psychology there are a range of definitions and understandings of what constitutes resilience. Resilience comes from the Latin *salire* to spring up and *resilire* meaning to leap or spring back, hence the bounce back concept of resilience.

Originally the term was used in 1818 to describe the property of timber to withstand load without breaking. More recently the term has been adopted by ecologists to describe settings like the family, community, and natural environments to withstand challenges or stress. Additionally it has moved into the individual and collectivist human domain rather than the original focus on environmental aspects.

The individual aspect of resilience arose from trauma research where there was an interest in an individual's capacity to rebound despite adversity. Resilience can be construed as a multifaceted dynamic process wherein individuals engage in positive adaptation despite experiences of significant adversity or trauma (Lutha & Cicchetti, 2000).

A summary of 73 definitions of resilience (Meredith et al., 2011) highlights that the majority of definitions focus on adaptation whilst only a few focus on growth. The construct might be captured best by Zautra and Reich (2010) who define **resilience** broadly as being the meaning, methods, and measures of a fundamental characteristic of human adaptation. They postulate that **resilience** is recovery, sustainability, and growth from an individual or collectivist perspective; from a single biological system to a person, an organisation, a neighbourhood, a community, a city, a state, or even a nation. Three features of this definition relate to recovery, sustainability, and growth. They acknowledge that 'our attention to these three features of resilience is best seen through the dynamic lens of coping and adaptation' (p. 175). Indeed, in that sense resilience is akin to coping.

Masten, a key researcher in the field of resilience, particularly as it relates to development, in her paper titled *Ordinary Magic: Resilience Process in Development* (Masten, 2001), notes that the study of resilience has 'turned on its head' many negative assumptions and deficit-focused models of human behaviour. In fact, this challenge to the negative and deficit approaches to the study of human endeavour has been gaining momentum over three decades or more. It is the positive approaches to human pursuit that the work of Seligman on positive psychology (2011), Maddi on hardiness (2002), Mayer and Salovey on emotional intelligence (1995), Lazarus (1993) and Hobfoll (1989) on coping, Dweck (2006, 2015) on mindset, and Duckworth and Eskreis-Winkler (2015) on grit, each capture from a different perspective. Masten's thesis examines the ordinariness of resilience. For her, resilience derives from the human 'adaptation system' through the process of development. What is promoted by the positive psychology movement and coping researchers is the capacity of humans to grow their adaptation capabilities through gaining insight into their experiences and participation in interventions that build the skills for resilience.

As resilience has come into the 'lingua franca', it has acquired a range of meanings that are best captured by Masten (2001), when she wrote that 'resilience refers to the class of phenomenon characterised by good outcomes in spite of serious threats to adaptation or development' (p. 228). Later Schoon (2006), citing Masten, pointed out that the central assumptions in resilience research are:

(a) a positive outcome despite adversity;
(b) continued positive or effective functioning in adverse circumstances; and
(c) recovery after significant trauma.

Masten (2001) refers to resilience as being an 'inferential and contextual construct that requires two major kinds of judgements' (p. 228). The first judgement focuses on the threat or risk of the inference, and the second involves the criteria by which adaptation or developmental outcomes are assessed. This approach is consistent with the appraisal processes in the coping literature whilst evaluating outcomes is more a feature of resilience research. For Masten, 'resilience doesn't come from rare or special qualities, but from everyday magic of ordinary, normative human resources, in the minds, brains, bodies of children, in their families and relationships, and in their communities' (p. 235).

Unlike coping, which consists of thoughts, feelings, and actions, and has a long-established history in measurement, the concept of resilience is not so readily quantifiable, particularly given there is a judgement implied about effective outcomes. Resilience is regarded as two dimensional: the first being the exposure to adversity and the second is the manifestation of successful adaptation. However, these dimensions are linked to normative judgements as to what constitutes desirable or positive outcomes. To conceptualise resilience as a trait rather than a state bears the danger of blaming the victim when things do not go well and ignoring the potential for growth.

Resiliency Versus Coping

The question as to whether the concept of resilience is too good to be true has been considered. For example, Lemay (2004) suggests that ' resiliency theory's proposition that ordinary day to day experiences are in most circumstances sufficient [to] overcome the developmental affects of severe adversity is hard to accept' (p. 11). Indeed if development alone was the intervention by which resilience is measured and the capacity to recover from adversity is inherent in the definition, then resilience as a construct falls short.

Coping on the other hand, as will be demonstrated in subsequent chapters, is readily operationalised and the theory takes account of the individual's resources, the context in which development has taken place, and the context in which the stressor occurs. Coping theory has the capacity to be used for prevention and intervention at primary, secondary, and tertiary stages: that is, as the first response to adversity, as the response to the impact on adversity, or as an outcome of an intervention.

Consistent with Masten's (2001) theorising, Garbarino (2002) points out that 'the concept of resilience rests on the research findings that, although there is a correlation between specific negative experiences and specific negative outcomes, in most situations, a majority (maybe 60–80 %) of children and youth will not display negative outcomes' (p. 247). Resilience is not an absolute as virtually every child, indeed every person, has a 'breaking point' (Lemay, 2004, p. 12); some are crushed by adversity, and others thrive. Early experiences alone do not predetermine an individual's life path. Resilience diminishes as risk accumulates. It is difficult or perhaps impossible to determine an individual's breaking point. Both personal history and situational determinants play a part. Additionally, since luck, good and bad, or happenstance, is commonplace, so is adversity and the likely outcome of resilience.

However, whilst an individual's resilience may be measured in terms of outcomes, that is, in gross terms, this indicator may obscure the inner life of an individual and a host of vulnerability factors. This is illustrated by the experience of the 34-year-old champion Australian surfer, Michael Eugene Fanning, nicknamed 'White Lightning', who won the 2007, 2009, and 2013 Association of Surfing Professional World Tours. In 2015, Fanning survived an encounter with what is suspected to be a great white shark during the J-Bay Open finals in Jeffreys Bay, South Africa. He subsequently performed well in the championship, having heard only hours earlier that his brother had died. In Fanning's case there would have been grit and determination to succeed despite having heard the devastating news of his brother's death.

Coping in essence is about an individual's capacity to respond to environmental demands, and professionals can facilitate the growth of that capacity and assist in reducing the impact of adversity to create the conditions for resilience to occur. There is a cost to adversity but 'Resilience is in part about putting adversity behind you and getting on with the hustle and bustle of life' (Lemay, 2004, p. 14).

Lemay's (2004) reflection on how survivors of the European holocaust in World War II often thought of themselves as lucky and the successful lives they made in America attests to the fact that 'Coping is the science of *remarkable people* whereas resilience is the story of how remarkable people can be' (p. 13).

Measuring Resilience

High level of interest in resilience has stimulated the development of measurement tools by psychometricians. Measurement of psychological constructs can be useful if there is clarity around what is being measured and what are the predictive capabilities and/or limitations of the instrument that is used. In the context of wanting to build resilience, both personal and collective, identifying constructs has to be of benefit for not only assessment and prediction but more importantly for helping to develop skills. However, the complexities inherent in defining the resilience construct have been widely recognised.

When Windle, Bennett, and Noyes (2011) reviewed 19 resiliency measures, all self-report measures that examined resilience constructs such as intrapersonal (e.g., resilience attitude) and interpersonal protective factors (e.g., family, community), no 'gold standard' was found amongst the measures reviewed. They point out that there are no benchmarks for resilience measures and that due consideration should be given to the purpose and context of assessment, and the need to ensure reliability is considered when measuring change.

A distinction has been made between 'resiliency' which is the contextual or environmental dimension and 'resilience' which refers to the qualities of the individual (Prince-Embury, 2011). Prince-Embury's Resiliency Scales for Children and Adolescents (RSCA) provides an assessment of the personal attributes of resiliency including Sense of Mastery, Sense of Relatedness, and Emotional Reactivity (Prince-Embury & Courville, 2008). The tool consists of 64 'Likert-type' items which are grouped into 10 scales that make up the 3 core constructs.

For example, the Vulnerability Index from the Prince-Embury instrument is a summary score that quantifies children's personal vulnerability as the relative discrepancy between their combined self-perceived resource (the Resource Index) and their fragility as described by emotional reactivity (the Emotional Reactivity scale score) (Prince-Embury, 2011). Sense of Mastery, one of the three core attributes, is aligned to self-efficacy which is linked to motivation and achievement, and includes adaptability and optimism. Whilst problem-solving skills are encouraged, as with coping, it is the *belief* in one's capacity to problem solve that matters (Frydenberg & Lewis, 2009).

Sense of Relatedness, the second core attribute, refers to the relational experience, and a sense of trust is considered to represent this most clearly. Access to Support, Social Comfort, and Tolerance of Difference are also subscales that contribute to this attribute. The third core attribute is Emotional Reactivity which is the capacity to regulate emotions. It is the 'risk' aspect of resiliency. There are strong relationships between the Vulnerability Index score and the Emotional Reactivity scale score and bullying, victimisation, and frequency of risk behaviours from the Beck Youth Inventory (Beck, Beck, Jolly, & Steer 2005). The resiliency scale can distinguish a clinical population and thus enable targeted interventions to be developed. As Prince-Embury points out it can be used as an outcome measure if the intervention is targeted to the tool. However, researchers must decide whether to focus on the context or environmental factors (resiliency), or personal attributes (resilience), or the interaction between the two.

Another perspective brought to the field comes from de Terte, Stephens, and Huddleston (2014) who developed a three-part model of psychological resilience. For them, like others, psychological resilience is defined as the ability of an individual to recover from a traumatic event or to remain psychologically robust when faced with an adverse event. A sample of 176 police officers was tested at the commencement of their training (1998/1999), 12 months later, and at the end of 2009 to determine what was helpful when dealing with difficult situations.

For example, a three-part model (Environment, Physical Behaviours, Cognitions) was used to demonstrate that social support, adaptive health practice, adaptive coping, and optimism were effective when police officers were faced with adversity. They measured outcomes using the Five-PR Model of Psychological Resilience (de Terte, Becker, & Stephens, 2009), namely, optimism, adaptive coping (Cognitions), emotional competence EQ (Emotions), adaptive health practices (Physical behaviours/reactions), and social support (Environment). Adaptive coping was measured by the four-item Brief Resilient Coping Scale (BRCS) and emotional competence by Mayer, Salovey, and Caruso (2012) MISCEIT which consists of 141 questions. The results highlight that there are two frequently used definitions of resilience: (1) the rebound or bounce back from adversity; and (2) the ability to maintain psychological and physical health despite adversity, such as when exposed to a traumatic event (Bonanno, 2004).

Whilst for some resilience is a return to homeostasis or sustainability, to Hobfoll (2010), a key coping researcher (see Chap. 3), resilience means two things:

> First, I refer to people's ability to withstand the most negative consequences of stressful challenges, even the traumatic challenges they face. Second, I refer to the extent people remain vigorous, committed, and absorbed in important life tasks… amidst significant challenge. (p. 128)

Hobfoll's approach clearly focuses on positive adaptation in the face of adversity.

There are various aspects of resilience. For example, the psychobiological aspect of resilience reflects physiological adaptation to stressors so as to maintain homeostatic stability. While genetic influences play a significant role in resilience, they are not considered necessary to have the foremost effect (Rutter, 2012). Developmental processes also play a significant part in resiliency research in the context of child development (Masten et al., 1999). Additionally, the focus has shifted from risk factors for psychopathology to psychosocial resources associated with resilience, strong healthy parental attachment, peer relationships, and language competence (Lutha, 2006).

In order to return to homeostasis so as to have psychological healthy adaptation within the individual, family, and community there is a set of fundamentals in the process of the life course (Schoon, 2006). As Schoon points out:

1. Human development is a lifelong process.
2. Individuals construct their own life course through choices (agency).
3. Life course is embedded and shaped by social structures.
4. There are antecedents and consequences;
5. Lives are lived interdependently.
6. There are transitions and turning points.

When considering resilience, factors such as educational transitions, individual characteristics, human agency, bounded agency (e.g., synchronising with desires and goals of others), biological dispositions, family influences, caregiver relationships, linked lives, neighbourhood, institutions, and cohort comparisons all need to be taken into account (Schoon, 2006).

Connor and Davidson (2003) acknowledge that 'resilience can be viewed as a measure of stress coping ability' (p. 76) and as such deem it useful for intervention. They describe a 25-item measure using a 5-point Likert scale (0–4). As with coping, resilience is seen as a 'multidimensional construct that varies with context, time, age, gender and cultural origin' (p. 76). Whilst the theoretical underpinnings seem well grounded, particularly citing the work of Rutter (1985) and Kobasa (1979), it is not until one looks closely at the items that they can be compared and contrasted with coping. Items mentioned in Connor and Davidson includes: *Able to adapt to change, Close and secure relationships, Sometimes fate or God can help, Can deal with what comes, Past success gives confidence for new challenge, See the humorous side of things, Coping with stress strengthens, Tend to bounce back after illness or hardship, Things happened for a reason, Best effort no matter what, You can achieve all your goals, When things look hopeless, I don't give up, Know where to turn for help, Under pressure focus and think clearly, Prefer to take the lead in problem solving, Not easily discouraged by failure, Think of self as a strong person, Making unpopular or difficult decisions, Can handle unpleasant feelings, Have to act on a hunch, Strong sense of purpose, Being in control of your life, I like challenges, You work to achieve your goals, Pride in your achievements.* The items read like a strong employment application hence encouraging the respondent to present themselves in a favourable light and likely to involve response bias.

Nevertheless items such as those above have predictive power and can be seen as assets that contribute to success. For example, knowing where to turn for help, having a purpose, and being in control of one's life are self-assessed positive attributes. However, when it comes to coping we know that it is not enough to just do more of the positive without reducing the use of negative strategies (Lewis & Frydenberg, 2004). All our coping research indicates that what is important is to do less of the negative whilst doing more of the positive (see Chap. 5).

There is a 'huge heterogeneity' in people's responses to all kinds of stresses and adversity (Rutter, 2013). However, resilience is an interactive phenomenon that indicates some individuals have a good outcome despite adversity. It is therefore important to identify the risk factors for individuals and communities in particular situations. Resilience can result from repeated brief exposure to negative experiences and can result in inoculation against stress. Individual differences in responses to adversity may reflect biological pathways that are influenced by genes.

For some researchers such as Resnick (2014) 'adversity is critical to the development of resilience. Humans have the ability to adapt in the face of adversity, it is a component of personality' (p. 155). Regardless of the influence from genes, personality, and personal history, it is possible to arm people with skills and resources to withstand adversity and thus learn from experience during their life course. This is best achieved through the lens of coping. Individuals can become effective evaluators of their own coping abilities so enabling them to have the insight to contribute to adaptation and growth.

In Chap. 2 a number of theories that contribute to coping and resilience are identified and described. Chapter 3 describes the major theoretical formulations of coping, and subsequent chapters consider measurement and what we know, particular approaches to coping, and the outcomes of interventions. Finally, some case studies highlight resilient individuals, their histories, and coping strategies.

References

Beck, J. S., Beck, A. T., Jolly, J. B., & Steer, R. A. (2005). *Beck youth inventories-second edition for children and adolescents manual.* San Antonio, TX: PsychCorp.

Bonanno, G. A. (2004). Loss, trauma, and human resilience: Have we underestimated the human capacity to thrive after extremely aversive events? *The American Psychologist, 59*(1), 20–28.

Connor, K. M., & Davidson, J. R. T. (2003). Development of a new resilience scale: The Connor-Davidson Resilience Scale (CD-RISC). *Depression and Anxiety, 18*(2), 76–82.

de Terte, I., Becker, J., & Stephens, C. (2009). An integrated model for understanding and developing resilience in the face of adverse events. *Journal of Pacific Rim Psychology, 3*(1), 20–26. doi:10.1375/prp.3.1.20.

de Terte, I., Stephens, C., & Huddleston, L. (2014). The development of a three part model of psychological resilience. *Stress and Health: Journal of the International Society for the Investigation of Stress, 30*(5), 416–424.

Duckworth, A. L., & Eskreis-Winkler, L. (2015). Grit. In J. D. Wright (Ed.), *International encyclopedia of the social and behavioral sciences* (2nd ed., pp. 397–401). Oxford, UK: Elsevier.

Dweck, C. (2015). Growth. *British Journal of Educational Psychology, 85*, 242–245. doi:10.1111/bjep.12072.

Dweck, C. S. (2006). *Mindset: The new psychology of success* (1st ed.). Carol S. Dweck. New York: Random House, c2006.

Frydenberg, E., & Lewis, R. (2009). Relationship among wellbeing, avoidant coping and active coping in a large sample of Australian adolescents. *Psychological Reports, 104*(3), 745–758.

Garbarino, J. (2002). Coping with resilience. *Contemporary Psychology: APA Review of Books, 47*(3), 247–248. doi:10.1037/001107.

Hobfoll, S. E. (1989). Conservation of resources: A new attempt at conceptualizing stress. *The American Psychologist, 44*(3), 513–524.

Hobfoll, S. E. (2010). *Conservation of resources theory: Its implication for stress, health, and resilience.* NewYork: Oxford University Press.

Kobasa, S. C. (1979). Stressful life events, personality, and health: An inquiry into hardiness. *Journal of Personality and Social Psychology, 37*(1), 1–11.

Lazarus, R. S. (1993). Coping theory and research: Past, present, and future. *Psychosomatic Medicine, 55*(3), 234–247.

Lemay, R. (2004). Resilience versus coping. *Child and Family, 8*(2), 11–15.

Lewis, R., & Frydenberg, E. (2004). Students' self-evaluation of their coping: How well do they do it? In E. Frydenberg (Ed.), *Thriving, surviving, or going under: Coping with everyday lives* (pp. 23–43). Connecticut: Information Age Publishing.

Luthar, S. S. (2006). Resilience in development: A synthesis of research across five decades. In D. Cicchetti & D. J. Cohen (Eds.), *Developmental psychopathology: Risk, disorder, and adaptation* (pp. 740–795). New York: Wiley.

Luthar, S. S., & Cicchetti, D. (2000). The construct of resilience: Implications for interventions and social policies. *Development and Psychopathology, 12*(4), 857–885.

Maddi, S. R. (2002). The story of hardiness: Twenty years of theorizing, research, and practice. *Consulting Psychology Journal: Practice and Research, 54*(3), 173–185. doi:10.1037/1061-4087.54.3.173.

Masten, A. S. (2001). Ordinary magic: Resilience processes in development. *American Psychologist, 56*(3), 227–238.

Masten, A. S., Hubbard, J. J., Gest, S. D., Tellegen, A., Garmezy, N., & Ramirez, M. (1999). Competence in the context of adversity: Pathways to resilience and maladaptation from childhood to late adolescence. *Development and Psychopathology, 11*(1), 143–169.

Mayer, J. D., & Salovey, P. (1995). Emotional intelligence and the construction and regulation of feelings. *Applied and Preventive Psychology, 4*(3), 197–208.

Mayer, J. D., Salovey, P., & Caruso, D. R. (2012). The validity of the MSCEIT: Additional analyses and evidence. *Emotion Review, 4*(4), 403–408.

Meredith, L. S., Sherbourne, C. D., Gaillot, S., Hansell, L., Ritschard, H. V., Parker, A. M., & Wrenn, G. (2011). *Promoting psychological resilience in the U.S. Military.* Santa Monica, CA: RAND Corporation.

Prince-Embury, S. (2011). Assessing personal resiliency in the context of school settings: Using the resiliency scales for children and adolescents. *Psychology in the Schools, 48*(7), 672–685.

Prince-Embury, S., & Courville, T. (2008). Measurement invariance of the resiliency scales for children and adolescents with respect to sex and age cohorts. *Canadian Journal of School Psychology, 23*(1), 26–40.

Resnick, B. (2014). Resilience in older adults. *Topics in Geriatric Rehabilitation, 30*(3), 155–163. doi:10.1097/TGR.0000000000000024.

Rutter, M. (1985). Resilience in the face of adversity: Protective factors and resistance to psychiatric disorder. *British Journal of Psychiatry, 147,* 598–611.

Rutter, M. (2012). Resilience as a dynamic concept. *Development and Psychopathology, 24*(2), 335–344. doi:10.1017/S0954579412000028.

Rutter, M. (2013). Annual research review: Resilience – Clinical Implications. *Journal of Child Psychology and Psychiatry, 54*(4), 474–487.

Schoon, I. (2006). *Risk and resilience: Adaptations in changing times.* Cambridge, MA: Cambridge University Press.

Seligman, M. E. P. (2011). *Authentic happiness. [Electronic resource]: Using the new positive psychology to realise your potential for lasting fulfilment.* London: Nicholas Brealey Publishing.

Windle, G., Bennett, K. M., & Noyes, J. (2011). A methodological review of resilience measurement scales. *Health and Quality of Life Outcomes, 9*(8), 1–18.

Zautra, A. J., & Reich, J. W. (2010). *Resilience: The meanings, methods, and measures of a fundamental characteristic of human adaptation.* New York: Oxford University Press.

2

Positive Psychology, Mindset, Grit, Hardiness, and Emotional Intelligence and the Construct of Resilience: A Good Fit with Coping

There are no failures. You just go back and give it your best.
(Tania, marathon swimmer)

I think IQ is changeable with the benefit of experience and exposure. If I had stayed in a small country town with a dad who was a bank manager and never been to a university, I would probably not be where I am today in the way I think and the level at which I think. (Carlie, company director)

There are multiple bodies of literature that contribute to our understanding of resilience. The psycho-philosophical orientations of positive psychology and the ecological framework of Bronfenbrenner underpin an understanding of resilience. These are complemented by the theories of coping that underscore much of this volume. Additionally evidence-based approaches such as mindset, grit, emotional intelligence, and hardiness also contribute to an understanding of resilience. Each of these complementary theories focuses on success and achievement. When these approaches are underpinned by a positive psychological orientation, they combine to become a powerful tool for building resilience in different ways, in diverse contexts, throughout the lifespan.

© The Author(s) 2017
E. Frydenberg, *Coping and the Challenge of Resilience,*
DOI 10.1057/978-1-137-56924-0_2

Positive Psychology

Positive psychology is the philosophical and psychological theory that underpins this volume. It is about building strengths, capacity, and personal growth. Each of the constructs considered contribute in some way to resilience, as does coping theory in all its applications.

For more than 60 years, psychology worked within the disease model and has succeeded in developing a scientific discipline with classifications, treatment plans, and interventions to make miserable people less miserable. This approach was recognised as being incomplete in the portrayals of humankind (Seligman, Parks, & Steen, 2004). Undeniably, the negative is part of humankind, but only a part, and what is viewed as negative in one group may be positive in another. For example, starting a new job can be exciting for a person or group but anxiety-provoking for another. Similarly, a child moving out of home can be a loss for some parents or a relief for those parents who wish to rediscover their own freedom.

Towards the end of the twentieth century, during his term as President of the American Psychological Association, Martin Seligman highlighted the cost of adopting a disease model of psychology. Psychiatrists and psychologists were viewed negatively as 'victimologists' and 'pathologisers', who failed to address the improvement of normal lives and the identification and nurturance of high talent. Rather than being guided by the thinking of 'what is wrong with our lives?', Seligman (2011) encouraged people to refocus on the subject matter and to look at 'what is right in people's lives?' This question is at the heart of positive psychology and has led to widespread international interest in research and practice in mental and physical health and the capacity to learn skills to enhance well-being in individuals and communities. Seligman and Csikszentmihalyi (2000) describe positive psychology in the following way:

> At the personal level positive psychology is about having experiences that are valued, having a sense of wellbeing, contentment, and satisfaction (in the past); hope and optimism (for the future); and happiness (in the present). At the individual level, it is about having a capacity for love and endeavour, courage, interpersonal skill, aesthetic sensibility, perseverance, forgiveness, originality, future mindedness, spirituality, high talent, and

wisdom. At the group level, it is about the civic virtues and the institutions that move individuals toward better citizenship: responsibility, nurturance, altruism, civility, moderation, tolerance, and work ethic. (p. 5)

This frequently cited definition highlights the fact that positive psychology is concerned with achieving a state of happiness and satisfaction as well as with good citizenship. It is about achieving pleasure from positive experiences and contributing to the greater good. At the child level, it is about bringing up children who are engaged with the world around them, retain curiosity to explore their environment, and gain satisfaction when tasks are accomplished.

The four pillars of positive psychology have been described as virtue, meaning, resilience, and well-being. At an institutional level, it seeks to explore the roots of happy and compassionate individuals, strong social bonds, and altruistic behaviour. In sum, it is the science or study of a meaningful life. Whilst positive psychology is an orientation that originated from studies with adult populations, the tenets and pillars have relevance and have been applied to children and adolescents in all settings.

Achieving well-being and a capacity to cope with life situations has been the concern of philosophers since Aristotle who is credited with saying that 'happiness depends upon ourselves'. But to learn the art of human existence requires an understanding of the dynamic process that involves the interaction between one's circumstances, activities, and psychological resources for growth, and ways of achieving a sense of meaning and satisfaction with life, within one's cultural context. In order that both adults and children may flourish four main components—goodness, generativity, growth, and resilience (Fredrickson & Losada, 2005)—are required.

Well-being itself is also a much-used concept. We all strive for well-being. It is not just the absence of ill health or disappointment when we do not achieve something that we strive for, it is about experiencing positive emotions, being able to savour the moment, and having satisfaction. Mihaly Csikszentmihalyi (2008), the co-founder of the Positive Psychology movement, pointed out that rather than happiness being something that just happens to us, it is something that we 'make happen'.

Happiness is ultimately the striving that is innate and not readily achieved, but according to Seligman on his website, the best recommendation for happiness is to locate your strengths and find new ways to deploy them. We can certainly do that for ourselves as adults and also help children to do that. All the evidence points to the fact that people clearly want to be happy. Indeed, what parents want for their children is also happiness (Seligman, 2011).

Whilst positive psychology has emphasised the experience of positive emotions, it does not imply that we are not interested in also identifying and labelling negative emotions. We learn to appreciate the good through negative experiences and losses. However, generally it is through the positive emotional experiences that we broaden and build our personal resources for living the good life (Fredrickson, 2004). As adults, we strive to build resources such as the physical, psychological, intellectual, and social. In sum, positive psychology is a philosophical orientation that underpins human endeavour; it focuses on what people can do rather than on what they cannot do.

Socio-ecological Model

Another theoretical orientation that underpins human endeavour is Bronfenbrenner's (1978) socio-ecological systemic approach which posits that the relationship between individuals and their environments is reciprocal in that individuals are influenced by their environments and in turn impact their environments. The micro system, such as family, school, workplace, and neighbourhood, bears a direct influence on the individual. This is complemented by the macro systems, that is, the sociocultural political context in which the individual is located. So both cultural contextual influences along with the more direct family, peer, school, and workplace are important. It is the environment in which individuals operate, taking account of both proximal (e.g., school, workplace) and distal (e.g., economic, cultural) factors. In the 1980s, Bronfenbrenner emphasised that both the ecological and development context are relevant. As with coping, there is an assumption that there is a **bidirectional** transaction between individuals and their environments, and in turn

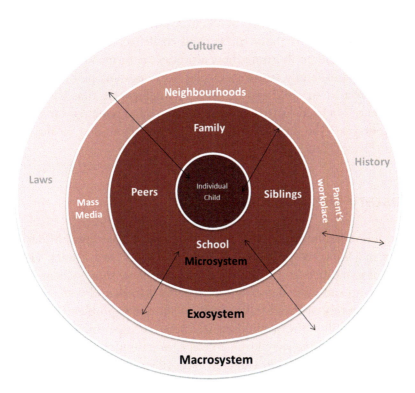

Fig. 2.1 Bronfenbrenner's socio-ecological model

there is an interplay between context and development. Thus, when it comes to resilience and coping, both the philosophical and sociocultural influences are relevant to take into consideration (Fig. 2.1).

Mindset

Mindset is a useful construct when it comes to considering adaptation and growth. Carol Dweck's work focuses on an understanding that intelligence is not fixed, but that there is a capacity for growth given a mindset or belief system (Dweck, 2006). Similarly Duckworth and Gross (2014) state that if you can change your mindset you can change your grit, and it follows that you can change your coping.

Mindset is one of the bodies of literature outside the traditional coping arena that informs us about success and challenge. Dweck's early work with school children illustrates how attitudes are formed at an early age, and school and family experiences play an important part. Her initial research related to children's theories of intelligence, that is, whether intelligence is a fixed entity or a capacity which has potential for growth. In recent years she has extended the concept of mindset to the adult world (Dweck, 2012).

Mastery Orientation

Some four decades ago, in their work on learned helplessness, Miller and Seligman (Miller & Seligman, 1975) and Diener and Dweck (1978) spelt out two different reactions to failure. There are those who are helpless (give up and show deterioration in performance) and there are those who are mastery-oriented (take action to surmount problems). It is not a matter of ability but of mindset. In a series of experiments by Diener and Dweck, students were given concept formation problems on which they initially succeeded but failed on subsequent more difficult tasks. An attribution questionnaire determined how they would ascribe failures. It was predicted that those who would attribute failures to lack of effort were likely to display a mastery-oriented response. The researchers were also interested in thoughts, feelings, and behaviours when confronting failure. Those in the helpless group denigrated their intellectual competence. Those in the mastery-oriented group did not analyse reasons for their failure but gave themselves instructions on how to improve their performance by concentrating harder or reviewing the feedback. Everyone expressed positive emotions when succeeding. The helpless group expressed sadness and boredom when failing, while the mastery group continued to enjoy the problems. Some displayed increased positive affect in the face of adversity: 'I love a challenge' and 'mistakes are our friends'. The helpless group deteriorated in problem solving, while the mastery group continued to improve (Dweck & Sorich, 1999).

In another study, Licht and Dweck (1984) gave fifth graders new material to master. The students were ascribed to mastery and helpless groups and half in each group given a confusing passage. Seventy per cent of the mastery-oriented group successfully completed the task, and only one-third of the helpless group was able to learn material when preceded by a confusing paragraph.

Elliott and Dweck (1988) established that the goals students set themselves gave rise to helpless or mastery-oriented responses. They identified two types of goals: performance goals (aim to gain favourable judgement of his or her own competence and avoid unfavourable judgements, that is, look smart) versus learning goals (where aim is to increase competence, that is, to get smarter) (p. 237). 'Both sets of goals are natural, necessary, and pretty much universal' (p. 238). Everyone wants his or her ability to be esteemed by others, and everyone wants to learn new things. They repeatedly observed that performance goals (i.e., by focusing students on measuring their ability by their performance) made them vulnerable to a helpless pattern in the face of failure. Learning goals, in contrast (i.e., by focusing on the effort and strategies students need for learning), foster a mastery-oriented stance towards difficulty (Ames & Archer, 1988; Dweck & Leggett, 1988; Roeser, Pintrich, & DeGroot, 1994).

Students' theories of intelligence are associated with their goals. That is, those with performance goals see intelligence as static while those with mastery goals consider that intelligence can be developed. These two theories of intelligence have been called entity and incremental theories (Dweck & Sorich, 1999). In a series of studies, Dweck and her colleagues demonstrated that different theories of intelligence set up different goals (Dweck & Leggett, 1988; Zhao, Dweck, & Mueller, 1998). Entity theory fosters performance goals and helpless response to failure and incremental theory fosters learning goals and a mastery response to failure. Entity theorists feel that if you have to work hard (show effort) you risk showing that you do not have ability.

The impact of mindset on achievement was examined in Dweck's study of transition to junior high school. Students' theories of intelligence were the best predictors of their seventh grade results. Entity theorists remained low achievers with a helpless pattern of response while incremental theorists showed a mastery-oriented pattern. Another study (Sorich & Dweck, 1997) found that both learning and performing were important goals, but when goals were placed in conflict (as in real life), incremental theorists were far more interested in learning than simply performing well. They wanted to meet challenges and acquire new skills rather than just have easy work to make them look smart. Entity theorists wanted to minimise effort. They had conflicting interests. They wanted to do well but had an aversion to the effort required. Incremental theorists believed that effort was a key ingredient to success. The mastery-oriented approach by incremental students yielded better results intellectually and emotionally.

These patterns begin as early as the preschool years with at least one-third of the students showing helpless response when experiencing failure (Cain & Dweck, 1995; Herbert & Dweck, 1985; Dweck, 1990). In kindergarten, helpless children felt not good and not nice. In their role play they showed more criticism and more punishment. In general the helpless individuals see intelligence as a fixed trait. Furthermore, helpless young children (Heyman, Dweck, & Cain, 1992) see badness as a stable trait. It is socialisation that makes a difference.

Socialisation

Adult feedback in the form of criticism that reflected on the child's traits fostered a stronger helpless reaction in response to later setbacks, as well as negative emotions, self-blame, and feelings of badness (Mueller & Dweck, 1998). Criticism that indicated that more effort was required or a new strategy was needed set up a mastery-oriented reaction (feedback that criticised the behaviour but not the child was in between).

In the study with kindergarteners and fifth graders, when praise was given for the child as a whole and praise was given for the child's traits (e.g., intelligence) after a job well done, significantly greater helpless response was created when the child failed (Mueller & Dweck, 1998). It was the strategy of praise for effort that created the most mastery-oriented coping response. There were three responses: the intelligence praise group, 'You got it right you must be smart', the effort praise group, 'You got it right. That's a good score and you must have tried hard' and the control group, 'You got it right. That's really good.' The intelligence praise group fell apart after failure. They also showed less enjoyment of the task after failure. They lied about their scores. The effort praise group felt that they needed to try harder. The effort praise group did best on the last task. After feedback was given and a choice of performance or learning goals made, the intelligence praise group just wanted to keep looking smart with the majority choosing performance tasks.

Labelling children as gifted or bright promotes the entity theory of intelligence. Giving young people a gifted status can make them sensitive to failure, that is, vulnerable and helpless. They show enthusiasm for the product rather than enthusiasm for the process. Those who believe in fixed traits differ from those who believe in malleable qualities not only in the way that they judge themselves but also in the way in which they judge others. The fixed entity theorists tend to stereotype others more than do the increment theorists.

It is clear then that a helpless mindset leads to a host of maladaptive thoughts, including fear of challenge and avoidance of effort, while the mastery-oriented young people focus on effort. They think about how to accomplish things, how to surmount challenges to achieve their goals, and how to increase their abilities. Children with incremental theory of intelligence were more successful in negotiating transitions while children with an entity theory of intelligence performed less well. If we give messages explicitly or implicitly that ability is fixed and ability can be measured from performance, we are very likely to undermine mastery-oriented inclinations and promote helplessness even when the message is couched in praise. The indications are that to maximise success we need to socialise people to see their ability as malleable and that there is a reward for effort.

The learning or schooling experience is all important in providing a basis for adult life. According to Dweck (2006), many people have the one consuming goal whether it is in the classroom, workplace or relationships: 'Will I succeed or fail? Will I look smart or dumb? Will I be accepted or rejected? Will I feel like a winner or loser?'(p. 6). But when it comes to resilience, it is those with a growth mindset who are likely to benefit from the capacity to learn and adapt to meet the challenges that are likely to arise throughout their lives.

Various cognitive and motivational self-regulatory processes need to be promoted to help individuals become their own teachers. Cues which elicit positive emotions, such as joy, contentment, satisfaction, or anticipated pride or interest, temporarily broaden the scope of attention, cognition, and action. In contrast, cues which elicit negative emotions (e.g., anxiety, fear, frustration, irritation, shame, or guilt) temporarily narrow the scope of attention, cognition, and action. Not all children choose challenging tasks when given the opportunity; rather 37 % choose to do the familiar and easy puzzle. However, the response they receive at the completion of the task determines whether they persevere (Smiley & Dweck, 1994). The interviewees in Chap. 11, particularly those interviewed in 2015, display a growth mindset. They have a belief in their capacities but also in their potential for growth.

In considering the notion of growth in general, Dweck (2015) pointed out that we need to consider small-scale studies in which we measure students' 'growth-relevant beliefs or goals' and closely observe their 'thoughts, feelings, actions, and outcomes' (i.e., much like coping) as they perform their tasks. What is also important is how much students value learning over looking smart; how much they value hard work; and how resilient they are in the face of adversity. Dweck cites a study using a computer game that has been developed to reward effort rather than performance on mathematics-related tasks. Students who were rewarded for effort tried more strategies, showed more sustained effort, and displayed greater persistence on the harder problems than the students who were rewarded for speed and performance.

People profit from an increased capacity to judge whether a particular action will lead to goal attainment, that is, whether increased effort and persistence will pay off. However, effort investment is related to perceived value of tasks and perceived competence to execute it. In a diverse and changing environment in the school or workplace, in a world where technology often provides the instruction, individuals are increasingly being called upon to be self-regulated performers. A distinction is made between self-regulators and self-controls in that the latter activates the punishment system while the former is associated with positive emotions. And emotions matter in task performance.

Emotional Intelligence

The term 'Emotional Intelligence' (EI) emerged in the 1990s from the work of Salovey and Mayer. Described as a social intelligence, EI involves 'the ability to monitor one's own and others' emotions, to discriminate among them, and to use the information to guide one's thinking and actions' (Salovey & Mayer, 1990, p. 189). It includes the expression and regulation of emotions in both the self and in others using both verbal and nonverbal cues. EI uses these emotional abilities to assist in solving problems. Similar to cognitive intelligence, different individuals will be more or less emotionally intelligent. Those individuals who are more aware of their own feelings and that of others are regarded as more emotionally intelligent. Emotionally intelligent individuals are also more open to both positive and negative emotions, have the ability to label emotions correctly, and can communicate these feelings appropriately.

High emotional awareness is argued to result in 'effective regulation of affect within themselves and others, and so contribute to well-being' (Mayer & Salovey, 1993, p. 440). A variety of measures have been developed to measure EI, and on the whole, empirical evidence lends support to EI being a 'predictor of significant outcomes across diverse samples in a number of real world domains' (Mayer, Roberts, & Barsade, 2008, p. 527). In children, research has found EI consistently predicts positive social outcomes along with negatively predicting problem behaviours such as internalising and hyperactivity (see Mayer et al., 2008).

In more recent years, Daniel Goleman (2005, 2011) has popularised EI to the point where it is readily acknowledged as a desirable quality in all relationships across the lifespan, from the early years through to late adulthood. Goleman's focus has been mainly on the workplace where leadership and relational success are critical to advancement in the hierarchy. In many roles that are people- or customer-focused, EI is essential to performance outcomes.

Hardiness

Historically, hardiness is an approach to achieving resilience. From an existential psychological perspective, life is a series of stresses starting with birth trauma, moving through childhood, and into adulthood (Maddi, 2002). 'Megatrends' such as globalisation, threat to the environment, rapid technological change all contribute to life as a series of stresses. Whilst the capacity to survive in the face of stress varies according to individuals, there is also the potential to thrive. Maddi's model identifies the stressful circumstances that involve mental and physical strain which for some lead to performance deficits, but for others it is about having a hardy attitude that involves commitment, being decisive, obtaining social support, and engaging in hardy health practices, such as relaxation and exercise. All these are features of good coping. There is a capacity to measure hardiness and to see how hardiness contributes to resilience in diverse populations. For example, it has been found that hardiness and optimistic attributional styles are predictors of mental health (Moosavi & Ahadi, 2011).

Athletes who were low in hardiness exacerbated and attenuated the impact of pre-injury negative life events (i.e., low hardiness was a significant predictor of sport injury and post-injury responses). Wadey, Evans, Hanton, and Neil (2012) found that athletes high on hardiness possessed a refined repertoire of problem- and emotion-focused coping strategies that they used pre- and post-injury whilst athletes low in hardiness used avoidance coping strategies that had long-term negative implications (Wadey et al., 2012).

Grit

Grit is another useful construct in the resilience and successful achievement domain. Grit is defined as perseverance and passion for long-term goals (Duckworth, Peterson, Matthews, & Kelly, 2007). It encompasses stamina, passion or interest, and effort. Only half the questions in the Grit Scale (Duckworth & Quinn, 2009) are about responding resiliently to failure. So more than being resilient in the face of adversity, it is about having a deep commitment and loyalty. Grit predicts success over and beyond talent. Therefore it is a useful educational and training construct. Most highly successful people are both talented and gritty. In commenting on Paul Tough's *How Children Succeed. Grit, Curiosity and the Hidden Power of Character*, Hong (2014) argues that noncognitive character traits are more important to success, or at least as important, as cognitive abilities. These are character strengths like gratitude, honesty, generosity, empathy, social intelligence, tact and charisma, and being proactive.

Tough's book emphasises that it is not so much about moral character, but rather about performance character.

Duckworth, building on the work of Seligman, considered the relationship between grit and resiliency, where resilience is construed as the capacity to 'bounce back' from adversity, whilst for Seligman it is more about optimism and seeing the possibilities of making changes in one's life. Grit is seen as a personality construct that identifies an individual's long-term drive and determination. Therefore, having goals and pursuits and seeing demands as challenges certainly is associated with grit. It is a relatively recent area of study with many unanswered elements. For example, Levy and Steele (2011) consider that there is an association between grit and attachment, both in the early years and even more so in the adult years. It is clear from successful achievers and from the interviews in Chap. 11 that grit and determination have been important in individuals achieving their successful outcomes and being resilient in the face of adversity.

Concluding Remarks

The essential thesis of this volume is that each of the constructs considered in this chapter contribute to coping and resilience. Generally they are underpinned by philosophical orientations such as positive psychology, elements that are teachable with heuristic devices that are operationalized in order that tools, such as those measuring hardiness for example, can be developed. The tools are comprised of constructs which have generally been derived factor analytically. Once identified, these constructs, can be used to underpin the teaching of skills in the social-emotional domain. However, because coping is a particular heuristic that encompasses a wide range of possible applications, it is well able to accommodate multiple concepts as a way of developing resilience. In sum, coping can accommodate numerous theoretical paradigms.

For example, the convergence of Maddi's theories of hardiness, Dweck's theory of mindset, Goleman's concept of emotional intelligence, and Duckworth's grit, along with Hobfoll's resource theory of coping (see Chap. 3), and Frydenberg and Lewis's approach to transactional coping (see Chap. 3) enable these complementary theories to be adapted for use by individuals and professional practitioners in order to benefit health and well-being.

Positive psychology and a sociocultural perspective of human endeavour underpin this volume as it focuses on coping skills in the pursuit of building resilience. Having a positive mindset about one's capacity to change is an important element when building a coping skills repertoire, as is the capacity to be hardy, and to have grit and tenacity. Emotions also play their part in how an individual adapts and thrives. Therefore, a focus on identifying emotions in oneself and others, and the increased usage of helpful emotions whilst reducing the use of the unhelpful emotions, is an important piece in the coping puzzle. As coping is considered in greater depth in the subsequent chapters, it will become evident how coping can be construed as a core set of constructs that serve to build resilience.

References

Ames, C., & Archer, J. (1988). Achievement goals in the classroom: Students' learning strategies and motivation processes. *Journal of Educational Psychology, 80*(3), 260.

Bronfenbrenner, U. (1978). The social role of the child in ecological perspective. *Diesoziale Rolle des Kindes in ökologischer Perspektive, 7*(1), 4–20.

Cain, K., & Dweck, C. S. (1995). The development of children's achievement motivation patterns and conceptions of intelligence. *Merrill-Palmer Quarterly, 41*, 24–52.

Csikszentmihalyi, M. (2008). *Flow : The psychology of optimal experience.* New York: Harper Perennial, c1990. 1st Harper Perennial Modern Classics ed.

Diener, C. I., & Dweck, C. S. (1978). *An analysis of learned helplessness: Continuous changes in performance, strategy, and achievement cognitions following failure. Journal of Personality and Social Psychology, 36*, 451–462.

Duckworth, A., & Gross, J. J. (2014). Self-control and grit: Related but separable determinants of success. *Current Directions in Psychological Science (Sage Publications Inc.), 23*(5), 319–325. doi:10.1177/0963721414541462.

Duckworth, A. L., Peterson, C., Matthews, M. D., & Kelly, D. R. (2007). Grit: Perseverance and passion for long-term goals. *Journal of Personality and Social Psychology, 96*(6), 1087–1101.

Duckworth, A. L., & Quinn, P. D. (2009). Development and validation of the short grit scale (Grit-S). *Journal of Personality Assessment, 91*(2), 166–174. doi:10.1080/00223890802634290.

Dweck, C. (2012). *Mindset: How you can fulfil your potential.* New York: Constable & Robinson.

Dweck, C. (2015). Growth. *British Journal of Educational Psychology, 85*, 242–245. doi:10.1111/bjep.12072.

Dweck, C. S. (1990). Self-theories and goals: Their role in motivation, personality, and development. *Nebraska Symposium on Motivation. Nebraska Symposium on Motivation, 38*, 199–235.

Dweck, C. S. (2006). *Mindset: The new psychology of success* (1st ed.). Carol S. Dweck. New York: Random House, c2006.

Dweck, C. S., & Leggett, E. L. (1988). A social-cognitive approach to motivation and personality. *Psychological Review, 95*(2), 256–273.

Dweck, C. S., & Sorich, L. A. (1999). Mastery-oriented thinking. In C. R. Snyder (Ed.), *Coping* (pp. 232–251). New York: Oxford University Press.

Elliott, E. S., & Dweck, C. S. (1988). Goals: An approach to motivation and achievement. *Journal of Personality and Social Psychology, 54*(1), 5–12.

Fredrickson, B. L. (2004). The Broaden-and-Build theory of positive emotions. *Philosophical Transactions of the Royal Society of London, 359*, 1367–1377.

Fredrickson, B. L., & Losada, M. F. (2005). Positive affect and the complex dynamics of human flourishing. *American Psychologist, 60*(7), 678–686.

Goleman, D. (2005). *Emotional intelligence.* New York: Bantam Books.

Goleman, D. (2011). *The brain and emotional intelligence: New insights.* Northampton, MA: More than sound LLC.

Herbert, C., & Dweck, C. (1985). *Mediators of persistence in pre-schoolers: Implications for development.* Unpublished manuscript, Harvard University.

Heyman, G. D., Dweck, C. S., & Cain, K. M. (1992). Young children's vulnerability to self-blame and helplessness: Relationship to beliefs about goodness. *Child Development, 63*, 401–415.

Hong, P. Y. P. (2014). How children succeed: Grit, curiosity, and the hidden power of character, Paul Tough. *Qualitative Social Work, 13*(3), 438–442, 435p. doi:10.1177/1473325014530940a.

Levy, J. M., & Steele, H. (2011). Attachment and grit: Exploring possible contributions of attachment styles (from past and present life) to the adult personality construct of grit. *Journal of Social and Psychological Sciences, 16*(2), 16.

Licht, B. G., & Dweck, C. S. (1984). Determinants of academic achievement: The interaction of children's achievement orientations with skill area. *Developmental Psychology, 20*(4), 628–636.

Maddi, S. R. (2002). The story of hardiness: Twenty years of theorizing, research, and practice. *Consulting Psychology Journal: Practice and Research, 54*(3), 173–185. doi:10.1037/1061-4087.54.3.173.

Mayer, J. D., Roberts, R. D., & Barsade, S. G. (2008). Human abilities: Emotional intelligence. *Annual Review of Psychology, 59*, 507–536.

Mayer, J. D., & Salovey, P. (1993). The intelligence of emotional intelligence. *Intelligence, 17*, 433–442.

Miller, W. R., & Seligman, M. E. P. (1975). Depression and learned helplessness in man, *Journal of Abnormal Psychology, 84*, 228–238.

Moosavi, E. A., & Ahadi, H. (2011). Hardiness and attributional styles as predictors of coping strategies and mental health. *Amity Journal of Applied Psychology, 2*(1), 3–10.

Mueller, C. M., & Dweck, C. S. (1998). Praise for intelligence can undermine children's motivation and performance. *Journal of Personality and Social Psychology, 75*(1), 33–52.

Roeser, R. W., Pintrich, P. R., & DeGroot, E. A. M. (1994). Classroom and individual differences in early adolescents' motivation and self-regulated learning. *Journal of Early Adolescence, 14*(2), 139–161.

Salovey, P., & Mayer, J. D. (1990). Emotional intelligence. *Imagination, Cognition, and Personality, 9*, 185–211. doi: 0.2190/DUGG-P24E-52WK-6CDG.

Seligman, M. E. P. (2011). *Authentic happiness. [Electronic resource]: Using the new positive psychology to realise your potential for lasting fulfilment.* London: Nicholas Brealey Publishing.

Seligman, M. E. P., & Csikszentmihalyi, M. (2000). Positive psychology: An introduction. *The American Psychologist, 5*(1), 5–14.

Seligman, M. E. P., Parks, A. C., & Steen, T. (2004). A balanced psychology and a full life. *Philosophical Transactions of the Royal Society of London. Series B, Biological Sciences, 359*(1449), 1379–1381.

Smiley, P. A., & Dweck, C. S. (1994). Individual differences in achievement goals among young children, *Child Development, 65*, 1723–1743.

Sorich, L. A., & Dweck C. (1997). *Psychological mediators of student achievement during the transition to junior high school.* Unpublished manuscript, Columbia University.

Wadey, R., Evans, L., Hanton, S., & Neil, R. (2012). An examination of hardiness throughout the sport-injury process: A qualitative follow-up study. *British Journal of Health Psychology, 17*(4), 872–893.

Zhao W., Dweck C., & Mueller C., (1998). *Implicit theories and depression like responses to failure.* Unpublished manuscript, New York University.

3

The Utility of Coping When Considering Resilience

In popular vernacular, resilience has acquired a meaning that is much like buoyancy, and the concept of 'bounce back' is frequently incorporated into the numerous definitions. It is applied to the economy, the community, and the individuals. Whilst well-validated approaches to measurement are yet to be developed, there is a greater clarity on how we assess individual resilience rather than collective or communal resilience. Assessment post-event can be an indicator of a resilient outcome whilst coping provides evidence of the process that leads to resilience. Moreover, coping has established predictive power for health and well-being (see series of studies in Chap. 5).

Resilience and coping are inextricably linked in that resilience generally refers to the ability to return to equilibrium despite adversity and exposure to setbacks. Having good coping resources is the key to the capacity for returning to equilibrium and achieving personal resilience. It is an asset that can be acquired.

According to Windle's (2011) definition, resilience is 'the process of effectively negotiating, adapting to, or managing significant sources of

---

How do you eat an elephant – one bite at a time. (Robyn, musician)

© The Author(s) 2017
E. Frydenberg, *Coping and the Challenge of Resilience*,
DOI 10.1057/978-1-137-56924-0_3

stress or trauma. Assets and resources within the individual, their life and environment facilitate this capacity for adaptation and recovery from adversity. During the life course, the experience of resilience will vary' (p. 153). Thus the definition recognises, as does coping theory, that individual assets and resources, as well as environmental ones, are critical for an outcome that can be considered to reflect resilience.

Trauma research and the interest in extreme stress have fuelled the initial focus on resilience over the past four to five decades. In recent years, coping theory has underpinned much of the interest in stress and resilience. Additionally, since there has been growing emphasis on the management of stress, the fields of stress, resilience, and coping have converged. Richard Lazarus's seminal book *Psychological Stress and the Coping Process* (Lazarus, 1966) showed the impact of stress on health-related outcomes such as anger, hostility, immune system, and vascular system, and demonstrated how to alleviate the impact of stress through coping. The field continued to grow for the next four to five decades until recent years when the focus on resilience has become dominant.

Historically, coping research has evolved from stress research and consistent with the positive psychology movement has moved from a deficit model of adaptation to exploring people's capacity to deal with life's circumstances and fulfil their potential rather than simply reacting to stress. Thus, increasingly coping research deals with how individuals can enhance their quality of life through use of effective coping strategies. There has been a shift in emphasis on the impact and outcome of stress to coping and how coping can mitigate the impact of stress.

The research field of coping has progressed significantly with the emergence of numerous ways to operationalise coping and utilising empirically developed tools so that it is possible to identify the ways in which coping can contribute to resilience and well-being.

Theories of Coping

Coping theory has dominated the literature for the last four decades as the interest on how humans adapt and manage the stresses that come their way has grown. These stresses range from the demands of everyday life through to major traumas that individuals may have to confront throughout the lifespan. As Chap. 2 illustrates coping theory can accommodate contemporary conceptualisations of positive psychology, hardiness, grit, mindset, and emotional intelligence. In simple terms, as noted in Chap. 1, coping is a dynamic process that relies on the interaction between persons and their environments and resilience can be construed as the outcome.

There are two major but complementary theories of how individuals cope with stress and trauma. The first is the transactional theory of Richard Lazarus and Susan Folkman (1984) who conceptualised coping as a transaction between individuals and their environments, and the second is the Conservation of Resources (COR) theory of Stevan Hobfoll (1989). Generally these broad but compatible theories can accommodate most contemporary research in the field. The two theories provide frameworks within which to understand coping.

Both major foundational approaches to coping research have evolved from conceptualisations of adult functioning and have subsequently been adapted and incorporated into the child and adolescent domains. The seminal transactional theory has been augmented by Stevan Hobfoll's COR theory and by future-oriented coping by Aspinwall and Taylor (1997) and proactive coping by Greenglass and Schwarzer (1998). Dyadic coping (Aldwin, 2010) has entered the literature (see Chap. 7) relatively recently. Coping research and practice has been applied in most contexts throughout the lifespan.

As was noted in Chap. 1, in the past five years resilience as a key term has outstripped coping in the research literature. Nevertheless, since coping is construed as the process and resilience the outcome the two constructs are inextricably linked. Much of the research in the last decade has focused on how individuals and groups deal with stress, adversities, loss, and challenging situations in life. The theoretical insights and practical applications of coping research have gone beyond the original goal of reducing stress to advance our understanding of human endeavour, facilitate well-being and resilience by measuring outcomes following interventions that are underpinned by sound theory.

Measurement has been, and remains, a significant feature of coping research and practice and is dealt with in detail in Chap. 4. Implications for practice and outcomes are considered in Chap. 5. This chapter focuses on the major theories of coping and discuss the relevance and significance of emotions. It also presents some directions as to how this vast field might continue to promote quality of life.

Similar to the early origins of resilience as the property of timber to withstand load without breaking, the term 'stress' has its origins in physics rather than in psychology and physiology. Essentially it was a term used in engineering to describe the effect of a mechanical force that places strain or pressure on an object. The physiological theories of stress focus on the arousal that occurs when an organism is under stress or threat and there is a response to the stress that may be adaptive in that there is an attempt to 'fight' or 'flee' the stress. If the stress persists, there is likely to be a harmful outcome for the organism (Cannon, 1989). Illness is often a result of the exertion or demand that is made on a particular physiological system. However, biological or genetic predisposition may play an important part in illness.[1]

Selye (1976, p. 472) described stress as 'the non-specific response of the body to any demands made upon it'. Selye makes the distinction between stress that mobilises the individual to effective performance, such as when there is heightened performance, which has been labelled 'eustress', and stress that is more negative and has been labelled 'distress'. He observed that the body would respond to any external biological source of stress with a predictable biological pattern in an attempt to restore the body's internal homeostasis. Stresses can be physical such as those pertaining to the environment, like extreme heat or cold, psychosocial stresses such as those experienced when relationships are not working, and daily hassles, such as having a disagreement with one's friend or partner. Early stress researchers such as Holmes and Rahe (1967) identified major life events as stresses. Since the mid-1960s, and particularly over the past three decades, there has been interest in how individuals deal with stress, that is, coping.

Coping emerged as a process in the latter half of the twentieth century through the work of theorists such as Pearlin and Schooler (1978),

---

[1] However, it should be noted that in recent years Shelley Taylor has challenged this theorising, saying that whilst it is true that in situations of extreme stress both males and females 'fight or flee', in situations which are not extreme females are more inclined to look after their young and join with their friends. She termed this 'tend and befriend' (Taylor, 2010).

Lazarus and Folkman (1984), Billings and Moos (1984), and Kobasa (1979) to name a few. A range of different approaches was devised to study the antecedents of, and the relationship between, coping and a given set of outcomes (e.g., personality characteristics) (Saklofske, Austin, Mastoras, Beaton, & Osborne, 2012), and the nature of stressful events (Shanan, De-Nour, & Garty, 1976; Weigold & Robitschek, 2011).

Appraisal Theory

Richard Lazarus launched the field with his seminal book *Psychological Stress and the Coping Process* (Lazarus, 1966) in which he had an interest in maximising immune functioning and removing harmful effects on the cardiovascular system. However, the impact of his interest in coping had a far wider reach in terms of influencing research agendas and output. In 1984, Lazarus and Folkman, in foreshadowing the theory on coping, described stress as the mismatch between the perceived demands of a situation and the individual's assessment of his or her resources to deal with these demands. Considering coping as 'constantly changing cognitive and behavioral efforts to manage specific external and/or internal demands that are appraised as taxing or exceeding the resources of the person' (Lazarus & Folkman, 1984, p. 141) remains the most frequently cited definition. This definition addresses the cognitive, affective, and behavioural aspects of the coping process and also focuses on the effort associated with an individual's response. Moving beyond the traditional view of coping as mastery over the environment, Lazarus and Folkman (1984) broaden the process of coping to include accepting, tolerating, avoiding, or minimising the stressors, and all purposeful attempts to manage stress regardless of their effectiveness. The key elements of this transactional theory of coping by Lazarus and Folkman are the person, the environment, and the appraisal process. Coping is hence viewed as a dynamic process that changes over time as it responds to demands, following appraisals, both objective and subjective.

The Lazarus and Folkman's conceptualisation rests firmly on the concept of appraisal which may occur unconsciously at an automatic level (Lazarus, 1991, 1993). During primary appraisal, one assesses whether a situation is one of threat (i.e., potential future harm); harm/loss (that has occurred) or challenges (i.e., how we can learn or gain confidence from this experience). The person then examines whether he or she has the resources (both internal and external) to cope (secondary appraisal) and followed by an evaluation of the coping strategy post coping (tertiary appraisal). The complex interaction between persons and their environments means that appraisal and coping actions are impacted by the environment and how one copes, which in turn impacts the environment. Emotions contribute to the dynamic and are in turn impacted by what happens between persons and their environments (Fig. 3.1).

Two dimensions of coping, emotion- and problem-based, are addressed by this model. Whilst emotion-based coping attempts to reduce negative emotion states or appraisal of demands through strategies such as avoiding, distancing, accepting or seeking emotional support, problem-based coping attempts to change negative emotions and stress through generating and evaluating alternative solutions that may involve learning new skills to manage stresses. As Folkman (2011) recently pointed out

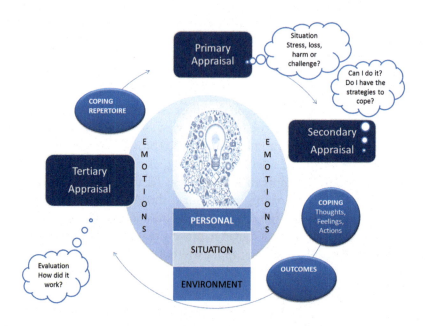

Fig. 3.1 Appraisal theory of coping

'coping is a critical point of entry for protecting mental and physical health from the harmful effects of stress' (p. 453). Folkman acknowledges that although the Lazarus and Folkman (1984) model of stress has stood the test of time, it is not free of problems and limitations. For example, there is an overlap of the primary and secondary appraisal processes. That is, a situation is more likely to be appraised as stressful if an individual does not perceive that they have the strategies to cope. Additionally, it could be difficult to label factors that determine stress. Folkman and Moskowitz (2000) identified meaning-focused coping (see Chap. 10), where positive emotions occur and meaning and purpose are ascribed to a stressful event, as the third function of coping as distinct from the problem- and emotion-focused conceptualisations. Folkman highlights the strength of the approach as being the fact that it is individualised, and it is preceded by antecedents such as biology, developmental stage, and in a particular setting with social and material resources (Folkman, 2010).

Conservation of Resources (COR)

The complementary, but equally important, conceptualisation of coping is the Conservation of Resources model, COR (Hobfoll, 1989, 2010), which is based on a single motivational tenet, that individuals seek to acquire, maintain, and protect that which they value. COR provides an integrated model of stress that complements the appraisal theory of coping. Stress occurs when there is a loss of resources, a threat of loss, or when the individual invests resources without getting adequate return for effort. An adequate return for investment fosters self-esteem and confidence by building up one's resource pool.

Resources include objects (e.g., home, clothes, food), personal characteristics (e.g., being optimistic, mastery), conditions that allow you to obtain other resources (e.g., being married, employed or living with someone provides social support, more financial security), and energies (e.g., time, money, knowledge). COR theory posits that people do not wait for disaster to strike. They invest in resources, that is, take out insurance or purchase future protection, for example, by investing time and energy in relationships. In that sense this aspect of the framework is proactive rather than reactive.

People strive to develop a resource surplus to offset the possibility of future loss. Resource surpluses are likely to be associated with eustress (positive well-being) rather than distress. Self-protection is about trying to protect against resource loss. We invest time and energy and love and affection in the expectation of the return of the same. Power and money are important resources that allow us to accumulate other resources. The concept of loss is central to COR theory. It posits that gain is important but secondary to loss. That is, the impact of loss is far stronger and longer lasting than the benefit of gain. In other words, we generally take grieve far longer when experiencing a setback or loss than when we celebrate our wins. Most severe stress events relate to loss. However, with COR theory there is the notion that individuals can shift the focus of attention from loss by reinterpreting a threat as a challenge, which can be construed as a positive aspect of coping. Stress occurs when there is a loss of resources, or a threat of loss. For example, the model proposes that work-family conflict leads to stress because resources (e.g., time, energy) 'are lost in the process of juggling both work and family roles' (p. 352), which in turn leads to job dissatisfaction, anxiety, and thoughts about quitting one's job. Individual difference variables, such as self-esteem, are treated as resources that may moderate the relationship between work-family conflict and stress.

This is essentially a 'balance sheet' or 'ledger' view of stress and coping that has its basis in existential and biological theories of human adaptation. It is the resource side of the balance sheet that needs to be monitored so that it can be augmented to a level that provides protection and enables advancement.

According to Hobfoll (1989), the emphasis of COR theory is on objective elements of threat and loss and 'common appraisals' by people who share a biology and culture. The emphasis is on the circumstances that occur rather than the appraisals. One of the core themes in COR is that the threat of loss leads to increased risk aversion and protection of assets. COR was born out of the study of how communities cope with natural disasters and how resource-challenged regions continually operate in a state of depleted resources. Yet, there are regions which demonstrate remarkable resilience in face of repeated disasters by engaging in proactive coping interventions such as increasing resource pools within the community (Zamani, Gorgievski-Duijvesteijn, & Zarafshani, 2006). This approach is aligned with positive psychology with a focus on how proactive coping through optimising of resources, contributes to resilience and capacity to thrive beyond survival. To assist with thriving there are 'caravan passageways', that is, the environmental conditions that support, foster, enrich and protect the resources of individuals, families, and organisations, or that detract, undermine, obstruct, or impoverish people's resource reservoirs. It is not the number of resources that alone matter but the way they combine in the 'caravan' to serve the individual.

One of Hobfoll's underlying principles is paradoxical, in that resource loss is more potent than resource gain, but the salience of gain increases under situations of resource loss (Wells, Hobfoll, & Lavin, 1999). Others have highlighted the detrimental effect of loss and the efforts that are required to overcome the impact. Gains have a positive connotation but losses are strongly negatively linked to poorer recovery. This is consistent with the work of others such as Kahneman and Tversky (2013) who demonstrated that it is more unpleasant to lose than it is pleasant to win. Whilst it is difficult to predict or identify that which is going to restore the equilibrium, socio-economic status is amongst the best predictors of mental health. Most neighbourhood factors supersede family factors (Rutter, 2012). Additionally, the impact of social support (see Chap. 6) is one of the most robust single markers of resiliency resources, after socio-economic status and race are accounted for (Schumm, Briggs-Phillips, & Hobfoll, 2006).

Consistent with their theoretical approaches, Lazarus and Folkman and Hobfoll have operationalised coping, the former with the Ways of Coping Questionnaire (WOC) (Folkman & Lazarus, 1980) and Hobfoll with the Strategic Approaches to Coping Scale (1998). However, emotions underpin both approaches in that emotions play a key part in the coping process.

Coping and Emotions

The relationship between coping and emotion is important in that coping is traditionally viewed as a response to emotion and as possessing the function of arousal or tension reduction. Studies have broadened this perspective based on cognitive and relational principles to explore the dynamic, and mutually reciprocal, relationship between emotions and coping (Folkman & Lazarus, 1988). In any encounter, there can be multiple emotions such as feeling sad and happy at the same time and each emotion determines how an encounter is appraised; so the outcome in turn determines the individual's emotional state both in the ongoing interaction and in future interactions. Folkman and Lazarus (1988) distinguish this from the Darwinian approach, where emotions, like fear and anger, are thought to stimulate behaviours that are conducive to survival in the face of threat and also from the ego psychological approach which includes reference to cognitive processes like denial, repression, suppression, intellectualisation, and problem solving in an effort to reduce stress and anxiety.

The ability to regulate emotions is addressed comprehensively in the developmental literature. Understanding the role of affect, that is, how different emotions such as fear, worry, anxiety, sadness, and anger promote or impede their efforts to appraise, manage, and respond to feedback on the success of an individual's efforts (Aspinwall, 2005).

Although there is no single definition of emotion there is general agreement that emotion is a complex psychological state that involves three distinct components: a subjective experience, a physiological response, and a response that is expressed through behaviour (Hockenbury & Hockenbury, 2001). The metaphoric representations of negative emotions such as anger or hate generally portray such emotions as an irresistible force. Thus in the literature on emotion-focused coping, much effort has been directed to examining maladaptive strategies that aim to reduce and manage the intensity of the negative and distressing emotions that a stressful situation has caused rather than solving the problematic situation itself. A more functionalist perspective of emotions has focused on the adaptive nature of emotions and how individuals can organise social communication, goal achievement, and cognitive processes from an early age (Mahoney, 1991; Thompson, 1994; Ekman, 1994; Greenberg & Safran, 1987; Izard, 1993; Smith, 1991). Research has also focused on how emotions are closely related to the regulation of actions and action tendencies, with less emphasis on modulating feeling or on controlling expression. Three theoretical constructs exemplify a functionalist view of emotions in personality research, namely, emotional competence (Saarni, 1997), emotional intelligence (Salovey & Mayer, 1990), and emotional creativity (Averill & Thomas-Knowles, 1991). All contribute to healthy interpersonal and intrapersonal functioning. Emotional competence is essentially self-efficacy in the context of 'emotion-eliciting social transactions' (Saarni, 1997, p. 38).

According to the broaden-and-build theory of positive emotions (Fredrickson, 2004), the positive affect provides the 'psychological lift' that allows individuals to broaden their awareness and encourages a range of thoughts and actions that are more inspiring, pleasant, and creative. In that way people are able to build resilience and protection against future negative events. The adaptational aspects of positive emotions during periods of chronic stress have been explored, particularly by Folkman and her colleagues as they examined emotions, coping, and resilience of caregivers in various settings. According to Fredrickson (2004), positive emotions broaden the scope of attention, cognition, and action and help build physical, intellectual, and social resources.

In line with the appraisal theory of coping (Lazarus and Folkman, 1984), the appraisal of a threat is associated with anxiety or fear and harm and loss with sadness, which are negative emotions, whilst challenge is associated with positive emotions such as excitement, eagerness, and confidence. Consistent with the appraisal conceptualisation, Richard Lazarus (2000) has argued for a more balanced approach to positive psychology where we take account of the negative emotions as well as the positive ones. Alternatively, one could argue that negative emotions are addressed comprehensively in the clinical literature and the interventions are heavily focused on their management.

The case for positive emotions in the stress process was highlighted by Folkman (2008). She pointed out that positive emotions have a distinct part to play that is different from those that regulate distress. Positive emotions have a restorative function with respect to physiological, psychological, and social coping resources. Positive emotions can generate benefit finding, reminding, adaptive goal processes, reordering priorities, and infusing meaning into normal events.

Indeed, Susan Folkman presaged the current interest in models of resilience in her work on coping as she focused on positive adaptations to stressful life experiences. Folkman's work on HIV/AIDS patients and their carers focused on positive emotions despite 'worst case scenarios'. Lazarus, Kanner, and Folkman (1980) reported three important adaptive functions of positive emotions, namely, sustaining coping efforts, providing a breather, and restoring depleted resources.

Stress, Positive Emotions, and Coping

Folkman (1997), in a study that monitored gay men who had been caregivers for partners with HIV/AIDS for more than five years reported positive affect as frequently as negative affect except immediately after the death of a partner (Folkman, 1997). Positive reappraisal provides opportunities for personal growth and seeing one's efforts as benefiting others. Positive reappraisal was associated with positive emotions. Problem-focused coping, such as developing a to-do list, created positive emotions. Creating positive events is like creating positive psychological 'time out' like enjoying the sunset, which infuses ordinary events with positive meaning. For example, 'smelling the roses' or finding humour in a situation reduces tension as well as giving pleasure.

However, the above study addressed the frequency of emotions rather than the duration, and there is evidence that positive emotions are less enduring than negative emotions (Folkman, Moskowitz, Ozer, & Park, 1997). Stressful conditions can make self-regulation behaviours more challenging. It could be that both positive and negative affect are experienced, and it is postulated that they could be a continuum (bipolar, i.e., at two ends of the continuum). They co-occur but not simultaneously.

Self-regulation is vital to performance in life (Baumeister & Exline, 2000). Both intensity and frequency of positive emotions may have helped overcome the effects of depletion and resulted in better performance on role functioning. Coping and emotions are both dynamic. There is inherent variability in terms of persons and situations. However, there is a reciprocal relationship in that when there is an experience of positive emotions, there is more likely to be positive coping and vice versa. There is a place for targeting emotions as well as teaching coping skills. When it has come to intervention studies, most interventions have not given much attention to positive emotions.

Seligman, Parks, and Steen (2004) also argue for a more balanced approach in positive psychology where we take account of the negative emotions as well as the positive ones. The longitudinal study of caregiving and bereavement in the context of HIV/AIDS conducted in 2009 with 253 gay men fuelled Folkman and Moskowitz's interest in studying the role of positive emotions. The findings since then have been replicated with maternal caregivers of children with HIV and other chronic illnesses (Moskowitz, Shmueli-Blumberg, Acree, & Folkman, 2012). Positive emotions do not only occur when people live under highly favourable circumstances. When it comes to high-stress, health-related situations, there is the possibility of both harm and benefit as the result of the experience. Harm or threat is usually accompanied by negative emotions such as anger, sadness, or worry whilst the appraisal of benefit is usually accompanied by positive emotions such as relief, gratitude, or happiness.

Concluding Remarks

In sum, there is a complex dynamic interaction between emotions and coping in social encounters and the process is multifaceted and continually evolving according to the changing status of the person-environment relationship. Coping is underpinned by the cognitive appraisal processes, before, during, and after an encounter. The early appraisal conceptualisation of coping has been augmented by resource theories of coping. Both can be applied to everyday life events as well as to high-stress, traumatic experiences. The more recent recognition of the important part that both positive and negative emotions play when the demands are high highlights the benefit of understanding emotions in the context of the coping process and how skills can be developed to better serve the individual in a range of circumstances.

References

Aldwin, C. (2010). Stress and coping across the lifespan. In *The Oxford handbook of stress, health, and coping* (pp. 15–34). Oxford, UK: Oxford University Press. doi:10.1093/oxfordhb/9780195375343.013.0002.

Aspinwall, L. G. (2005). The psychology of future-oriented thinking: From achievement to proactive coping, adaptation, and aging. *Motivation and Emotion, 29*(4), 203–235.

Aspinwall, L. G., & Taylor, S. E. (1997). A stitch in time: Self-regulation and proactive coping. *Psychological Bulletin, 121*(3), 417.

Averill, J. R., & Thomas-Knowles, C. (1991). Emotional creativity. In K. T. Strongman (Ed.), *International review of studies on emotion* (Vol. 1, pp. 269–299). New York: Wiley.

Baumeister, R. F., & Exline, J. J. (2000). Self-control, morality, and human strength. *Journal of Social and Clinical Psychology, 19*(1), 29–42.

Billings, A. G., & Moos, R. H. (1984). Coping, stress, and social resources among adults with unipolar depression. *Journal of Personality and Social Psychology, 46*(4), 877–891.

Cannon, W. B. (1989). *Wisdom of the body* (Special ed.). Birmingham, AL: Classics of Medicine Library.

Ekman, P. (1994). All emotions are basic. In P. Ekman & R. J. Davidson (Eds.), *The nature of emotion: Fundamental questions* (pp. 15–19). New York: Oxford University Press.

Folkman, S. (1997). Positive psychological states and coping with severe stress. *Social Science & Medicine, 45*(8), 1207–1221, 1215.

Folkman, S. (2008). The case for positive emotions in the stress process. *Anxiety, Stress, and Coping, 21*(1), 3–14.

Folkman, S. (2010). Stress, coping, and hope. *Psycho-Oncology, 19*(9), 901–908. doi:10.1002/pon.1836.

Folkman, S. (2011). *The Oxford handbook of stress, health, and coping.* Oxford/New York: Oxford University Press.

Folkman, S., & Lazarus, R. S. (1980). An analysis of coping in a middle-aged community sample. *Journal of Health and Social Behavior, 21*, 219.

Folkman, S., & Lazarus, R. S. (1988). The relationship between coping and emotion: Implications for theory and research. *Social Science & Medicine (1982), 26*(3), 309–317.

Folkman, S., & Moskowitz, J. T. (2000). Stress, positive emotion, and coping. *Current Directions in Psychological Science, 9*(4), 115–118. doi:10.1111/1467-8721.00073.

Folkman, S., Moskowitz, J. T., Ozer, E. M., & Park, C. L. (1997). Positive meaningful events and coping in the context of HIV/AIDS. In B. H. Gottlieb (Ed.), *Coping with chronic stress* (pp. 293–314). New York: Plenum.

Fredrickson, B. L. (2004). The Broaden-and-Build theory of positive emotions. *Philosophical Transactions of the Royal Society of London, 359*, 1367–1377.

Greenberg, L. S., & Safran, J. D. (1987). *Emotion in psychotherapy: Affect, cognition, and the process of change.* New York: Guilford.

Greenglass, E., & Schwarzer, R. (1998). The Proactive Coping Inventory (PCI). In R. Schwarzer (Ed.), *Advances in health psychology research* (CD-ROM). Berlin, Germany: Free University of Berlin. Institut for Arbeits, Organizations- und Gesundheitspsychologie. (IBN 3-00-002776-9).

Hobfoll, S. E. (1989). Conservation of resources: A new attempt at conceptualizing stress. *The American Psychologist, 44*(3), 513–524.

Hobfoll, S. E. (1998). *Stress culture and community: The psychology and philosophy of stress.* New York: Plenum Press.

Hobfoll, S. E. (2010). *Conservation of resources theory: Its implication for stress, health, and resilience.* New York: Oxford University Press.

Hockenbury, D. H., & Hockenbury, S. E. (2001). *Discovering psychology.* New York: Worth Publishers.

Holmes, T. H., & Rahe, R. H. (1967). The social readjustment rating scale. *Journal of Psychosomatic Research, 11*(2), 213–218.

Izard, C. E. (1993). Organizational and motivational functions of discrete emotions. In M. Lewis & J. Haviland (Eds.), *Handbook of emotions* (pp. 631–641). New York: Guilford.

Kahneman, D., & Tversky, A. (2013). Prospect theory: An analysis of decision under risk. In L. C. MacLean & W. T. Ziemba (Eds.), *Handbook of the fundamentals of financial decision making. Part I, World scientific handbook in financial economics series* (Vol. 4, pp. 99–127). Hackensack, NJ/Singapore: World Scientific.

Kobasa, S. C. (1979). Stressful life events, personality, and health: An inquiry into hardiness. *Journal of Personality and Social Psychology, 37*(1), 1–11.

Lazarus, R. S. (1966). *Psychological stress and the coping process.* New York: McGraw-Hill.

Lazarus, R. S. (1991). *Emotion and adaption.* New York: Oxford University Press.

Lazarus, R. S. (1993). Coping theory and research: Past, present, and future. *Psychosomatic Medicine, 55*(3), 234–247.

Lazarus, R. S. (2000). Toward better research on stress and coping. *The American Psychologist, 55*(6), 665–673.

Lazarus, R. S., & Folkman, S. (1984). *Stress, appraisal, and coping.* New York: Springer.

Lazarus, R. S., Kanner, A., & Folkman, S. (1980). Emotions: A cognitive phenomenological analysis. In R. Plutchik & H. Kellerman (Eds.), *Emotion- Theory research and experience: Vol. I. Theories of emotion.* New York: Academic Press.

Mahoney, M. J. (1991). *Human change processes: The scientific foundations of psychotherapy.* New York: Basic Books.

Moskowitz, J. T., Shmueli-Blumberg, D., Acree, M., & Folkman, S. (2012). Positive affect in the midst of distress: Implications for role functioning. *Journal of Community and Applied Social Psychology, 22*(6), 502–518. doi:10.1002/casp.1133.

Pearlin, L. I., & Schooler, C. (1978). The structure of coping. *Journal of Health and Social Behavior, 19*(1), 2–21.

Rutter, M. (2012). Resilience as a dynamic concept. *Development and Psychopathology, 24*(2), 335–344. doi:10.1017/S0954579412000028.

Saarni, C. (1997). Emotional competence and self-regulation in childhood. In P. Salovey & D. Sluyter (Eds.), *Emotional development and emotional intelligence: Educational implications* (pp. 35–66). New York: Basic Books.

Saklofske, D. H., Austin, E. J., Mastoras, S. M., Beaton, L., & Osborne, S. E. (2012). Relationships of personality, affect, emotional intelligence and coping with student stress and academic success: Different patterns of association for stress and success. *Learning and Individual Differences, 22*, 251–257. doi:10.1016/j.lindif.2011.02.010.

Salovey, P., & Mayer, J. D. (1990). Emotional intelligence. *Imagination, Cognition, and Personality, 9*, 185–211 .doi: 0.2190/DUGG-P24E-52WK-6CDG.

Schumm, J. A., Briggs-Phillips, M., & Hobfoll, S. E. (2006). Cumulative interpersonal traumas and social support as risk and resiliency factors in predicting PTSD and depression among inner-city women. *Journal of Traumatic Stress, 19*(6), 825–836.

Seligman, M. E. P., Parks, A. C., & Steen, T. (2004). A balanced psychology and a full life. *Philosophical Transactions of the Royal Society of London. Series B, Biological Sciences, 359*(1449), 1379–1381.

Selye, H. (1976). *Stress in health and disease.* Boston, MA: Butterworths, c1976.

Shanan, J., De-Nour, A. K., & Garty, I. (1976). Effects of prolonged stress on coping style in terminal renal failure patients. *Journal of Human Stress, 2*(4), 19.

Smith, C. A. (1991). The self, appraisal, and coping. In C. R. Snyder & D. R. Forsyth (Eds.), *Handbook for social and clinical psychology: The health perspective* (pp. 116–137). Elmsford, NY: Pergamon.

Taylor, S. E. (2010). *Health handbook of social psychology.* Hoboken: Wiley.

Thompson, R. A. (1994). Emotion regulation: A theme in search of definition. *Monographs of the Society for Research in Child Development, 59*, 25–52.

Weigold, I. K., & Robitschek, C. (2011). Agentic personality characteristics and coping: Their relation to trait anxiety in college students. *American Journal of Orthopsychiatry, 81*(2), 255–264.

Wells, J. D., Hobfoll, S. E., & Lavin, J. (1999). When it rains, pours: The greater impact of resource loss compared to gain on psychological distress. *Personality and Social Psychology Bulletin, 25*(9), 1172–1182.

Windle, G. (2011). What is resilience? A review and concept analysis. *Reviews in Clinical Gerontology, 21*(2), 152–169, 118p. doi:10.1017/S0959259810000420.

Zamani, G. H., Gorgievski-Duijvesteijn, M. J., & Zarafshani, K. (2006). Coping with drought: Towards a multilevel understanding based on conservation of resources theory. *Human Ecology, 34*, 677.

4

The Measurement of Coping

Resilience has been variously defined as the capacity to successfully adapt in the face of adversity with a capacity for growth (see Chap. 1). Resilience, like coping, is reliant on both internal and external resources and the capacity to go beyond recovery. It is about identifying and developing the internal resources and the capacity to access external resources in the service of the individual. In contrast to coping, the measure of resilience has been elusive, mainly because it is difficult to predict how an individual will react in any given situation. However, when it comes to coping it is possible to be situation specific as well as consider how one would adapt in general. It is both possible to measure coping and utilise its predictive powers. Furthermore, what makes it such a useful construct is that it is possible to build an individual's coping resources so as to enhance their capacities to adapt. Thus, coping is an applied construct that has relevance to the diverse social and cultural contexts in which individuals find themselves. The process determines the resilient outcomes.

I believe in the glass table. If you have an issue and you keep it under the table you can't see it or touch it so it can't be deal with. I say at every meeting 'put the issue on the table because then we can all see it and deal with it and move it. You're not going to get rid of it by ignoring it.' (Doug, company director)

© The Author(s) 2017
E. Frydenberg, *Coping and the Challenge of Resilience*,
DOI 10.1057/978-1-137-56924-0_4

The measurement of resilience is a relatively recent phenomenon with a range of instruments that are diverse in what they measure. In contrast, coping measurement is well developed with a range of valid and reliable tools available to assess skills across the lifespan. Coping can be assessed in children, adolescents, and adults both to provide an understanding of population trends and differences and with an explicit intent to provide resources for self-reflection and help identify thoughts, emotions, and actions that can be changed to develop an individual's coping responses. The extensions of the heuristic devices that represent coping are reflected in the tools that have been available for the past three to four decades to measure the construct. This chapter builds on the conceptualisation of coping by Folkman and Lazarus as reflected in their original Ways of Coping Questionnaire (WOC) (Folkman & Lazarus, 1980) and that of Hobfoll's Strategic Approaches to Coping Scale (1998) which was based on the multi-axial model of coping (Hobfoll, Dunahoo, Ben-Porath, & Monnier, 1994).

More specifically, this chapter will focus on several measurement tools, namely, the Adolescent Coping Scale (ACS, ACS-2; Frydenberg & Lewis, 1993, 2011) and the Coping Scale for Adults (CSA, CSA-2; Frydenberg & Lewis, 1997, 2014). These tools have been widely used for both research and clinical purposes and provide rich insights into what is known about coping and how coping skills can be best developed. Additionally, the more recent Children's Coping Scale (Yeo, Frydenberg, Northam, & Deans, 2014) is a parent-reported instrument that provides a picture of children's coping. In subsequent chapters, particularly in Chap. 5, the key findings using these measurement tools for assessment and evaluation will be highlighted as exemplars of what we know in the field of coping. Overall the focus is on how these tools can be used in the service of developing resilience.

Coping is a complex multidimensional construct that is sensitive to the demands and resources available in the environment, the appraisal of the stressor and the appraisal of the individual of his/her own resources or capacities to cope (Folkman & Moskowitz, 2003; Folkman, 2004). Both the nature of the stressor and the characteristics of the individual influence the outcome (2004).

Skinner, Edge, Altman, and Sherwood (2003) reviewed 1000 different coping category systems and found that only four were empirically constructed, theory based, and subjected to confirmatory statistical techniques rather than exploratory analytic methodologies that are guided by ad hoc and intuitive judgements.

As early as 1978 Pearlin and Schooler pointed out that 'Coping, in sum, is certainly not a unidimensional behaviour. It functions at a number of levels and is attainted by a plethora of behaviours, cognitions and perceptions' (pp. 7–8). Early measurement of coping focused on adult populations. Interest in the assessment of how younger people cope emerged in the late 1980s when the coping literature turned its attention to coping in childhood (Compas, 1987). In their comprehensive review of coping scales, Aldwin and Werner (2007) identified 200 references to different coping scales with 51 of these being in the child and adolescent arena. Generally, coping instruments have been developed through self-reports, semistructured interviews, daily diary recordings, observation of behaviour, and the reports of significant others, such as parents, teachers, and peers. The many ways to assess coping generally have in common a set of descriptions or single actions which are grouped into coping strategies where there is a similarity of concept or ideation. These in turn can be further grouped more broadly into everyday practice. The most common categorisation or grouping of approaches to coping is the dichotomous grouping of strategies by Lazarus and Folkman (1984) and Lazarus (1993), which identifies problem- and emotion-focused coping. Alternative categorisations range from groupings of eight to ten strategies or scales (e.g., Spirito, Overholser, & Stark, 1989).

The first two levels of coping, actions and strategies, encompass an exceptionally wide range of thoughts and behaviours (see Skinner et al., 2003) for a comprehensive summary of strategies. In order to create parsimonious research tools and conceptualisations of the coping construct, researchers have undertaken inductive measures (e.g., Exploratory Factor Analysis) to construct smaller scales of coping strategies. The Coping Scale for Adults (CSA, CSA-2; Frydenberg & Lewis, 1997, 2014) outlines 19 coping strategies for the CSA and 20 for the CSA-2. Similarly the Adolescent Coping Scale (ACS, ACS-2; Frydenberg & Lewis, 1993, 2011) has 19 strategies for the ACS and 20 strategies in the ACS-2 (see Table 4.1).

Coping actions are the first level; coping strategies are the second level, and perhaps the most difficult level of coping to categorise is the

Table 4.1 Coping strategies on ACS-2 and CSA-2 and their conceptual definitions

ACS-2	CSA-2
Productive (problem-solving) style: 11 coping strategies	Productive coping style: Eight coping strategies
Social support (SocSup) is represented by items which indicate an inclination to share the problem with others and enlist support in its management, e.g., *look for support and encouragement from others*	**Wishful thinking (WishThink)** is characterised by items which are based on hope and anticipation of a positive outcome, e.g., *imagine that things will work out well*
Focus on solving the problem (SolvProb) is a strategy which tackles the problem systematically by learning about it, taking into account different points of view or options, e.g., *work out a way of dealing with the problem*	**Improve relationships (ImpRel)** is about improving close relationships, e.g., *get into or improve on existing special relationships: partner, spouse, boy/girl friend*
Physical recreation (PhysRec) is characterised by items which relate to playing sport and keeping fit, e.g., *keep fit and healthy: play a sport.*	**Ignore the problem (Ignore)** is characterised by items which reflect a conscious blocking out of the problem, e.g., *put the problem out of my mind.*
Seek relaxing diversions (Relax) is about relaxation in general rather than about sport. It is characterised by items which describe leisure activities such as reading and painting, e.g., *relax: watch TV, play computer games, go for a walk*	**Humour (Humour)** consists of items involving entertaining others, e.g., *try to be funny*
Invest in close friends (Friends) is about engaging in a particular intimate relationship, e.g., *spend more time with a good friend*	**Seek spiritual support (Spirit)** is comprised of items which reflect prayer, and belief in the assistance of a spiritual leader or higher power, e.g., *pray for help and guidance so that everything will be all right*
Work hard and achieve (Work) is a factor describing commitment, ambition (achieve well), and industry, e.g., *work hard*	**Protect self (ProtSelf)** involves improving one's self-image by looking after oneself, particularly through one's appearance, e.g., *improve my appearance*

Table 4.1 (continued)

ACS-2	CSA-2
Productive (problem-solving) style: 11 coping strategies	Productive coping style: Eight coping strategies
Focus on the positive (*FocPos*) is represented by items which indicate a positive and cheerful outlook on the current situation. This includes seeing the 'bright side' of circumstances and seeing oneself as fortunate, e.g., *look on the bright side of things and think of all that is good*	**Focus on the positive (*FocPos*)** is represented by items which indicate a positive and cheerful outlook on the current situation. This includes seeing the 'bright side' of circumstances and seeing oneself as fortunate, e.g., *look on the bright side of things and think of all that is good*
Accept one's best efforts (*Accept*) is characterised by items which indicate an acceptance of having done one's best and therefore there is nothing further to be done, e.g., *accept things as they are because I've done my best*	**Seek relaxing diversions (*Relax*)** is about relaxation in general rather than about sport. It is characterised by items which describe leisure time with friends and family such as reading, watching a movie, or listening to music, e.g., *make time for friends or family*
Social action (*SocAct*) is about letting others know your concerns and enlisting support by writing petitions or organising an activity such as a meeting or a rally, e.g., *join with others to deal with the problem: organise a petition, attend a meeting*	
Seek professional help (*ProfHelp*) denotes the use of a professional adviser, such as a teacher or counsellor, e.g., *ask a teacher or other professional person for help.*	
Humour (*Humour*) is characterised by items which involve entertaining others, e.g., *try to be funny*	
***Nonproductive (passive avoidant) style*: Nine strategies**	***Nonproductive coping style*: Five strategies**
Worry (*Worry*) is characterised by items, which indicate concern about the future in general terms or more specifically concern with happiness in the future, e.g., *worry about what will happen to me*	**Dwell on the negative (*DwellNeg*)** is a strategy whereby a person focuses on the negative, e.g., *I keep thinking about my failures*

(continued)

Table 4.1 (continued)

ACS-2	CSA-2
Nonproductive (passive avoidant) style: Nine strategies	*Nonproductive coping style*: Five strategies
Wishful thinking (*WishThink*) is characterised by items which are based on hope and anticipation of a positive outcome, e.g., *wish a miracle would happen to make things turn out well*	**Self-blame (*SelfBlame*)** is characterised by items which indicate that an individual sees him/herself as responsible for the concern or worry, e.g., *blame myself*
Not coping (*NotCope*) consists of items which reflect the individual's inability to deal with the problem and the development of psychosomatic symptoms, e.g., *I get sick*	**Worry (*Worry*)** is described by items which indicate concern about what is happening and what may happen in the future, e.g., *worry about what is happening*
Ignore the problem (*Ignore*) is a style which reflects a conscious blocking out of the problem and resignation coupled with an acceptance that there is no way of dealing with it, e.g., *shut myself off from the problem so I can try and ignore it*	**Not coping (*NotCope*)** consists of items which reflect the individual's inability to deal with the problem and the development of psychosomatic symptoms, e.g., *I get sick*
Keep to self (*KeepSelf*) is characterised by items which reflect the individual's withdrawal from others and wish to keep others from knowing about concerns, e.g., *don't let others know about my problem.*	**Tension reduction (*TensRed*)** is a strategy which focuses on making oneself feel better by releasing tension, e.g., *find a way to let off steam: cry, scream, drink, take drugs*
Self-blame (*SelfBlame*) is characterised by items which indicate that an individual sees him/herself as responsible for the concern or worry, e.g., *blame myself*	
Act up (*ActUp*) is characterised by items which reflect an attempt to make oneself feel better by releasing tension, e.g., *act up and make life difficult for those around me*	*Problem solving style*: Four strategies
Seek spiritual support (*Spirit*) is comprised of items which reflect prayer and belief in the assistance of a spiritual leader or Lord, e.g., *pray to God to look after me*	**Focus on solving the problem (*SolvProb*)** is a strategy which analyses and tackles the problem, e.g., *develop a plan of action*

Table 4.1 (continued)

ACS-2	CSA-2
Nonproductive (passive avoidant) style: Nine strategies	**Nonproductive coping style**: Five strategies
Tension reduction (*TensRed*) is an attempt to make oneself better by releasing tension, e.g., *letting off steam, crying, screaming, using alcohol, cigarettes, or drugs*	**Seek professional help (*ProfHelp*)** denotes consultation with a professional adviser, such as a counsellor, e.g., *discuss the problem with qualified people*
	Social action (*SocAct*) is about letting others know what is of concern and enlisting support by attending or organising activities such as meetings or rallies, e.g., *go to meetings which look at the problem*
	Social support (*SocSup*) is represented by items indicating an inclination to share the problem with others and enlist support in its management, e.g., *talk to other people about my concern to help me sort it out*
	Other
	Work hard and achieve (*Work*) is a factor describing increasing one's focus on his or her work, commitment, ambition (achieve well), and industry, e.g., *focus on my work*
	Physical recreation (*PhysRec*) is characterised by items which relate to playing a sport and keeping fit, e.g., *play a sport*
	Keep to self (*KeepSelf*) is characterised by items which reflect the individual's wish to keep concerns to himself or herself, e.g., *don't let others know how I am feeling*

third level—coping styles. This level aims to provide the simplest, most 'full' account of coping into which all lower instances can be organised. Skinner et al. (2003) assert that this level of coping must also 'meaningfully link these [coping] actions with longer term processes of adaptation and development, and categories must be organised with respect to their function' (p. 217). Various frameworks have attempted this task, including those proposing functional distinctions, for example, problem-focused versus emotion-focused coping (Folkman & Lazarus, 1980; Lazarus & Folkman, 1984), topological distinctions, for example, approach versus avoidance (Anshel & Si, 2008; Moos & Schaefer, 1993), and distinctions that identify higher order action categories, for example, productive versus nonproductive coping (Frydenberg & Lewis, 1993, 1997, 2002a, b). Each of these categorisations offer advancements and limitations in how coping is measured and conceptualised, and together provide important insight into the complex coping construct.

Productive and Nonproductive Coping

In psychological research, distinctions which facilitate improved well-being are of high value. The distinction between productive and nonproductive coping is one such example. Productive strategies refer to coping efforts (either emotion-focused or problem-focused) that are generally helpful in dealing with a problem (e.g., problem solving, seeking social support, physical recreation), whereas nonproductive strategies appear largely unhelpful in dealing with stress (e.g., self-blame, worry, and tension reduction) (Frydenberg & Lewis, 2014). This distinction is supported by studies that have found a significant positive correlation between productive coping strategies and higher self-esteem (Evert, 1996), higher internal locus of control (Goble, 1995), deeper learning (McDonald, 1996), and greater well-being (Lewis & Frydenberg, 2004), and a significant negative association between nonproductive coping strategies and the inverse of the above. Some of the poorest personal outcomes are associated with the self-blame coping strategy (Lewis & Frydenberg, 2004). See Chap. 5 for a more comprehensive range of insights on coping. When trying to assist individuals in improving their coping skills, the literature highlights the need to increase the use of productive strategies while simultaneously decreasing the use of nonproductive strategies (Frydenberg & Lewis, 2002b).

While the conceptual dichotomy between 'productive' and 'nonproductive' coping is attractively simple and supported by a significant body of research, it must be noted that coping cannot be classified as universally adaptive or maladaptive across all situations, without consideration of personal and situational factors (Matthews, Roberts, & Zeidner, 2004). For example, while physical recreation is commonly understood to be a 'productive' coping strategy, a sky-diving obsession in the face of financial pressure, or joining multiple sports clubs to avoid resolving relationship conflict, may well result in negative consequences. As such, coping strategies should be categorised and interpreted with caution, with considerable reference to the individual and the context wherever possible.

From the work of Frydenberg and Lewis, coping is conceptualised as thoughts, behaviours, and actions that arise in response to demands placed upon an individual. Some strategies attempt to remove or to remedy the source of the demand (e.g., problem solving), others help individuals to accommodate to it (e.g., wishful thinking). Additionally, there are strategies that demonstrate an inability to deal with the demand (e.g., despair and get sick) (Frydenberg, 2008). The tools that Frydenberg and Lewis have developed provide measures of all three types of responses and have been used to both identify correlates and determine outcomes. To date, Frydenberg and Lewis's research has identified conceptual areas of coping for three age groups: adolescent population (ACS/ACS-2; Frydenberg & Lewis, 1993, 2011), adult populations (CSA/CSA-2; Frydenberg & Lewis, 1997, 2014), and young children (CCS; Yeo et al., 2014).

The Adolescent Coping Scale (ACS)

The original *Adolescent Coping Scale* was published in Australia by the Australian Council for Educational Research (ACER), and reviewed by the *Mental Measurements Yearbook* of the Buros Institute, the most eminent reviewer of psychology tests in print. It was primarily intended for the use of adolescents between the ages of 12 and 18 years and can be administered by a range of professionals who work with adolescents, including teachers, counsellors, and associated health professionals. In addition to research applications, the tools provide impetus for self-directed behavioural change. The ACS was developed to assist with understanding adolescent coping behaviour, both generally and in response to particular stressors, and as a means for determining how adolescents cope with a range of life concerns and circumstances. There are two forms of the ACS, a Long Form which can be used in both a general and specific manner, and a Short Form, which consists of one item from each group that make up a particular strategy that can be used as an indicator of coping strategies used by adolescents. Since the publication of the original ACS, and its use in a range of local and international contexts, its predictive validity has been greatly strengthened as has the reliability of its scales.

In 2011, the *Adolescent Coping Scale* was revised to further improve its construct validity and predictive capacity and *ACS-2* was published. The *ACS-2* is a self-report inventory (online and paper-based) comprising 60 items which reliably assesses 20 conceptually and empirically distinct coping strategies (see Table 4.1 for details): the Long Form (which can be used as both a 'general' and a 'specific' scale) with three items per scale, and the Short Form with one item for each scale. The Short Form is a useful indicator of a respondent's performance on the Long Form and is recommended for situations where the longer questionnaire proves to be too involved or time-consuming, though the longer form remains the more functionally effective and accurate of the two formats of the instrument.

The Short Form of the original *ACS-2* scale was subjected to further analysis and found to group into two reliable dimensions, Productive Coping (PC) and Nonproductive Coping (NPC) styles, with the exception of Humour and Spirit which failed to load significantly to either style. The Productive Coping style effectively integrates the earlier styles of 'problem solving' and 'reference to others' from ACS into the one style, while the Nonproductive Coping Style remains essentially intact.

Whilst adult measures of coping were the first to emerge (Folkman & Lazarus, 1980; Hobfoll, 1989), an adolescent measure was, at the time of development, what was required. However, having developed the ACS and utilised it with young adults in the university and college settings, it became evident that the constructs and approach would be equally useful in the adult domain. Indeed, as much of the work with adolescents had been utilised in educational settings it was timely for adults, particularly teachers, parents, and administrators, to have the opportunity to utilise an instrument which paralleled the ACS in language and content, whilst having its own empirical integrity. It was deemed important to utilise the same concepts, constructs, and language so that comparisons could be made and teaching tools could be developed for the various age groups. After all, in expecting young people to cope productively it was important for the adults around them to do the same.

Coping Scale for Adults (CSA)

The initial measures of coping were in the adult domain, so the adolescent tool was developed to meet the need to understand and contribute to the world of adolescents. The Coping Scale for Adults followed the development of the Adolescent Coping Scale. Adults in a family play an important role in influencing how children and adolescents cope with challenges in life. The CSA (and revised version CSA-2 in 2014) was devised with the intention of aiding a range of interested parties in understanding adult coping behaviour, both generally and in response to particular stressors, and as a means for determining how adults coped with a range of life concerns and circumstances. Similar to the ACS, there are two forms of the CSA: a Long Form which could be used with either a general or specific focus, and a Short Form, which consisted of one item from each group of the 20 strategies which can be used as an indicator of the coping strategies used by adults. It was found that in addition to 20 coping strategies, 3 styles of coping were common amongst adults: productive coping style, nonproductive coping style, and problem-solving coping style (see Table 4.1 for details). The coping scales, both in the short and the long form together with the self-evaluation of coping provided by the CSA-2 afford useful measures both for researchers and practitioners. Table 4.1 illustrates the different coping styles, the 20 coping strategies alongside their conceptual definitions which underpinned ACS-2 and CSA-2.

A range of variables were found to impact on adult coping: gender, age, culture, perceptions of the self, perception of the ability by others, supportive workplace climates, and the experience of stress in the family (see Chap. 5). The original CSA was distinct from other similar instruments in that it identified a wider array of conceptual areas of coping, allowing administrators to essentially profile an individual's or a group's coping styles and strategies. This provided a basis upon which adults could be assisted to reflect upon their coping actions in a meaningful way, thus providing the opportunity for functional behavioural change.

Well-being and resilience can be achieved through multiple approaches. There is strong evidence that resources matter (Hobfoll, 2010). Those who have more resources such as jobs, cohesive family, friendship, and support from others do better. However, there is also strong evidence that having the capacity to examine and reflect on one's coping is of value in determining which strategies may be helpful in a particular circumstance, and which are not. We can generally do what we do better. That is increasingly true of coping. When it comes to coping, reducing the bad and increasing the good is the general principle that needs to be put into practice.

A range of studies utilising the Long and the Short Forms and the Specific and General forms of both the ACS and the CSA are reported in Chap. 5.

In both the ACS-2 and CSA-2 it is possible to assess how one copes in general and how one deals with a specific nominated issue. An individual may complete two forms: one for general coping responses and one for a specific concern.

Thus on each questionnaire, two types of responses are available:

1. Usage—how often each of the coping strategies described in the items provided are used by the respondent; and
2. Helpfulness—an evaluation of how helpful the strategy was perceived to be when it was used.

These appear in both the Long Form and the Short Form (for each of the two forms: General and Specific; Usage and Helpfulness). In this Second Edition, individuals are encouraged to consider the frequency of usage and the effectiveness of the coping strategies they have used.

The relevant consideration is whether the strategy is effective and, therefore, whether the frequency of use should be increased. This is a worthwhile endeavour if the strategy is a productive or problem-solving one. However, if the strategy is a nonproductive one, but is considered by the individual to be helpful, it is likely to be more challenging for the individual to reduce the use of this strategy.

Although these taxonomies of coping have been used in research with children and adolescents, the study of coping in children requires a developmental perspective as broad adult-based dimensions of coping are not generally applicable to younger age groups. In a review of 12 coping measures (9 self-report and 3 observational methods) in paediatric populations by Blount et al. (2008), only 6 met the criteria of 'well established' that broaden understanding and guide treatment.

Factor-analytic studies on coping in children have yielded more factors than the conventional two-factor models used to describe adult coping. In a study on primary school students aged 8–12 and using a self-report questionnaire, five factors were extracted using confirmatory factor analysis—approach, avoidance, support seeking, aggression, and crying (Röder, Boekaerts, & Kroonenberg, 2002).

Using a sample of children aged 9–13 years, Ayers, Sandier, West, and Roosa (1996) found that a four-factor model of coping consisting of active coping, social support, distraction, and avoidance provided a better fit with the data as compared with adult-derived, two-factor models representing problem- versus emotion-focused coping and approach versus avoidance coping (Ayers et al., 1996).

Coping in Early Childhood

Despite the relative paucity of research to date, the study of coping in preschoolers is deemed to be viable. It was considered important to have the tools with which to assess and develop input at an early stage of a child's development. It has been established that children aged 4–5 were able to articulate up to 36 different coping responses (Deans, Frydenberg, & Tsurutani, 2010). These responses were then categorised conceptually into three categories: active (what children do), passive (how they withdraw or avoid difficult situations), and relational (how they dealt with situations involving others), as suggested by Zimmer-Gembeck, Lees, and Skinner (2011). In another study by Blair, Denham, Kochanoff, and Whipple (2004), the authors proposed 3 types of coping in preschool children based on a questionnaire of 13 coping items. These three coping dimensions were constructive coping (e.g., 'talks with someone to help find a solution'), emotional venting (e.g., 'uses verbal and physical aggression to release feeling'), and passive coping (e.g., 'denial').

Studies conceptually categorise preschoolers' coping responses into preconceived dimensions derived from models pertaining to older age groups. This method may disguise important differences in the nature and function of coping in young children (Compas et al., 2001). Empirically derived taxonomies through the use of factor analyses can provided information specific to preschoolers' coping that is not confounded by the imposition of adult theoretical models.

The Children's Coping Scale-Revised (CCS-R) is a parent-reported measure of coping strategies that their children use. It consists of 29 items and can be used to measure general as well as situation-specific coping. This scale was derived empirically from the literature and parents and children generated descriptions of age-appropriate coping strategies (Deans et al., 2010). The CCS-R requires parents to rate how frequently their child uses the 29 strategies listed to cope with problems, on a 3-point Likert scale (i.e., *never, sometimes, a lot*). Some examples of items on the scale include 'notice what others are doing', 'keep feelings to self', and 'ask a teacher for help'. One hundred and twenty-nine parents of preschoolers whose ages ranged from 48 to 60 months responded to the CCS-R. Coping dimensions were derived through principal components analysis (PCA) to reduce the 29 items to smaller groupings.

Situation-Specific Coping

In a subsequent study (Yeo et al., 2014), the same strategies were presented for situation-specific coping questions in which parents rated how often the child used each of the strategies in two different situations: separating from parents and being asked to do something he/she doesn't like. These two situations were selected as they were common stressful situations for this population of children. In addition, they are thought to represent a low-control situation (separating from parents) and a high-control situation (doing something he/she doesn't like).

These derived components were tentatively labelled and subjected to reliability analyses. The first component, referred to as positive coping, was composed of 13 items with a Cronbach's alpha of 0.87. The second component, referred to as negative coping-emotional expression, was composed of eight items with a Cronbach's alpha of 0.73. The third component, referred to as negative coping-emotional inhibition, was composed of five items with a Cronbach's alpha of 0.66.

In a subsequent study, the two sets of data were combined to conform the factor structure of the Children's Coping Scale-Revised, using PCA and parallel analysis, with orthogonal rotation for use in this study (Pang, Frydenberg, & Deans, 2015). One hundred and nineteen (70 % Anglo-Australian, 30 % from other countries) parents of preschoolers enrolled at an Early Learning Centre (ELC) were the subjects of the study. The mean age of the preschoolers was 54.6 months (M = 54.6 months, SD = 6.48), and comprised of 67 (57.8 %) females and 49 (42.2 %) males. PCA (SPSS Version 21.0) with parallel analysis and Cattell's scree plot as the decision criteria was used to analyse the CCS-R. Both promax (oblique) and varimax (orthogonal) rotations were performed and similar component loadings were derived. Hence, a varimax rotation was deemed appropriate as oblique and orthogonal rotation methods will generally produce near-identical results if the factors are uncorrelated (Fabrigar, Wegener, MacCallum, & Strahan, 1999; Schmitt, 2011).

A three-component solution using varimax rotation explained 38.9 % of the variance, and minimum retained loadings were 0.36 (Tabachnick & Fidell, 2007). These components were labelled Positive Coping, Negative Coping-Emotional Expression, and Negative Coping-Emotional Inhibition (Table 4.2).

The three coping dimensions derived in the current study correlate the findings in Yeo et al. (2014) and also closely resemble those of other studies that were derived on data that had not been subjected to factor analysis (Blair et al., 2004; Eisenberg, Fabes, & Guthrie, 1997), as well as

Table 4.2 Three components of the CCS-R (rotated component matrix for the three-component model of the children's coping scale)

Component	Items (factor loadings)
Positive coping (component 1–13 items)	Notice what others are doing
	Play
	Try
	Chat to friends
	Hope
	Try to help others
	Get a teacher or grown-up to help
	Work hard
	Work with others
	Be happy with the way things are
	Have fun, play sport, draw, play games
	Spend a lot of time with a good friend
	Go out and play and forget about their problem
Negative coping-emotional expression (component 2–8 items)	Worry
	Cry or scream
	Keep away from other children
	Feel sad
	Feel bad
	Get mad with themselves
	Blame themselves when things go wrong
	'Lose it'—cy, scream, or fight
Negative coping -emotional inhibition (component 3–5 items)	Do nothing
	Give up
	Keep feelings to self/not show others how he/she feels
	Don't let others know how they are feeling
	Get sick

those that had been subjected to factor analysis and utilised different factor extraction methods (e.g., Tsurutani, 2009). These considerations give increased confidence to the number and type of coping dimensions that preschoolers utilise to cope with stressful situations. The derivation of two emotion-focused coping dimensions in the current study is consistent with previous research findings where the use of emotion-focused coping strategies emerge during the preschool years and begin to develop during early childhood (Kopp, 2009). In addition, the convergence of empirically derived components with previous studies and the moderate to high reliabilities (0.64 to 0.86) of these components suggests the CCS-R has construct validity and internal consistency respectively.

Concluding Remarks

Whilst the tools have reliability and validity that enable the measures to be used for research purposes that involve population data gathering, the adolescent and adult tools have a further explicit aim of being useful for counselling and clinical practice as tools for self-awareness and engagement in behavioural change.

Much of the psychometrically valid instruments have been used exclusively for research rather than intervention; yet the tools lend themselves to clinical applications because the very identification of the individual's coping characteristics can lead to reflection and behavioural change. Unlike the measurement of resilience, the measurement of coping has been long established and accepted as useful. Despite the diversity of nomenclature and classification, there is considerable consensus on what is helpful coping and what is not when dealing with life's circumstances.

References

Aldwin, C. M., & Werner, E. E. (2007). *Stress, coping, and development: An integrative perspective/Carolyn M. Aldwin; foreword by Emmy E. Werner.* New York: Guilford Press. 2.

Anshel, M. H., & Si, G. (2008). Coping styles following acute stress in sport among elite Chinese athletes: A test of trait and transactional coping theories. *Journal of Sport Behavior, 31*(1), 3.

Ayers, T. S., Sandier, I. N., West, S. G., & Roosa, M. W. (1996). A dispositional and situational assessment of children's coping: Testing alternative models of coping. *Journal of Personality, 64*(4), 923–958.

Blair, K. A., Denham, S. A., Kochanoff, A., & Whipple, B. (2004). Playing it cool: Temperament, emotion regulation, and social behavior in preschoolers. *Journal of School Psychology, 42*(6), 419–443.

Blount, R. L., Simons, L. E., Devine, K. A., Jaaniste, T., Cohen, L. L., Chambers, C. T., & Hayutin, L. G. (2008). Evidence-based assessment of coping and stress in pediatric psychology. *Journal of Pediatric Psychology, 33*(9), 1021–1045.

Compas, B. E. (1987). Coping with stress during childhood and adolescence. *Psychological Bulletin, 101*(3), 393–403.

Compas, B. E., Connor-Smith, J. K., Saltzman, H., Thomsen, A. H., & Wadsworth, M. E. (2001). Coping with stress during childhood and adolescence: Problems, progress, and potential in theory and research. *Psychological Bulletin, 127*(1), 87–127.

Deans, J., Frydenberg, E., & Tsurutani, H. (2010). Operationalising social and emotional coping competencies in kindergarten children. *New Zealand Research in Early Childhood Education Journal, 13*, 113–124.

Eisenberg, N., Fabes, R. A., & Guthrie, I. K. (1997). Coping with stress: The roles of regulation and development. In S. A. Wolchik & I. Sandler (Eds.), *Handbook of children's coping: Linking theory and intervention* (pp. 41–70). New York: Plenum.

Evert, H. (1996). *Gender, culture, psychological and social resources and their influence on coping behaviour in physiotherapy students.* Unpublished Master of Educational Psychology thesis, University of Melbourne, VIC.

Fabrigar, L. R., Wegener, D. T., MacCallum, R. C., & Strahan, E. J. (1999). Evaluating the use of exploratory factor analysis in psychological research. *Psychological Methods, 4*(3), 272–299. doi:10.1037//1082-989X.4.3.272.

Folkman, S. J. T. (2004). COPING: Pitfalls and promise. *Annual Review of Psychology, 55*(1), 745–774. doi:10.1146/annurev.psych.55.090902.141456.

Folkman, S., & Lazarus, R. S. (1980). An analysis of coping in a middle-aged community sample. *Journal of Health and Social Behavior, 21*, 219.

Folkman, S., & Moskowitz, J. T. (2003). Positive psychology from a coping perspective, *Psychological Inquiry, 14(2)*, 121–125.

Frydenberg, E. (2008). *Adolescent coping: Advances in theory, research and practice.* Hoboken, NJ: Taylor and Francis.

Frydenberg, E., & Lewis, R. (1993). *Manual, The adolescent coping scale.* Melbourne, VIC: Australian Council for Educational Research.

Frydenberg, E., & Lewis, R. (1997). *Coping scale for adults.* Melbourne, VIC: Australian Council for Educational Research.

Frydenberg, E., & Lewis, R. (2002a). Do managers cope productively? A comparison between Australian middle level managers and adults in the general community. *Journal of Managerial Psychology, 17*, 640–654.

Frydenberg, E., & Lewis, R. (2002b). Adolescent wellbeing: Building young people's resources. In E. Frydenberg (Ed.), *Beyond coping: Meeting goals, vision and challenges* (pp. 175–194). Oxford, UK: Oxford University Press.

Frydenberg, E., & Lewis, R. (2011). *Adolescent coping scale – Second Edition (ACS-2).* Melbourne, VIC: Australian Council for Educational Research (ACER Press).

Frydenberg, E., & Lewis, R. (2014). *Coping scale for adults – Second Edition (CSA-2)*. Melbourne, VIC: Australian Council for Educational Research. (ACER Press).

Goble, G. (1995). *Assessment of coping strategies*. Unpublished research report, Monash University, Melbourne, VIC.

Hobfoll, S. E. (1989). Conservation of resources: A new attempt at conceptualizing stress. *The American Psychologist, 44*(3), 513–524.

Hobfoll, S. E. (1998). *Stress culture and community: The psychology and philosophy of stress*. New York: Plenum Press.

Hobfoll, S. E. (2010). *Conservation of resources theory: Its implication for stress, health, and resilience*. NewYork: Oxford University Press.

Hobfoll, S. E., Dunahoo, C. L., Ben-Porath, Y., & Monnier, J. (1994). Gender and coping: The dual-axis model of coping. *American Journal of Community Psychology, 22*(1), 49–82.

Kopp, C. B. (2009). Emotion-focused coping in young children: Self and self-regulatory processes. *New Directions for Child and Adolescent Development, 2009*(124), 33–46. doi:10.1002/cd.241.

Lazarus, R. S. (1993). Coping theory and research: Past, present, and future. *Psychosomatic Medicine, 55*(3), 234–247.

Lazarus, R. S., & Folkman, S. (1984). *Stress, appraisal, and coping*. New York: Springer.

Lewis, R., & Frydenberg, E. (2004). Students' self-evaluation of their coping: How well do they do it? In E. Frydenberg (Ed.), *Thriving, surviving, or going under: Coping with everyday lives* (pp. 23–43). Connecticut: Information Age Publishing.

Matthews, G., Roberts, R. D., & Zeidner, M. (2004). Seven myths about emotional intelligence, *Psychological Inquiry, 15*, 179–196.

McDonald, A. (1996). *Approaches to learning of tertiary students: The role of coping, developmentally-related variables and study stressors*. Unpublished Master of Educational Psychology Thesis, University of Melbourne, Melbourne, VIC.

Moos, R. H., & Schaefer, J. A. (1993). Coping resources and processes: Current concepts and measures. In L. Goldberger & S. Breznitz (Eds.), *Handbook of stress: Theoretical and clinical aspects* (pp. 234–257). New York: Free Press.

Pang, I., Frydenberg, E., & Deans, E. (2015). The relationship between anxiety and coping in preschoolers. In P. Buchenwald & K. Moore (Eds.), *Stress anxiety* (pp. 27–36). Berlin, Germany: Verlag.

Röder, I., Boekaerts, M., & Kroonenberg, P. (2002). The stress and coping questionnaire for children (school version and asthma version): Construction, factor structure, and psychometric properties. *Psychological Reports, 91*(1), 29–36.

Schmitt, T. A. (2011). Current methodological considerations in exploratory and confirmatory factor analysis. *Journal of Psychoeducational Assessment, 29*(4), 304–321. doi:10.1177/0734282911406653.

Skinner, E. A., Edge, K., Altman, J., & Sherwood, H. (2003). Searching for the structure of coping: A review and critique of category systems for classifying ways of coping. *Psychological Bulletin, 129*(2), 216–269.

Spirito, A., Overholser, J., & Stark, L. J. (1989). Common problems and coping strategies II: Findings with adolescent suicide attempters. *Journal of Abnormal Child Psychology, 17*(2), 213–221.

Tabachnick, B. G., & Fidell, L. S. (2007). *Using multivariate statistics* (5th ed.). Boston, MA: Pearson Education.

Tsurutani, H. (2009). *A multi-informant approach to understanding the coping behaviours of preschool children: A comparative study of teachers' and parents' observations.* Unpublished master's thesis, University of Melbourne, Melbourne Graduate School of Education.

Yeo, K., Frydenberg, E., Northam, E., & Deans, J. (2014). Coping with stress among preschool children and associations with anxiety level and controllability of situations. *Australian Journal of Psychology, 66*(2), 93–101. doi:10.1111/ajpy.12047.

Zimmer-Gembeck, M. J., Lees, D., & Skinner, E. A. (2011). Children's emotions and coping with interpersonal stress as correlates of social competence. *Australian Journal of Psychology, 63*, 131–141. doi:10.1111/j.1742-9536.2011.00019.x.

5

What We Know About Coping

On January 24, 2016, a young relatively unknown 20-year-old tennis player, Daria 'Dasha' Gavrilova was playing in the fourth round of the Australian Open Grand Slam Tennis Tournament. To date, that was the furthest she had advanced in a Grand Slam. In the weeks before, she had won numerous matches and smiled during the course of the matches, particularly when she was the victor. She won the crowds over; the media loved her. She breezed through the first set effortlessly with a 6-0 score. But then things unravelled. She lost the next two sets 6-3 and 6-2. At the end of the match she sunk to her knees in disappointment. Having lost one point after another she looked to her coach's box, pleading for support. The coach's face was rather stern. Daria pulled out a folded sheet of paper as she sat between matches on which were some motivational texts she had written to herself. Following the loss she described herself as having been very 'emotional and going crazy…I got myself emotionally fried and crazy. I was going mad at myself.' Her positive self-scripts did not appear to help. Instead she was visibly blaming herself. Self-blame is the

---

As a tennis player you are guaranteed to lose every week of the year. You always look to the tournament next week. (Justin, tennis player)

© The Author(s) 2017
E. Frydenberg, *Coping and the Challenge of Resilience*,
DOI 10.1057/978-1-137-56924-0_5

coping strategy that is most clearly associated with low well-being. Rather than staying calm and focused, she invested energy in self-denigration. In contrast, her opponent, Carla Suerez Navarro described her own performance as having started too relaxed in the first set but then, 'You have to believe. I try, I fight, I was there…I just believed that I can (win) and until the last point I fight' (McGowan, 2016).

Elite sporting performances often provide good illustrations of resilience and the coping strategies at work. Support from peers, coaches, or others who matter is helpful. But the use of self-blame is generally not. Additionally the belief in one's capacity to cope or to succeed is often more important than ability per se.

Theoretical Understandings

Coping Theory

Coping can be distinguished from competence and resilience. Coping is the process of adaptation; competence refers to characteristics and resources required for successful adaptation, and resilience refers to outcomes to which competence and coping have been put into action in response to stress and adversity. Theoretically, there is no right or wrong coping. It is the situation and the context that determines the outcome. However, we do know, from research (see Chap. 4), what is generally helpful coping and unhelpful coping. Nevertheless, the self-evaluation of the individual in relation to outcomes determines what is effective and what is not, given the circumstance. Self-assessment of efficacy and capacity in terms of resources determines whether the individual or group undertakes to change. Efficacy is what is implied in resilience as it is the outcome that is considered, either objectively or subjectively. Coping mobilises resources, and resilience is the successful outcome.

Folkman and Lazarus's theorising, drawn from their research with adults, emphasises the context in which coping actions occur, the attempt rather than the outcome, and the fact that coping is a process that changes over time, as the person and the environment are continuously in a dynamic, mutually influential relationship (Lazarus & Folkman, 1984; Folkman & Lazarus, 1988). This is generally known as the Transactional Model of Coping. Lazarus (1993) defined coping as a response to the 'ongoing cognitive and behavioural demands that are taxing or exceeding the resources of the person' (p. 237).

The utility of the coping construct has long been appreciated. From the early work of psychodynamic researchers who used qualitative interview techniques to explore the construct, through to the explosion of measurement tools and research conducted during the past 50 or so years, we have learnt to appreciate that coping represents what we do in our everyday lives and in particular how we deal with stress.

From our work, and drawing upon the Transactional Model of stress and coping articulated by Richard Lazarus, coping is a function of situational determinants, the individual's characteristics, perception of the situation, and coping intentions. The individual brings a host of biological, dispositional, personal, and family characteristics to the encounter. How these impact upon the perception of the situation and the response to the stress or concern is of interest. Following an appraisal of the situation, the individual assesses the likely impact of the stress, that is, whether the consequences are likely to lead to 'loss', 'harm', 'threat', or 'challenge', and what resources (personal or interpersonal) are available to the individual to deal with it (Frydenberg, 2008). The intent of the action, along with the action, determines the outcome. Following a response, the outcome is reviewed or reappraised (tertiary appraisal or reappraisal), and another response may follow. There may be a subsequent development in an individual's coping repertoire. There is a circular mechanism, or feedback loop, which determines whether the strategies are likely to be tried again or rejected for future use. Which outcome will be adopted is consequent on the effectiveness of the outcome after the deployment of a strategy, as judged by an individual. Both coping intentions and beliefs about the self can be accommodated within this model (see Frydenberg, 2008).

Coping is an important and useful construct because of its association with self-regulation, the links with health and well-being, and because coping is a mediator and moderator of the impact of stress on present and future functioning.

More recently the Conservation of Resources (COR) approach has addressed the complex interaction of situational, individual, and cultural factors in understanding stress and stress responses. In this approach, individuals are motivated to retain, protect, and build their resources in order to cope (Hobfoll, 1989). The four types of resources are object resources (tangible commodities), condition resources surrounding the person (e.g., a supportive group), personal resources such as skills or attributes, and energy resources involving enabling factors such as finances. According to Hobfoll (1998), the mainstream study of stress has been individualistic and mentalistic, reflecting a Western view of the self that is isolated from others, and consequently valuing self-reliance and individualism. The individualistic emphasis on coping and the cognitive behavioural approaches that focus on the individual's appraisal of a situation and teaches different ways to appraise the situation, by positive reframing, optimistic self-talk, and the like have been criticised. According to Hobfoll, such theories have concentrated on the reality 'in the mind' rather than taking into account the 'other' and the collective.

Whilst challenging the neglect of the environment in the appraisal approach, Hobfoll acknowledges that perceptions are reality based and that appraisals are generally products of real occurrences. The COR theory has focused on the complex ecology that affects how humans deal with the stresses that confront them and the social context of coping, which prescribes rules, guidelines, and expectations for both behaviour and thinking. Coping behaviour is designed to modify psychological distress by increasing needed resources (Freedy & Hobfoll, 1994). Those individuals with greater resources will be safer from threats to resources and in a stronger position to make further gains.

Coping has traditionally been defined in terms of reaction, that is, how people respond after or during a stressful event, which seems to relate to reactive aggression. But more recently just as aggression has been defined in terms of reactive and proactive, coping is being defined more broadly to include reactive coping, anticipatory coping, preventive coping, and proactive coping (Schwarzer & Taubert, 2002). Proactive coping, described by Greenglass (2002) as future oriented, has the main features of planning, goal attainment, and the use of resources to obtain goals. The proactive coper takes initiative, uses others, and takes the credit for successes, but does not blame himself or herself for failures. The proactive coper chooses actions according to how they imagine the future (Schwarzer & Taubert, 2002) (see Chap. 7).

Patterns of coping in childhood are a precursor to adaptation in adulthood. An individual's development contributes to resources and limits coping responses. Interventions provide prevention of pathology and help maximise capacity and outcome. In order to promote a more positive social and emotional development, there needs to be a change in the language that we use: by reducing the use of words that promote hopelessness and despondency. Talking about coping instead of focusing on stress, helplessness, and despair and utilising a language that embraces optimism and ability is moving in a positive direction. The way an individual thinks usually directs their feelings. Developing a language of coping, in conjunction with utilising appropriate coping skills, enables the acquisition of support and resources that can potentially sustain positive well-being for the individual.

Adult Coping

There is substantial research that provides evidence for correlates of coping such as age, gender, ethnicity, and culture. Additionally, there are the situational factors that impact how individuals cope. All these need to be taken into account in the context of resilience. This chapter presents what we have learnt from decades of research, with the Coping Scale for Adults (Frydenberg & Lewis, 1997) and the Adolescent Coping Scale (Frydenberg & Lewis, 1993a). Additionally, the Children's Coping Scale (Yeo, Frydenberg, Northam, & Deans, 2014) identifies several key correlates of children's coping and provides research insights.

Research with the CSA

The CSA has been used to identify coping responses of, particularly, subsets of the adult population, such as, teachers, hearing impaired, anorexics, anxious adults, and domestic violence victims, those with brain injury, or more generally professionals or mediators in a number of settings. It has also been used to evaluate outcomes in coping following an intervention such as cognitive behavioural therapy, leadership and parenting programmes. The studies include the following:

- stress in the workplace context;
- traumatic brain injury patients;
- tertiary students;
- MBA students;
- victims of domestic violence;
- people with eating disorders (anorexic girls and mothers);
- mediators;
- teachers in Australia, China, and Israel;
- post-injury patients;
- hearing impaired adults; and so on.

These studies reinforce the contention that significant relationships exist between a range of socially significant variables and the nature of coping in a range of settings. Broadly speaking, greater use of 'nonproductive' strategies—such as keep to self, tension reduction, worry, and self-blame—are associated with greater dysfunction. Conversely, lesser use of these strategies is typically associated with greater academic performance and academic self-concept in young adults. Moreover, greater use of some productive strategies—such as work hard, solve the problem, and seek social support—also associate with greater well-being and better outcomes, as does their perceived effectiveness (Table 5.1).

Adolescent Coping

When it comes to adolescence the influence of factors such as temperament, environmental contexts, physiological determinants, social relationships, and personal experiences (Compas, 2009, 1998; Skinner & Zimmer-Gembeck, 2009a; Zimmer-Gembeck & Skinner, 2008) has been well established. It is common for the source of stressors and the buffers that may aid in the amelioration of their effects to derive from

Table 5.1 Studies using CSA

Study	Test	N	Group	Key findings
Anson and Ponsford (2006)	CSA (short form), HADS RSE	33	Traumatic brain injury patients	Nonproductive coping (*avoidance, worry, wishful thinking, self-blame, and using drugs and alcohol*) associated with higher levels of anxiety, depression, and psychosocial dysfunction and lower levels of self-esteem Dealing with the problem/adaptive coping (*actively working on the problem and using humour and enjoyable activities to manage stress*) associated with higher self-esteem
Din, Bee, Subramania, and Oon (2010)	CSA PTSD	40	Women who experienced domestic violence and sought help from two shelters in Malaysia	Greater use of optimism coping style, less occurrence of PTSD
Evert (1996)	CSA Self-esteem Stress	200	Tertiary students	High self-esteem more *social support, problem focus, improving relationships, physical recreation, humour, relaxation and focus on the positive and less worry, keep to self, self-blame, tension reduction, ignoring the problem, not coping, and wishful thinking* Feeling overwhelmed more *wishful thinking, work hard, worry, keep to self, ignoring problem, not cope, self-blame and less tension reduction and seeking relaxing diversions*

(continued)

Table 5.1 (continued)

Study	Test	N	Group	Key findings
Frydenberg and Lewis (2002a)	CSA	137	Australian middle managers and community-based adults	Managers: more social action, work hard and achieve and less focus on positive, self-blame, wishful thinking, seek spiritual support and ignore the problem
Goble (1995)	CSA Locus of control	240	Tertiary students	Higher internal locus of control, more usage of productive coping style Higher external locus of control, more usage of nonproductive coping style
Gould, Ponsford, Johnston, and Schonberger (2011)	CSA, HADS	122	Traumatic brain injury patients with post-injury psychiatric disorder	Unproductive coping style associated with the experience of depressive and anxiety disorders at one year post-injury
Jones (1997)	CSA Trait Anxiety	160	Psychology 1 Students	Higher trait anxiety more worry, not cope, self-blame, keep to self, tension reduction, ignoring the problem, and seeking spiritual support
Jones (1997)	CSA Academic stress	170	Psychology 1 Students	Academic stress and self-blame, worry, keep to self, tension reduction, not cope and ignoring problem, wishful thinking, and seeking spiritual support

Table 5.1 (continued)

Study	Test	N	Group	Key findings
Lewis, Roache, and Romi (2011)	CSA Student misbehaviour and concern Classroom discipline strategies	515	Australian teachers	Three coping styles (*social problem solving, passive avoidant coping, and relaxation*) play a significant role in mediating the relationship between teachers' concerns about student misbehaviour and their use of classroom management techniques E.g., more socially oriented problem-solving coping strategies, more inclusive management techniques (discussion, involvement, hinting, and rewarding), more productive classroom management
Lewis et al. (2011)	CSA Student misbehaviour and concern Classroom discipline strategies	515	Australian teachers	Three coping styles (*social problem solving, passive avoidant coping, and relaxation*) play a significant role in mediating the relationship between teachers' concerns about student misbehaviour and their use of classroom management techniques. E.g., more socially oriented problem-solving coping strategies, more inclusive management techniques (discussion, involvement, hinting, and rewarding), more productive classroom management

(continued)

Table 5.1 (continued)

Study	Test	N	Group	Key findings
Lyneham (1996)	CSA	14	Anorexic girls and mothers	Anorexics more *not cope, self-blame, protect self, worry, seeking professional help, tension reduction,* and *wishful thinking* Mothers more *not cope, worry* and *self-blame* than population
Marshall (2008)	CSA EQ-i	43	Mediators	Strong associations between EQ-i variables (*self-regard, emotional self-awareness, assertiveness, independence, self-actualisation, empathy, social responsibility, interpersonal relationship, stress tolerance, impulse control, reality testing, flexibility, problem solving, optimism, happiness*) and coping strategies such as problem focus, humour, not worrying, not ignoring the problem or keeping it to oneself, or blaming oneself Negative associations between stress management, adaptability, intrapersonal and nonproductive coping styles Positive association between interpersonal, general mood, and the coping style of dealing with problem

Table 5.1 (continued)

Study	Test	N	Group	Key findings
McDonald (1996)	CSA Learning approaches	105	Tertiary students	Deep learning approaches, more work hard Surface learning approaches, less *focus on solving the problem and more physical recreation* Identity achievement and more solving *the problem, working hard, engaging in physical recreation, and focus on the positive* Identity achievement and less *self-blame, tension reduction, keep to self, ignore the problem, wishful thinking and not cope*
Richards (2012)	CSA (adapted items) STRESS	1, 201	Kindergarten through Grade-12 US teachers	Productive coping strategies used by teachers to cope with stress include *positive attitudes, humour, time for solitude/reflection, exercise/hobbies and in particular, building strong relationships with supportive family and friends*

(continued)

Table 5.1 (continued)

Study	Test	N	Group	Key findings
Romi, Lewis, and Roache (2013)	CSA Classroom management strategies	772	Teachers from a range of schools in Australia, China, and Israel	Use of more productive management techniques in Australia and Israel related to coping strategies associated with addressing the problem (e.g., *ProbSolve, ProfHelp, WorkHard and SocAction*)
				Use of *focuspos* relates to the use of both discussion and recognition in Australia
				Use of *worry* in Israel relates to under-assertion and aggression
				Use of *workhard* and *focuspos* relate to less use of aggression and punishment in China whereas *humour and self-blame* relate to more use of them
				Psychosomatic illness (*get sick*) relates to the use of aggression in Australia, Israel, and China, and to punishment in China
Skok (1996)	CSA	67	Hearing impaired	Hearing impaired, more *focus on the positive and less solving the problem, protect self, social support, seeking relaxing diversions, tension reduction, work hard, and physical recreation*
Spanjer (1999)	CSA	77	MBA students	External locus of control associated with nonproductive coping

Table 5.1 (continued)

Study	Test	N	Group	Key findings
Wilson (2012)	ASD Survey, CSA, CORE	172	Teachers from 21 Victorian government schools who have/had student(s) with autism spectrum disorder (ASD)	Teachers with higher personal resources reported greater use of productive coping than teachers with lower personal resources Teachers with lower personal resources reported significantly more nonproductive coping strategies than teachers with higher personal resources Teachers with inadequate ASD training use more nonproductive coping strategies than those with adequate ASD training Teachers low on personal resources use less nonproductive coping when provided with adequate ASD training

Table adapted from *Coping Scale for Adults—Second Edition (CSA-2)* (Frydenberg & Lewis, 2014) the same origins, that is, a situation that places great pressure on how adolescents respond to stressors, build their capacities, and marshal their resources may come from families, peer groups, and/or schools.

An adolescent's subjective cognitive appraisal of stressors, their evaluation of a stressor's potential to impact or threaten their well-being (Lazarus, 1991), can have a significant influence on the outcome of stressful life experiences, as can the lessons learnt in past experiences and how effective at coping an adolescent perceives himself or herself to be (Skinner & Zimmer-Gembeck, 2009b; Lewis & Frydenberg, 2007). Through such cognitive appraisal, an individual determines if a particular experience is relevant to his or her personal well-being and, if so, in what way. The first two steps in the coping process are, primary appraisal and secondary appraisal. The former determines what is at stake (e.g., self-esteem, or physical risk, to self or other) and the latter determines what, if anything, can be done to overcome or prevent the harm or improve the benefits (Folkman, Lazarus, Gruen, & DeLongis, 1986). These are, though, far from the only mitigating factors involved in coping. Not only is adolescence a period in which individuals build wider and deeper networks of social relationships with peers and adults other than parents, which represent fundamental sources of information and emotional consolation (Compas, 1998), it is also the time of life in which they also develop the increasingly complex set of cognitive strategies, such as abstract reasoning and hypothetical thinking, that they will utilise in managing their own emotions and their coping responses (Compas, 1998, 2009).

Stressful experiences are just that because they threaten or challenge our sense of self-efficacy and control, and they influence our feelings of autonomy and our place within groups with which we seek to belong. These are also three central elements in adolescence, paralleling as they do the development of self-identity, increased levels of emotional, behavioural, and personal autonomy, and the growing involvement in peer groups and nonparental relationships (Zimmer-Gembeck & Collins, 2003).

Adolescence thus becomes both a particularly stressful period of life and a very significant time to develop and practise personal coping skills. It is the time in life in which a developmental shift occurs in stress reaction and coping predicated upon major biological and cognitive changes, including neurochemical, hormonal, steroidal, and structural changes in the body and brain (Spear, 2000a, b). Research into these biological bases of stress vulnerability in adolescents has begun to shed considerable light on the various risk factors affecting adolescents and warrants extensive discussion.

Research with the ACS

The studies reported in Table 5.2 reflect a range of insights we have obtained regarding the relationship between characteristics of the adolescent population and coping. Studies include the following:

• Personality
• Self-efficacy and self-concept
• Decision making
• Problem solving
• Learning disability
• Giftedness
• Bullying
• School connectedness
• Depression

Gender is not the only factor influencing stress reactions and the selection of coping strategies by adolescents. Ethnicity, the age of the adolescent, the national setting, socio-economic status of the family, and the family's past experiences with coping, all play a part (Frydenberg & Lewis, 1991, 1996a; Lewis & Frydenberg, 2004a, b; Wilson, Pritchard, & Revalee, 2005; Compas, 1987; Seiffge-Krenke & Shulman, 1990; Stark, Spirito, Williams, & Guevremont, 1989). The ACS itself has been used in a range of cultural settings, as can be seen in the list of validity studies provided in Table 5.2, and has shown the often significant variation in usage of coping responses in differing national settings, though factors such as gender have often remained consistent in areas such as reported levels of concern, perceptions of efficacy, levels of self-esteem, and so on, all of which influence strategy selection (Frydenberg, 1994; Frydenberg et al., 2000, 2003). That

Table 5.2 Studies for the ACS

Study	Test(s)	N	Group(s)	Key findings
Barron, Castilla, Casullo, and Verdu (2002)	ACS BIEPS	417	Relationship between coping and well-being	The relationships between age, coping, and psychological well-being were not close Adolescent girls used a greater variety of strategies but were less skilful in coping with problems than boys
Boldero, Frydenberg, and Fallon (1993)	ACS SDQ II	208	Adolescents' view of themselves—high and low self-concept	Poor self-concept in the area of parent and same-sex relationships predicted nonproductive coping behaviour, namely, worry and self-blame High self-concept in the area of physical abilities was related to use of physical recreation and social action High academic self-concept was related to use of focus on solving the problem, work hard and achieve; low academic self-concept was related to not cope
Chesire and Campbell (1997)	ACS	60	Learning disabled versus non-learning disabled	Learning disabled less likely to relax, work hard, focus on the positive Less solve problem More wishful thinking and more not cope

Table 5.2 (continued)

Study	Test(s)	N	Group(s)	Key findings
Cogan and Schwannauer (2011)	ACS Demographic Q. YRBS – modified TDQ NDS	407	Links between personality, coping style, and risk behaviours, 14–17 years old, of mixed gender, primarily Scottish	Analysis indicated that adolescents with high scores on negativistic dominance strongly predicted engagement in health-risk behaviours. Adolescents with high scores on productive coping style and reference to others and low scores on nonproductive coping style were less likely to engage in health-risk behaviours. Coping style was found to mediate the relationship between state dominance and violence, sadness and suicidality, while a mediation effect was not found for substance misuse or physical inactivity
Cunningham (1997)	ACS (Short General), CDI and Teacher depression rating	94 students 47 teachers	High- versus low-risk depression	Nonproductive coping style predictive of depression. Active problem-focused coping style (inversely) predictive of depression
Davies (1995)	ACS II	25	12–14 year gifted accelerated programme	Rigid beliefs about self, more nonproductive coping. More worry, seek to belong, wishful thinking, self-blame and keep to self

(continued)

Table 5.2 (continued)

Study	Test(s)	N	Group(s)	Key findings
Fallon, Frydenberg, and Boldero (1993)	ACS FES	108	Perceived family functioning and coping	Adolescents from families who make frequent use of personal growth dimensions (achievement, intellectual/cultural orientation, moral/religious emphasis) use more work hard, social support, and solve the problem strategies
				Adolescents who report frequent family conflict and control report high use of tension reduction strategies
Frydenberg and Lewis (1993b)	ACS	643	Use of particular coping strategies by adolescents	Irrespective of gender, young people attempt to solve problems to the same extent
				Coping strategies varied by number and type depending on age, ethnicity and gender
				Girls used more tension reduction, seek social support, and wishful thinking more than boys, who in turn used recreation
				Anglo-Australians used more tension reduction and less hard work than other groups, whilst Southeast Asian-Australians used more social action, hard work, and seek professional help, and European-Australians used more spiritual support than both other groups

Table 5.2 (continued)

Study	Test(s)	N	Group(s)	Key findings
Frydenberg and Lewis (1996a)	ACS	576	Replication study, secondary school students (Years 7, 9, and 11)	Replicated the construct validity of 16 of the 18 ACS scales; scales appeared sufficiently unique from one another to warrant separate usage
				The Long Form of the ACS provided more reliable measures of three distinct styles: (1) attempting to solve the problem whilst remaining physically fit and socially connected, (2) referring to others in a bid to deal with the concern and (3) avoidance strategies generally associated with poor coping
				Adolescent coping varies according to perceptions of self, perceptions of others, and family environment
				Age, gender, and origin of family are concomitants of coping

(continued)

Table 5.2 (continued)

Study	Test(s)	N	Group(s)	Key findings
Frydenberg and Lewis (1999)	ACS	829	Secondary School students	Girls seek more social support, tension reduction, self-blame, and worrying, but less seeking of professional advice, than boys, whilst boys were more likely to use relaxing, recreation, ignoring, and keeping problems to themselves Students generally increased the number of inefficient strategies used with age, whilst also decreasing the number of productive coping strategies
Frydenberg, Care, Freeman, and Chan (2009)	ACS In-class survey	536	Interrelationships between coping styles, emotional well-being, and school connectedness	Productive coping styles positively relate to a student's sense of well-being and to school connectedness (though to a lesser extent) A nonproductive coping style was inversely related to a student's sense of well-being and to school connectedness Emotional well-being was positively related to school connectedness Both risk factors and positive factors need to be taken into account when focusing on well-being and connectedness in school contexts

Table 5.2 (continued)

Study	Test(s)	N	Group(s)	Key findings
Frydenberg, Lewis, Ardila, Cairns, and Kennedy (2000)	ACS	399	Study of effects of four concerns across three national settings	Variations seen across national settings and genders in level of concern with social issues. Community violence was of greatest concern in all three settings. National and community contexts influence selection of coping strategies, though there is a relatively consistent gender difference across the cultures in the types of strategies chosen
Frydenberg, Lewis, Kennedy, Ardila, Frindte, and Hannoun (2003)	ACS	572	Comparative study across four countries	Variations found across cultures in usage of particular coping strategies, e.g., Australian youth use physical recreation and relaxation to a greater extent than youth from the other three countries. Certain strategies cross national boundaries, e.g., self-blame. National settings and inherent levels of stress may mediate the effectiveness of coping strategies. Need to take into account community settings when interpreting coping styles of youth

(continued)

Table 5.2 (continued)

Study	Test(s)	N	Group(s)	Key findings
Jenkin (1997)	ACS	134	Year 8 ± Outward Bound programme	High general self-efficacy, more work hard, solving the problem, focus on the positive
Lewis and Frydenberg (2007)	ACS	801	Effects of perceived efficacy in problem solving on adolescent coping	Girls who reported less efficacy in problem-solving ability were more likely to give up, acknowledge defeat, keep the issue to themselves, and use self-blame Both boys and girls who reported high self-efficacy in problem-solving ability employed the following productive coping strategies: accepting one's best efforts, focusing on the positive, and engaging in social action Boys specifically used more humour and spent time with friends, and girls relied more on social support, physical recreation, and worked hard

Table 5.2 (continued)

Study	Test(s)	N	Group(s)	Key findings
Mann, Nota, Soresi, Ferrari, and Frydenberg (2011)	ACS MDMQ	566	Explore links between coping and decision-making styles in Italian 14–17 year olds	Decision-making style and coping strategies are both significantly and similarly related to self-efficacy. The magnitude of the relationships between coping strategies and decision-coping patterns differed for boys and girls but were not systematic in difference. Small correlations between coping strategies and decision-coping patterns indicated that coping strategies and decision-coping patterns are related but separate concepts
McTaggart (1996)	ACS	32	Mainstream and teaching unit (problem behaviour)	Teaching unit more worry, ignore, keep to self, tension reduction
Neill (1996)	ACS Self-esteem scale	126	Southeast Asian Year 11 students studying in Australia compared to Australian students	Students with low self-esteem use more nonproductive coping, namely, not cope, worry, self-blame, keep to self. Southeast Asian students, more reference to others

(continued)

Table 5.2 (continued)

Study	Test(s)	N	Group(s)	Key findings
Noto (1995)	ACS	90 girls and 374 boys	High achievers (regardless of gender and IQ)	High achievers more work hard, solve the problem, social support, focus on the positive
				Less not cope, tension reduction, ignore the problem
				Achievement negatively related to invest in close friends
Parsons, Frydenberg, and Poole (1996)	ACS	374 boys	Overachieving versus other boys	Overachieving boys used more social support, less not cope
Poot (1997)	ACS YSR, BDI and self-esteem	50	Intervention programme for young with problems	Nonproductive coping associated with more problems, lower self-concept, greater depression
Poynton and Frydenberg (2011)	ACS About Me & School Quest	352 girls	Evaluated coping skills of girls facing bullying at school	Female adolescents who are frequently bullied use more nonproductive coping styles (including more reference to others)
				Bullied females experience higher levels of anxiety compared to females who are not victims of bullying
				Coping styles can be used as an indicator to differentiate between those at high risk of bullying and those at a low risk

Table 5.2 (continued)

Study	Test(s)	N	Group(s)	Key findings
Stevenson (1996)	ACS (Short Specific) SDQ III PSS	162	High and low perceived stress and academic self-concept	Negative academic self-concept, more nonproductive coping Lower perceived stress, more solving the problem
Szczepanski (1995)	ACS DRL Homesickness	77	High and low homesickness for boarding-school girls	Less adaptive, more tension reduction, keep to self, less focus on the positive Less homesickness, more solve the problem, focus on the positive, relax, physical recreation Less homesick, more productive coping

Table adapted from *Adolescent Coping Scale—Second Edition (ACS-2)* (Frydenberg & Lewis, 2011) the ACS remains functionally informative in regard to all these variables rests on the array of factors it assesses through the various scales and plethora of items, all of which enable it to maintain predictive validity across a range of situations (Frydenberg & Lewis 1996a).

As a consequence of these various sources of stress, coping strategies, and external and internal influences on coping ability, it is helpful to have an understanding of how an individual or group copes as an essential starting point in developing appropriate interventions that can lead to behavioural change (Frydenberg & Lewis, 1996b). Such interventions can take a range of formats from individual support and behavioural change, through programmes in a universal class or group setting for an identified population (such as those experiencing some difficulty), to systemic or school-based programmes that seek to alter both the interpersonal and environmental stressors affecting all adolescents. Many of these approaches have been greatly influenced by less medically inspired models of individual health that seek to balance the neuropsychological approach. Whilst the neuropsychological perspective on adolescence allows for greater depth of insight into the physiological, neurochemical, and ontogenetic factors affecting adolescence, it needs to be balanced with other perspectives that consider the lived experience of adolescent life.

The neurophysiological perspective stems from a tradition of psychology that has as its focus the 'disease model' (Seligman & Csikszentmihalyi, 2000) of psychology, which has its limitations however informative it may be. Those theorists, psychologists, and educationalists linked to what is commonly known as the 'positive psychology' movement believe that the disease model needs to be complemented with an approach that seeks to investigate how to build an individual's capacities and experiences, rather than only focusing on illness and treatments. The focus shifts to prevention rather than cure, with an emphasis on the 'human strengths' that can act as buffers to psychological illness, strengths such as 'courage, future mindedness, optimism, interpersonal skill, faith, work ethic, hope, honesty, perseverance, and the capacity for flow and insight' (Seligman & Csikszentmihalyi, 2000, p. 7).

In Table 5.3 some outcomes of interventions evaluated using the ACS are reported. See Chap. 6 for a comprehensive discussion regarding interventions.

Table 5.3 Outcomes studies using CSA/ACS

Study	Test	N	Group	Key findings
Anson and Ponsford (2006)	CSA (short form)	31	Traumatic brain injury patients	Increase in adaptive coping followed a cognitive behaviour therapy-based intervention programme
Gulliford, Deans, Frydenberg, and Liang (2015)	CSA	14	Parents of preschoolers	Significant decrease in the use of nonproductive coping strategies after the completion of a parenting programme
Hsieh et al. (2012)	CSA (short form), DASS	27	Patients with moderate-to-severe traumatic brain injury	Participants who received MI showed greater response to CBT, in terms of reduction in anxiety, stress, and nonproductive coping, compared to participants who received nondirective counselling
Andrews, Ainley, and Frydenberg (2011)	ACS Custom designed software— BTL	166	Relationships between coping style and responses to problem-solving task Mean age 14.07 years	Two higher order coping factors, maladaptive coping style and adaptive coping style, were found The adaptive coping style was positively related to self-efficacy, pre-task interest, and post-task interest. In addition, self-efficacy triggered pre-task interest, which, subsequently, was positively related to task performance and post-task interest The findings suggest that such programmes should be designed to promote the use of adaptive coping strategies, as well as to reduce the use of maladaptive coping strategies

(continued)

Table 5.3 (continued)

Study	Test	N	Group	Key findings
Frydenberg and Lewis (2002b)	ACS 'State-of-being' Scale	1264	Evaluated a number of coping skills programmes for adolescents	Avoidant or nonproductive coping strategies were associated with dysfunction Productive coping strategies were associated with well-being Future preventative interventions should focus more on the reduction of maladaptive coping strategies, particularly self-blame, rather than just focus on increasing problem-based coping

There is a growing consensus when it comes to adolescent coping in the general population as to what contributes to success and well-being. In a meta-analysis of 63 studies of child and adolescent coping, Compas, Connor-Smith, Saltzman, Thomsen, and Wadsworth (2001) found that overall the ways in which young people cope with stress is related to psychological adjustment, internalising and externalising symptomatology, and academic competence. Engagement and problem-focused strategies including problem solving, cognitive restructuring, and positive reappraisal of the stressful situation were significantly associated with indicators of greater mental health and well-being. Conversely, disengagement and emotion-focused coping strategies, including avoidance and withdrawal, resigned acceptance, emotional discharge, wishful thinking, and self-blame were associated with poorer mental health and well-being (Lewis & Frydenberg, 2004b).

Whilst the correlates of coping highlight the relationship between various constructs and coping, there are some stand-out insights that provide clarity about what should be taught and when. For example, in the adolescent arena the longitudinal studies of coping have highlighted that age and gender differences in coping have been consistently identified in the Australian context both in cross-sectional (Frydenberg & Lewis, 1999) and longitudinal studies (Frydenberg & Lewis, 2000). In the main, it is females who turn to each other and utilise more social support than males, and at the same time females are more inclined to declare their inability to cope and are more likely to utilise strategies such as tension reduction, self-blame, and worry. In contrast, boys, at least in the Australian context, are more likely to utilise physical recreation and relaxation strategies than are girls. Older adolescents, particularly girls, are more inclined to report their use of nonproductive coping strategies. When the same young people are followed through from age 12, through to 15, and from 15 through to 17 years, it was found that girls particularly report a greater inability to cope during the 14–16 year period than they did 2 years previously (Frydenberg & Lewis, 2000). That is one of the reasons why we recommend teaching coping skills in the early adolescent years and then providing booster sessions in the later adolescent years with a particular focus on what is of greatest importance to young people at a particular time in their lives.

Again when the relationship between well-being and coping is examined, there is a significant relationship between the use of negative avoidant coping styles with lesser well-being and greater distress. It was not just about the frequency of the coping strategy but once again the perceived effectiveness of the coping strategy that was also deemed to be important (Frydenberg & Lewis, 2009a, b). The interrelationships between coping styles, emotional well-being, and school connectedness using both well-being and coping was examined with a sample of 870 students (age 12–16 years) from eight Metropolitan Government schools (55% female) who completed the short form of the ACS and the 12-item State of Being questionnaire (Reynolds, 2001).

The effectiveness of coping and the frequency of coping strategy use were also considered (Frydenberg & Lewis, 2009a, b). Inherent in the State of Being scale was one construct that referred to well-being and used positive coping styles such as 'I had fun with my friends' and a second construct related to items that were associated with a more negative terminology and strategies (e.g., 'I felt depressed, I was very lonely'). It was found that when it comes to well-being there is a clear association so that those who use less self-blame have higher levels of well-being (Lewis & Frydenberg, 2004a, b).

Another clear insight is that belief in one's capacities is all important. We know from grit research (Perkins-Gough, 2013) and goal research (Moskowitz & Grant, 2009) that motivation and determination are important but when it comes to, for example, problem solving it is the belief in one's capacities to do so that is important. Self-efficacy is intrinsically related to coping, although the two bodies of theory have not been frequently linked in the literature. A belief in one's capacity to change behaviour has implications for how coping skills are acquired and subsequently employed. Self-efficacy is a regulatory process through which an individual shapes his or her responses to the environment (Bandura, 2012).

Given the probable links of coping with self-efficacy and the importance of problem solving in the educational context, Frydenberg and Lewis (2009a) examined the relationship between adolescents' sense of problem solving and their use of productive and nonproductive coping strategies. Using data from two studies, namely, Study 1 sample comprising 1047 adolescents (460 males: 587 females) and Study 2 sample comprising 870 adolescents (392 males: 478 females) where coping was measured using the ACS, it was found that there was a significant positive relationship between self-perceived efficacy of problem solving and a productive coping style. These findings suggest that focusing on the positive and accepting one's best effort can assist in problem-solving efficiency in adolescents. It is not only problem-solving skills per se that are important but the belief in one's efficacy and the capacity to judge one's coping as efficacious that are also of benefit.

Children's Coping

A children's measure of coping was introduced in Chap. 4. Using the Children's Coping Scale it was possible to demonstrate a clear association between children's coping and anxiety and how coping varies according to the situation that is of concern. As with adults, the use of coping strategies by children can be influenced by many variables. Of particular interest for researchers is anxiety level and the controllability of the stressful situation.

Within anxiety research, it is well established that avoidance is a central feature of anxiety in children (Baldwin & Dadds, 2007; Beesdo, Knappe, & Pine, 2009). There are several mechanisms by which avoidant behaviours may develop into a characteristic coping style for anxious children. Research indicates that anxious children tend to have a behaviourally inhibited temperament that manifests in observable behaviours such as refraining from exploration and approaching other children (Biederman et al., 2001; Kagan, 1997). Because temperament is largely stable (Kagan, Snidman, Arcus, & Reznick, 1994; Sanson, Pedlow, Cann, Prior, & Oberklaid, 1996), these early behavioural responses to unfamiliar situations form the template for avoidant coping in stressful situations in later life. There is also evidence that parents of anxious children may foster an avoidant approach to stressful situations (Barrett, Rapee, Dadds, & Ryan, 1996; McClure, Brennan, Hammen, & Le Brocque, 2001). These studies introduce an interesting empirical question of whether anxious children are more inclined towards emotion-focused, passive/inhibited, withdrawal types of coping, as opposed to problem-focused and active/ approach response styles.

Controllability of the situation was first investigated by Lazarus and Folkman (1984) in their conceptualisation of problem- and emotion-focused coping. Controllability refers to how much an individual believes that he/she has the ability to exert objective control over the event. Lazarus and Folkman (1984) suggested that when the stressor is controllable, adults tend to use problem-focused coping whereas when the stressor is uncontrollable, emotion-focused coping predominates. Band and Weisz (1988) were among the first investigators to report that preschoolers evidenced a similar ability to use different coping strategies in response to different situations. They found that six-year-old children tend to use more primary coping (attempts to alter objective conditions) in contrast to secondary control coping (attempts to adjust oneself to objective conditions), in controllable situations (e.g., separation from a friend, peer difficulty, and school failure) than in less controllable situations (e.g., medical procedures or physical accidents). This finding was replicated in later research with preschoolers (Chalmers, Frydenberg, & Deans, 2011; Pincus & Friedman, 2004). Chalmers et al. (2011) found that situations in which preschoolers generated most primary-control coping strategies included 'being left out of a game', 'choosing between friends', and 'choosing between things that the child doesn't like' as opposed to situations in which secondary control predominated such as 'night fears' and 'being told off by the teacher'. Thus, it appears that preschoolers were able to discriminate between situations and differentially utilise coping strategies.

The use of primary-control or problem-focused coping is not always associated with positive psychosocial outcomes. Studies on children with parents in conflict have demonstrated that the use of problem-focused coping (such as intervening in parental conflict) increased children's risk for adjustment problems (Jenkins, Smith, & Graham, 1989; Nicolotti, El-Sheikh, & Whitson, 2003) while avoidance coping appeared to be a buffer for adjustment problems (Kerig, 2001; O'Brien, Bahadur, Gee, Balto, & Erber, 1997). Some authors have suggested that when problem-focused or primary-control coping was applied to uncontrollable events (such as parental conflict), it increased psychological distress, because these strategies were likely to be ineffective. Conversely, the use of emotion-focused or secondary control in non-modifiable events fostered a sense of acceptance and vicarious control, which restored a sense of well-being (Compas, 1998; Frydenberg & Deans, 2011a). This suggests that children who are most effective at coping with stressful situations were those who not only possess a repertoire of coping strategies, but who were also able to differentiate between controllable and uncontrollable situations and then flexibly apply different strategies to different situations.

Relationship Among Coping, Anxiety, and Controllability

Anxious children, however, may possess less flexibility in modifying their coping responses. First, anxious children are characterised by a reliance on avoidance responses in most anxiety-provoking situations (Rapee, 2002). They may either have a more limited repertoire of coping strategies or a greater unwillingness to employ approach strategies. Second, anxious children tend to underestimate their ability to cope in anxiety-provoking situations (Dadds & Barrett, 2001; Suveg & Zeman, 2004) and rely on maladaptive ways of coping. Third, anxious children tend to have a heightened attentional capacity for threatening situations, to appraise ambiguous situations in threatening ways, and to overestimate threat in situations (Hadwin, Garner, & Perez-Olivas, 2006; Rapee, Schniering, & Hudson, 2009). These cognitive appraisals and beliefs may foster a sense of lack of control in the events of their lives even when situations may be more controllable than they perceive. In sum, anxious children may be characterised by an overreliance on avoidant or emotion-focused coping, thus limiting their ability to flexibly utilise the range of coping strategies demonstrated by nonanxious age peers.

In a sample of 100 preschoolers (Yeo et al., 2014) it was found that preschoolers were capable of using positive coping strategies to cope with stressors regardless of their level of anxiety. However, those who experienced elevated anxiety levels were also more likely to use emotionally expressive coping strategies that may be less adaptive. The findings of this study are also consistent with other studies where gender differences in anxiety symptoms were not observed during the preschool years (Egger and Angold, 2006; Furniss et al., 2006; Spence, Rapee, McDonald, & Ingram, 2001).

Three distinct coping dimensions were identified by Yeo et al. (2014): positive coping, negative coping-emotional expression, and negative coping-emotional inhibition. Preschoolers who were rated higher on anxiety were more likely to engage in negative forms of coping, specifically behaviours that expressed their emotions. An early pattern of maladaptive coping among anxious preschoolers was observed and the gender differences were not evident. There are implications for early mental health prevention and intervention and even more so for the building of resilience.

As a follow-up Cornell (2015) investigated the relationship between coping and anxiety in preschoolers to see whether the situation and the anxiety type would make a difference. Coping in general and in two specific situations (saying goodbye; doing something he or she does not like) was used. The Preschool Anxiety Scale: Parent Rating Form (PAS) measured children's total level of anxiety along with their generalised anxiety, social anxiety, obsessive-compulsive anxiety, specific fears, and separation anxiety. Seventy-two mothers of preschoolers who attended the same Early Learning Centre as Yeo et al.'s study completed the PAS. Correlations were conducted between the coping styles and anxiety types and were supplemented by a series of standard regression analyses. It was found that as preschoolers' total anxiety increased, so did their negative coping however different styles were used across specific situations. The relationship between coping and generalised anxiety was variable across the situations; however, a clear pattern emerged for social anxiety with children engaging in more negative coping-emotional inhibition. For separation anxiety, the relationship between coping and anxiety was only found in the goodbye specific-situation with children engaging in more negative coping-emotional expression. This study's findings suggest that coping styles used by anxious preschoolers can vary according to the situation and the anxiety experienced, suggesting it is important to go beyond children's general coping and overall anxiety. It follows that to build resilience in anxious children, teaching effective coping skills is a worthwhile avenue for intervention and prevention.

Concluding Remarks

Overall, when it comes to resilience, whether it is in the adolescent, adult, or child populations, it is clear that more productive coping is associated with better outcomes, like well-being and that more nonproductive coping is associated with poorer outcomes such as anxiety and distress (Lewis & Frydenberg, 2004b). Age and situation matter, as does one's belief in one's capacity to cope.

References

Andrews, M., Ainley, M., & Frydenberg, E. (2011). Adolescent coping styles and task-specific responses: Does style foreshadow action? In G. Reevy & E. Frydenberg (Eds.), *Research on stress and coping in education Volume VI: Personality, stress, and coping: Implications for education* (pp. 3–23). Charlotte, NC: Information Age Publishing.

Anson, K., & Ponsford, J. (2006). Evaluation of a coping skills group following traumatic brain injury. *Brain Injury, 20*(2), 167–178.

Baldwin, J. S., & Dadds, M. R. (2007). Reliability and validity of parent and child versions of the multidimensional anxiety scale for children in community samples. *Journal of the American Academy of Child and Adolescent Psychiatry, 46*(2), 252–260.

Band, E. B., & Weisz, J. R. (1988). How to feel better when it feels bad: Children's perspectives on coping with everyday stress. *Developmental Psychology, 24*(2), 247–253.

Bandura, A. (2012). Guest editorial: On the functional properties of perceived self-efficacy revisited. *Journal of Management: JOM, 38*(1), 9–44.

Barrett, P. M., Rapee, R. M., Dadds, M. M., & Ryan, S. M. (1996). Family enhancement of cognitive style in anxious and aggressive children. *Journal of Abnormal Child Psychology, 24*(2), 187–203.

Barron, R. G., Castilla, I. M., Casullo, M. M., & Verdu, J. B. (2002). Relationship between coping strategies and psychological wellbeing in adolescents. *Psicothema-Oviedo, 14*(2), 363–368.

Beesdo, K., Knappe, S., & Pine, D. S. (2009). Anxiety and anxiety disorders in children and adolescents: Developmental issues and implications for DSM-V. *The Psychiatric Clinics of North America, 32*(3), 483–524.

Biederman, J., Hirshfeld-Becker, D. R., Rosenbaum, J. F., Herot, C., Friedman, D., Snidman, N., et al. (2001). Further evidence of association between behavioral inhibition and social anxiety in children. *The American Journal of Psychiatry, 158*(10), 1673–1979.

Boldero, J., Frydenberg, E., & Fallon, B. (1993, September–October). Adolescents' view of themselves as predictors of their coping strategies. Paper presented at the *28th Annual Conference of the Australian Psychological Society*, Gold Coast, QLD.

Chalmers, K., Frydenberg, E., & Deans, J. (2011). An exploration into the coping strategies of preschoolers: Implications for professional practice. *Children Australia, 36*(3), 120–127. doi:10.1375/jcas.36.3.120.

Cheshire, G., & Campbell, M. (1997). Adolescent coping: Differences in the styles and strategies used by learning disabled students compared to non-learning disabled students. *Australian Journal of Guidance and Counselling, 7*(1), 65–73.

Cogan, N., & Schwannauer, M. (2011). Understanding adolescent risk-taking behaviour: Exploring the motivations, personalities and coping styles of young people in a school-based population. In *Personality and coping, Series on stress and coping in education* (pp. 91–110). Greenwich, CT: Information Age Publishing.

Compas, B. E. (1987). Coping with stress during childhood and adolescence. *Psychological Bulletin, 101*(3), 393–403.

Compas, B. E. (1998). An agenda for coping research and theory: Basic and applied developmental issues. *International Journal of Behavioral Development, 22*, 231–237.

Compas, B. E. (2009). Coping, regulation, and development during childhood and adolescence. *New Directions for Child and Adolescent Development, 2009*(124), 87–99. doi:10.1002/cd.245.

Compas, B. E., Connor-Smith, J. K., Saltzman, H., Thomsen, A. H., & Wadsworth, M. E. (2001). Coping with stress during childhood and adolescence: Problems, progress, and potential in theory and research. *Psychological Bulletin, 127*(1), 87–127.

Cornell, C. (2015). *The relationship between coping and anxiety in preschoolers: Does situation and anxiety types make a difference?* Unpublished Masters manuscript. Graduate School of Education, University of Melbourne, Melbourne, VIC.

Cunningham, E. (1997). *A model of predicting adolescent depressive syndromes using teacher and self-evaluations.* Unpublished Bachelor of Science (Honours), Department of Psychology, Monash University, Melbourne, VIC.

Dadds, M. R., & Barrett, P. M. (2001). Practitioner review: Psychological management of anxiety disorders in childhood. *Journal of Child Psychology and Psychiatry, 42*(8), 999–1011.

Davies, S. (1995). *The relationship between beliefs held by gifted students and the strategies they use. Unpublished Master of Educational Psychology project.* University of Melbourne, Melbourne, VIC.

Din, N. C., Bee, S. S., Subramaniam, P., & Oon, N. L. (2010). The prevalence and factors influencing posttraumatic stress disorders (PTSD) among help-seeking women experiencing domestic violence in Malaysia. *ASEAN Journal of Psychiatry, 11*(2), 158–170.

Egger, H. L., & Angold, A. (2006). Common emotional and behavioral disorders in preschool children: Presentation, nosology, and epidemiology. *Journal of Child Psychology and Psychiatry, 47*(3–4), 313–337.

Evert, H. (1996). *Gender, culture, psychological and social resources and their influence on coping behaviour in physiotherapy students.* Unpublished Master of Educational Psychology thesis, University of Melbourne, VIC.

Fallon, B., Frydenberg, E., & Boldero, J. (1993, September–October). Perception of family functioning and coping in adolescents. Paper presented at the *28th Annual Conference of the Australian Psychological Society,* Gold Coast, QLD.

Folkman, S., & Lazarus, R. S. (1988). The relationship between coping and emotion: Implications for theory and research. *Social Science & Medicine (1982), 26*(3), 309–317.

Folkman, S., Lazarus, R. S., Gruen, R. J., & DeLongis, A. (1986). Appraisal, coping, health status, and psychological symptoms. *Journal of Personality and Social Psychology, 50*(3), 571–579.

Freedy, J. R., & Hobfoll, S. E. (1994). Stress inoculation for reduction of burnout: A conservation of resources approach. *Anxiety, Stress, and Coping, 6*(4), 311.

Frydenberg, E. (1994). Adolescent concerns: The concomitants of coping. *Australian Journal of Educational and Developmental Psychology, 4*, 1–11.

Frydenberg, E. (2008). *Adolescent coping: Advances in theory, research and practice.* Hoboken, NJ: Taylor and Francis.

Frydenberg, E., Care, E., Freeman, E., & Chan, E. (2009). Interrelationships between coping, school connectedness and wellbeing. *Australian Journal of Educational Research, 53*(3), 261–276.

Frydenberg, E., & Deans, J. (2011a). Coping competencies in the early years: Identifying the strategies that preschoolers use. In P. Buchwald, K. A. Moore, & T. Ringeisen (Eds.), *Stress and anxiety: Application to education and health* (pp. 17–26). Berlin, Germany: Logos.

Frydenberg, E., & Deans, J. (2011b). *The early years coping cards.* Melbourne, VIC: Australian Council for Educational Research.

Frydenberg, E., & Lewis, R. (1991). Adolescent coping: The different ways in which boys and girls cope. *Journal of Adolescence, 14*(2), 119–133.

Frydenberg, E., & Lewis, R. (1993a). *Manual, The adolescent coping scale.* Melbourne, VIC: Australian Council for Educational Research.

Frydenberg, E., & Lewis, R. (1993b). Boys play sport a nd girls turn to others: Age, gender and ethnicity as determinants of coping. *Journal of Adolescence, 16*(3), 253–266.

Frydenberg, E., & Lewis, R. (1996a). A replication study of the structure of the adolescent coping scale: Multiple forms and applications of a self-report inventory in a counselling and research context. *European Journal of Psychological Assessment, 12*(3), 224–235.

Frydenberg, E., & Lewis, R. (1996b). Social issues: What concerns young people and how they cope. *Peace and Conflict, 2*(3), 271–283.

Frydenberg, E., & Lewis, R. (1997). *Coping scale for adults.* Melbourne, VIC: Australian Council for Educational Research.

Frydenberg, E., & Lewis, R. (1999). Academic and general wellbeing: The relationship with coping. *Australian Journal of Guidance and Counselling, 9*(1), 19–36.

Frydenberg, E., & Lewis, R. (2000). Teaching coping to adolescents: When and to whom? *American Educational Research Journal, 37*, 727–745.

Frydenberg, E., & Lewis, R. (2002a). Do managers cope productively? A comparison between Australian middle level managers and adults in the general community. *Journal of Managerial Psychology, 17*, 640–654.

Frydenberg, E., & Lewis, R. (2002b). Adolescent wellbeing: Building young people's resources. In E. Frydenberg (Ed.), *Beyond coping: Meeting goals, vision and challenges* (pp. 175–194). Oxford, UK: Oxford University Press.

Frydenberg, E., & Lewis, R. (2009a). Relationship among wellbeing, avoidant coping and active coping in a large sample of Australian adolescents. *Psychological Reports, 104*(3), 745–758.

Frydenberg, E., & Lewis, R. (2009b). The Relationship between problem-solving efficacy and coping amongst Australian adolescents. *British Journal of Guidance and Counselling, 37*(1), 51–64.

Frydenberg, E., & Lewis, R. (2011). *Adolescent coping scale – Second Edition (ACS-2).* Melbourne, VIC: Australian Council for Educational Research (ACER Press).

Frydenberg, E., & Lewis, R. (2014). *Coping scale for adults – Second Edition (CSA-2).* Melbourne, VIC: Australian Council for Educational Research (ACER Press).

Frydenberg, E., Lewis, R., Ardila, R., E., & Kennedy, G. (2000). Adolescent concern with social issues: An exploratory comparison between Australian, Colombian, and northern Irish students. *Peace and Conflict: Journal of Peace Psychology, 7*(1), 59–76.

Frydenberg, E., Lewis, R., Kennedy, G., Ardila, R., Frindte, W., & Hannoun, R. (2003). Coping with concerns: An exploratory comparison of Australian, Colombian, German and Palestinian adolescents. *Journal of Youth and Adolescence, 32*(1), 59–66.

Furniss, T., Beyer, T., & Guggenmos, J. (2006). Prevalence of behavioural and emotional problems among six-years-old preschool children. *Social Psychiatry and Psychiatric Epidemiology, 41*(5), 394–399. doi:10.1007/s00127-006-0045-3.

Goble, G. (1995). *Assessment of coping strategies.* Unpublished research report, Monash University, Melbourne, VIC.

Gould, K., Ponsford, J., Johnston, L., & Schönberger, M. (2011). Predictive and associated factors of psychiatric disorders after traumatic brain injury: A prospective study. *Journal of Neurotrauma, 28*(7), 1155–1163.

Greenglass, E. (2002). Chapter 3. Proactive coping. In E. Frydenberg (Ed.), *Beyond coping: Meeting goals, vision, and challenges* (pp. 37–62). London: Oxford University Press.

Gulliford, H., Deans, J., Frydenberg, E., & Liang, R. (2015). Teaching coping skills in the context of positive parenting within a preschool setting. *Australian Psychologist, 50*(3), 219–231. doi:10.1111/ap.12121.

Hadwin, J. A., Garner, M., & Perez-Olivas, G. (2006). The development of information processing biases in childhood anxiety: A review and exploration of its origins in parenting. *Clinical Psychology Review, 26*(7), 876–894.

Hobfoll, S. E. (1989). Conservation of resources: A new attempt at conceptualizing stress. *The American Psychologist, 44*(3), 513–524.

Hobfoll, S. E. (1998). *Stress culture and community: The psychology and philosophy of stress.* New York: Plenum Press.

Hsieh, M., Ponsford, J., Wong, D., Schönberger, M., Taffe, J., & Mckay, A. (2012). Motivational interviewing and cognitive behaviour therapy for anxiety following traumatic brain injury: A pilot randomised controlled trial. *Neuropsychological Rehabilitation, 22*(4), 585–608.

Jenkin, C. (1997). *The relationship between self-efficacy and coping: Changes following an Outward Bound program. Unpublished Master of Educational Psychology project.* University of Melbourne, Melbourne, VIC.

Jenkins, J. M., Smith, M. A., & Graham, P. J. (1989). Coping with parental quarrels. *Journal of the American Academy of Child and Adolescent Psychiatry, 28*(2), 182–189.

Jones, B. (1997). *The transition from secondary school to university: Who needs help coping with academic stress and when.* Unpublished Master of Educational Psychology thesis, University of Melbourne, Melbourne, VIC.

Kagan, J. (1997). Temperament and the reactions to unfamiliarity. *Child Development, 68*(1), 139–143.

Kagan, J., Snidman, N., Arcus, D., & Reznick, J. S. (1994). *Galen's prophecy: Temperament in human nature.* New York: Basic Books.

Kerig, P. K. (2001). Children's coping with interparental conflict. In I. J. J. Grych & H. Fincham (Eds.), *Interparental conflict and child development* (pp. 213–248). New York: Cambridge University Press.

Lazarus, R. S. (1991). *Emotion and adaption.* New York: Oxford University Press.

Lazarus, R. S. (1993). Coping theory and research: Past, present, and future. *Psychosomatic Medicine, 55*(3), 234–247.

Lazarus, R. S., & Folkman, S. (1984). *Stress, appraisal, and coping.* New York: Springer.

Lewis, R., & Frydenberg, E. (2004a). Students' self-evaluation of their coping: How well do they do it? In E. Frydenberg (Ed.), *Thriving, surviving, or going under: Coping with everyday lives* (pp. 23–43). Connecticut: Information Age Publishing.

Lewis, R., & Frydenberg, E. (2004b). Thriving, surviving or going under, which coping strategies relate to which outcomes? In E. Frydenberg (Ed.), *Thriving, surviving or going under: Coping with everyday lives, Series, research on stress and coping in education* (pp. 3–24). Greenwich, CT: Information Age Publishing.

Lewis, R., & Frydenberg, E. (2007). Adolescent problem-solving efficacy and coping strategy usage in a population of Australian adolescents. In G. S. Gates (Ed.), *Emerging thought and research on student, teacher and administrator stress and coping* (pp. 35–48). Greenwich, CT: Information Age Publishing.

Lewis, R., Roache, J., & Romi, S. (2011). Coping styles as mediators of teachers' classroom management techniques. *Research in Education, 85*(1), 53–68.

Lynham, S. (1996). *Comparison between coping styles of young women with anorexia nervosa and coping styles of mothers and daughters with anorexia nervosa: An exploratory investigation.* Unpublished Master of Education thesis, La Trobe University, Melbourne, VIC.

Mann, L., Nota, L., Soresi, S., Ferrari, L., & Frydenberg, E. (2011). The relationship between decision-making style and coping strategies in adolescence. In G. Reevy & E. Frydenberg (Eds.), *Personality and coping, Series on stress and coping in education* (pp. 25–48). Charlotte, NC: Information Age Publishing.

Marshall, P. (2008). *Stress and coping among professional mediators.* Melbourne, VIC: Faculty of Education, University of Melbourne.

McClure, E. B., Brennan, P. A., Hammen, C., & Le Brocque, R. M. (2001). Parental anxiety disorders, child anxiety disorders, and the perceived parent–child relationship in an Australian high-risk sample. *Journal of Abnormal Child Psychology, 29*(1), 1–10.

McDonald, A. (1996). *Approaches to learning of tertiary students: The role of coping, developmentally-related variables and study stressors.* Unpublished Master of Educational Psychology Thesis, University of Melbourne, Melbourne, VIC.

McGowan, M. (2016, January 25). Australian Open 2016: Spain's Carla Suarez Navarro beats Australia's Daria Gavrilova in fourth round. Herald Sun. Retrieved from http://www.news.com.au/

McTaggart, H. (1996). *Students at risk of school exclusion: How they cope.* Unpublished Master of Educational Psychology project. University of Melbourne, Melbourne, VIC.

Moskowitz, G. B., & Grant, H. (2009). *The psychology of goals/edited by Gordon B. Moskowitz, Heidi Grant.* New York: Guilford Press, c2009.

Neill, L. (1996). *Ethnicity, gender, self-esteem and coping styles: A comparison of Australian and South-East Asian adolescents.* Unpublished Graduate Diploma of Counselling Psychology project, Royal Melbourne Institute of Technology.

Nicolotti, L., El-Sheikh, M., & Whitson, S. M. (2003). Children's coping with marital conflict and their adjustment and physical health: Vulnerability and protective functions. *Journal of Family Psychology, 17*(3), 315–326.

Noto, S.S. (1995). *The relationship between coping and achievement: A comparison between adolescent males and females.* Unpublished Master of Educational Psychology project, University of Melbourne, Melbourne, VIC.

O'Brien, M., Bahadur, M. A., Gee, C., Balto, K., & Erber, S. (1997). Child exposure to marital conflict and child coping responses as predictors of child adjustment. *Cognitive Therapy and Research, 21*(1), 39–59.

Parsons, A., Frydenberg, E., & Poole, C. (1996). Overachievement and coping strategies in adolescent males. *British Journal of Educational Psychology, 66*(1), 109–114.

Perkins-Gough, D. (2013). The significance of grit: A conversation with Angela Lee Duckworth. *Educational Leadership, 71*(1), 14–20.

Pincus, D. B., & Friedman, A. G. (2004). Improving children's coping with everyday stress: Transporting treatment interventions to the school setting. *Clinical Child and Family Psychology Review, 7*(4), 223–240.

Poot, A. C. (1997). *Client factors which moderate outcome in an adolescent psychotherapy treatment program.* Unpublished Master of Counselling, School of Education, La Trobe University, Melbourne, VIC.

Poynton, E., & Frydenberg, E. (2011). Coping styles and anxiety amongst female victims of bullying. In G. Reevy & E. Frydenberg (Eds.), *Personality and coping, Series on stress and coping in education* (pp. 67–89). Greenwich, UK: Information Age Publishing.

Rapee, R. M. (2002). The development and modification of temperamental risk for anxiety disorders: Prevention of a lifetime of anxiety? *Biological Psychiatry, 52*(10), 947–957.

Rapee, R. M., Schniering, C. A., & Hudson, J. L. (2009). Anxiety disorders during childhood and adolescence: Origins and treatment. *Annual Review of Clinical Psychology, 5*, 311–341.

Reynolds, W. M. (2001). *Reynolds adolescent adjustment screening inventory.* Odessa, FL: PAR (Psychological Assessment Resources, Inc.).

Richards, J. (2012). Teacher stress and coping strategies: A national snapshot. *The Educational Forum, 76*(3), 299–316. Retrieved from http://search.proquest.com.ezp.lib.unimelb.edu.au/docview/102 7918073?accountid=12372

Romi, S., Lewis, R., & Roache, J. (2013). Classroom management and teachers' coping strategies: Inside classrooms in Australia, China and Israel. *Prospects (00331538), 43*(2), 215. doi:10.1007/ s11125-013-9271-0.

Sanson, A., Pedlow, R., Cann, W., Prior, M., & Oberklaid, F. (1996). Shyness ratings: Stability and correlates in early childhood. *International Journal of Behavioral Development, 19*(4), 705–724.

Schwarzer, R., & Taubert, S. (2002). Tenacious goal pursuits and striving toward personal growth: Proactive coping. In E. Fydenberg (Ed.), *Beyond coping: Meeting goals, visions and challenges* (pp. 19–35). London: Oxford University Press.

Seiffge-Krenke, I., & Shulman, S. (1990). Coping style in adolescence: A cross-cultural study. *Journal of Cross-Cultural Psychology, 21*(3), 351–377.

Seligman, M. E. P., & Csikszentmihalyi, M. (2000). Positive psychology: An introduction. *The American Psychologist, 5*(1), 5–14.

Skinner, E. A., & Zimmer-Gembeck, M. (2009a). Challenges to the developmental study of coping. *New Directions for Child and Adolescent Development, 2009a*(124), 5–17. doi:10.1002/cd.239.

Skinner, E. A., & Zimmer-Gembeck, M. J. (Eds.) (2009b). Introduction: Challenges to the developmental study of coping, *Perspective on children's coping with stress as regulation of emotion, cognition and behavior. New directions in child and adolescent development series* (Issue 124, pp. 5–17). New York: Wiley.

Skok, M. (1996). Hearing impairment: Coping and social support. Unpublished Master thesis, University of Melbourne, Melbourne, VIC.

Spanjer, K. (1999). The relationship between locus of control and coping constructs as predictors of academic performance in an adult sample. Unpublished research report, Monash University, Melbourne, VIC.

Spear, L. P. (2000a). Neurobehavioral changes in adolescence. *Current Directions in Psychological Science, 9*(4), 111–114.

Spear, L. P. (2000b). The adolescent brain and age-related behavioral manifestations. *Neuroscience and Biobehavioral Reviews, 24*(4), 417–463.

Spence, S. H., Rapee, R., McDonald, C., & Ingram, M. (2001). The structure of anxiety symptoms among preschoolers. *Behaviour Research and Therapy, 39*, 1293–1316.

Stark, L. J., Spirito, A., Williams, C. A., & Guevremont, D. C. (1989). Common problems and coping strategies: Findings with normal adolescents. *Journal of Abnormal Child Psychology, 17*(2), 203–212.

Stevenson, R. (1996). *Academic self-concept, perceived stress and adolescents' coping styles in the VCE*. Unpublished Bachelor of Social Science (Family Studies), Australian Catholic University.

Suveg, C., & Zeman, J. (2004). Emotion regulation in children with anxiety disorders. *Journal of Clinical Child and Adolescent Psychology, 33*(4), 750–759.

Szczepanski, H. (1995). *A study of homesickness phenomenon among female boarding high school students*. Unpublished Master of Educational Psychology project, University of Melbourne, Melbourne, VIC.

Wilson, G. S., Pritchard, M. E., & Revalee, B. (2005). Individual differences in adolescent health symptoms: The effects of gender and coping. *Journal of Adolescence, 23*(3), 369–379.

Wilson, H. (2012). *Teaching children with autism: The resources and coping styles of teachers*. Unpublished Master of Educational Psychology thesis. University of Melbourne, Melbourne, VIC.

Yeo, K., Frydenberg, E., Northam, E., & Deans, J. (2014). Coping with stress among preschool children and associations with anxiety level and controllability of situations. *Australian Journal of Psychology, 66*(2), 93–101. doi:10.1111/ajpy.12047.

Zimmer-Gembeck, M. J., & Collins, W. A. (2003). Autonomy development during adolescence. In G. R. Adams & M. Berzonsky (Eds.), *Blackwell handbook of Adolescence* (pp. 175–204). Oxford, UK: Blackwell.

Zimmer-Gembeck, M. J., & Skinner, E. A. (2008). Adolescents coping with stress: Development and diversity. *The Prevention Researcher, 15*(4), 3–7.

6

Social Support, Proactivity, and Related Approaches

When it comes to resilience there are key elements of coping that contribute in a major way to prediction of successful outcomes, depending on the circumstances in which an individual finds himself or herself in. This chapter focuses on two particular approaches to coping that are highly linked to resilience. The first is the notion of affiliation and support from others and the second relates to particular forms of coping that help to put the individual or the group in a healthy situation to benefit from good outcomes.

Affiliation with others is a basic human response which is linked to the use of social support and related constructs such communal and dyadic coping. As with all coping these approaches vary according to culture and context. Whilst coping has traditionally been defined in terms of appraisal, transaction between the individual and the environment, and

---

I focus on positive outcomes. It's the projection of how it's going to feel when you've succeeded. Specifically, when I'm playing, and very nervous about it (you should be nervous to do it well, it's a normal part of it), I make myself as nervous as possible at the piano during the rehearsal so that on stage I do the reverse, I make myself as calm as possible. The piano looks the same, the music is the same. I flip it and it becomes normal and comfortable on stage, just as it became normal to be nervous at rehearsals. (Robyn, concert pianist)

© The Author(s) 2017   **111**
E. Frydenberg, *Coping and the Challenge of Resilience*,
DOI 10.1057/978-1-137-56924-0_6

reaction, that is, how people respond after or during a stressful event, more recently the generic construct has become extended to include particular aspects of the coping process such as proactive coping, anticipatory coping, and preventive coping. The proactive anticipatory and preventative approaches are key elements of resilience.

Affiliation is a biological response that occurs among both men and women as a buffer against stress. In response to their affiliative efforts, people commonly experience social support. There are benefits of affiliation for mental and physical health. Women are likely to respond to stress by protecting the self and their offspring. This has come to be known as the 'tend and befriend' approach (Taylor, 2010) that is in contrast to the 'fight or flight' approach which has come to be regarded as a more male gendered approach to stress.

Not all research shows beneficial effects of affiliation in challenging circumstances. There are cultural influences. For example, certain adverse impacts of social support are experienced by East Asians more acutely than European Americans. That is, East Asians and Asian Americans are more reluctant to explicitly ask for social support (Taylor et al., 2004).

Social Support

There is a distinction between explicit (use of social networks) and implicit social support, that is, receiving comfort from friends without necessarily disclosing or discussing problems.

Social support has been a key index of successful coping and an interest of many researchers (Greenglass & Fiksenbaum, 2009; Lelorain, Tessier, Florin, & Bonnaud-Antignac, 2012; Thoits, 1986, 1995). Some researchers like Greenglass (2002) have linked social support and coping in their theoretical discussions of coping. For example, when discussing proactive coping, Greenglass notes that there is an integral relationship between social support and coping. Moreover, social support is considered to be an essential resource for the development of proactive forms of coping (Greenglass, 2002). This approach recognises the importance of resources in others, which can be incorporated into the behavioural and cognitive coping repertoire of the individual (Greenglass & Fiksenbaum, 2009).

It has been pointed out that research has emphasised the social aspects of coping more from a cultural-sociological perspective than from solely a coping skills perspective (Hobfoll, 2002). Hobfoll considers the communal aspects of coping, that is, when coping is about coping together with others rather than the common understandings where individual effort is responsible for the desired outcomes. An independent style may be more efficient for the individual, but not necessarily for the group. Hobfoll and colleagues (Hobfoll, Johnson, Ennis, & Jackson, 2003) explored the notion that personal agency was more related to individualised action than to social coping and use of social support. They found that self-mastery was strongly associated with lower levels of anger and depressive mood. They explained that the likely reason being that there is a cost of connectedness such as, compromise or conforming to group expectations or needs. Nevertheless, those high on communal mastery, use less antisocial modes of coping, with women reporting higher levels of communal coping. Overall, the conclusion from three separate studies was that 'communal mastery appears to be related to greater concern for others, less alienation from social relationships, and more close attachments to a supportive social network from which satisfaction can be derived' (Hobfoll, 2002, p. 71). Hobfoll notes that the overreliance on personal agency in the stress literature limits our understanding of the role of attachment and relationships in a cultural context.

This has implications for resilience in that there is likely to be greater success in many endeavours when there is support and input from others.

As Bandura (1997) noted 'the strength of families, communities, organisations, social institutions, and even nations lies partly in people's sense of collective efficacy that they can solve the problem they face and improve their lives through unified effort, groups and organisations' (cited in Brandan et al., 2013, p. 477).

Communal Coping

Hobfoll (1998) emphasised that we are all socially connected individuals who are culturally linked to 'families and tribes' rather than seeing individuals as completely self-reliant. Resilience is often considered in terms of the individuals' mastery of situations with which they are confronted. But clearly there are benefits to 'sharing' the load and being able to call on others and much to be gained from receiving the tangible support and assistance of others. Belonging to a group in itself can promote resilience if the participants are accepting or able to share their experiences. 'Together' rather than 'alone' is the better option. Hobfoll calls this, communal coping, a reappraisal of stressors to 'our issues' as opposed to 'your issues'. Research has shown a positive association between communal coping and health outcomes, problem solving, and marital satisfaction.

Hobfoll (2010) in his chapter on 'Conservation of Resources Theory: Its Implications for Stress, Health and Resilience' highlights how COR theory focuses on the common or communal appraisals of threat and loss in 'individuals who share a common biology or culture'. The focus is on circumstances rather than individual appraisal. This is consistent with the fact that COR theory was born out of major traumatic stress. He talks of caravans of resources (see Chap. 3) that individuals and families can develop and maintain. In his studies of post-traumatic growth, a concept that refers to the positive psychological change that can be construed as an outcome of adversity such as post ill health, loss, or disasters (Tedeschi & Calhoun, 2004), Hobfoll concluded that growth was experienced in some of their studies, but it was greater when those individuals experienced greatest psychosocial and economic resource loss. He also explores the relationship between engagement defined as a persistent, pervasive, and positive affective-motivational state of fulfilment in individuals who are reacting to challenging situations. For him individuals need a 'strong armamentarium of material, social, personal and energy resources'. It is postulated that supportive environments create passageways for engagement. Psychosocial resource loss was the predictor of PTS and depression symptoms.

Dyadic Coping

An extension of the focus on community and the notion of support from individuals or collectives is dyadic coping. Much of the research in this field has addressed couples in the context of married life. Issues of spousal support in the context of marital or step-parenting conflict, chronic pain, illnesses such as rheumatoid arthritis and cancer have been reported extensively (Coyne & Smith, 1991; Englbrecht, Wendler, & Alten, 2012; King & DeLongis, 2014). Overall, there is strong evidence of empathic coping contributing to relationship building (Herzberg, 2013; O'Brien, DeLongis, Pomaki, Puterman, & Zwicker, 2009) and as a way of reducing marital tension. DeLongis and O'Brien (1990), in their examination of how families cope with Alzheimer's disease, discuss how interpersonal factors may be important as predictors of the individual's ability to cope with the situation. They talk about the importance of drawing on the resources of others for coping with difficult situations.

More recently, researchers are beginning to unpack the relationship between individual and dyadic coping. For example, Herzberg (2013) found that while there are mutual influences in a couple relationship on 'pragmatic' coping, this is not the case for emotion-related coping. The resilient individual is likely to draw on the resources of themselves and others. He or she is likely to be engaged with others in helpful and productive ways. Additionally he or she is likely to anticipate events and prepare for them in advance as they are best able.

Proactive Coping

Proactive coping is future oriented. It has the main features of planning, goal attainment, and the use of resources to obtain goals. The proactive coper takes initiative, uses others and takes the credit for successes, and does not blame himself or herself for failures. The proactive coper chooses actions according to how he or she imagines the future. In that sense it is closely aligned to resilience. Schwarzer and Knoll (2003) draw a distinction between reactive coping (dealing with an event that has just happened such as an accident), anticipatory coping (dealing with an event that is highly likely to happen such as a rainstorm that has been predicted) and preventative coping (where protections are made against potential threat of loss, such as taking out insurance). The conceptualisation of coping that emphasises the amassing of resources is highly consistent with that of Aspinwall and Taylor (1997) and Hobfoll (1989).

Anticipatory coping and preventative coping, whilst distinguishable from proactive coping, are often incorporated into the proactive coping construct and the instruments that measure it. Anticipation of loss, threat, harm, and challenge is central to the transactional theory of coping, but most research has focused on the ways in which individuals deal with stress rather than anticipate the future occurrence of events. However, Aspinwall and Taylor (1997) considered a more future-oriented approach to coping that predicts how an individual may adjust to a future event. They labelled this as 'proactive coping'.

Proactive coping is the process of anticipating potential stressors and act-ing 'in advance either to prevent them or to mute their impact' (Aspinwall & Taylor, 1997, p. 417). As such, proactive coping blends activities typi-cally considered to be coping (activities undertaken to master, reduce or tolerate environmental or intrapsychic demands perceived as represent-ing potential threat, existing harm, or loss) (Folkman & Lazarus, 1985; Lazarus & Folkman, 1984) with those considered to be self-regulation (the process through which people control, direct, and correct their own actions as they move towards or away from various goals (Aspinwall, 2005; Carver & Scheier, 1998; Fiske & Taylor, 1991). Proactive coping combines these two processes by examining people's emotions, thoughts, and behaviours, as they anticipate and address potential sources of adver-sity that might interfere with the pursuit of their goals) (Aspinwall & Taylor, 1997, pp. 334–335). Aspinwall and Taylor's (1997) proactive coping model is like that of Hobfoll (see Chap. 2). Essentially it is about building of personal and financial resources, screening the environment for danger and asking oneself, 'What can I do?' Which is really similar to the question, 'Do I have the strategies to cope?' Proactive coping is about taking an active effort to predict events and prepare for them and as such it is more helpful than avoidant behaviour.

According to Aspinwall and Taylor (1997) proactive coping is effica-cious where the resource cost is modest so that chronic stress can be kept under control by building resources, but there is a cost if the stresses do not materialise after an investment of resources. Proactive is differ-ent from anticipatory which is about bracing oneself for expected conse-quences of a known or imminent stress.

There are four components of the proactive coping process. Firstly, there is an emphasis on building reserves, including temporal, financial, and social resources. This is similar to that of Hobfoll's (1989) focus on amassing of resources and protection of resources so that losses do not occur. That is, coping is proactive or preventative of future loss. Secondly, there is a recognition of future stresses which anticipates what might change in the environment or in the circumstances. Thirdly, there is an initial appraisal of potential stresses which call on preliminary coping efforts and the soliciting of feedback about one's efforts (Aspinwall, 2005).

Some like Greenglass (2002), Schwarzer (2001), and Schwarzer and Taubert (2002) consider that proactive coping creates opportunities for personal growth and the building up of resources whilst others like Aspinwall (2005) and Aspinwall and Taylor (1997) focus more on the prevention of future threats rather than advancing personal goals.

Situational aspects are more important in shaping proactive coping behaviour than individual characteristics. In a vignette study among adults preparing for ageing (Ouwehand, Ridder, & Bensing, 2006) 123 adults aged 50–70 years were exposed to three situations, namely, health, social relationships, and personal finance. Proactive coping was used most frequently in health-related situations. Socio-demographic variables, such as age, gender, and education did not contribute significantly. Proactive coping varies within persons and situational factors, that is, type of stressor, how the threat is appraised, and the capacity for resources and assets to protect against future loss.

In contrast, preventative coping is about efforts to offset potential problems (Greenglass, 2002; Greenglass, Schwarzer, & Taubert, 1999; Schwarzer, 2001). Related terms are also used such as personal initiative to describe efforts to both overcome problems and develop new opportunities (Frese, Kring, Soose, & Zempel, 1996). In that sense, proactive coping can be both prevention focused and promotion focused. Achievement is about goals and proactive coping has gone beyond that, particularly when it comes to health and ageing (Table 6.1).

Table 6.1 Definition and function of proactive, anticipatory, and preventive coping

	Definition[a]	Function	Example
Proactive coping	An effort to build up general resources that facilitate the achievement of challenging goals and promote personal growth	Goal management—to construct a path of action for risks and demands and create opportunities for growth in the future	I visualise my dream to be an entrepreneur and try to find ways and support to achieve them
Anticipatory coping	An effort to deal with imminent threat in a near future event	Solving the actual problem at hand—such as increasing effort, getting help, or investing other resources	When I feel threatened by an upcoming public speaking event, I imagine success scenarios and seek help from experienced speakers
Preventive coping	An effort to build up general resistance resources that reduce the severity of the consequences of *possible* stressors, and lessen the likelihood of the onset of stressful events in the first place	Risk management—to manage various unknown risks in the distant future	I maintain a healthy lifestyle to buffer myself against stressors in life

[a]Definitions adapted from Greenglass (2002)

Proactive coping has four advantages over reactive coping:

1. Proactive coping is directed at avoiding future stress or minimising its effect, and feelings of distress may also diminish as a consequence.
2. Chronic stress is kept under control.
3. The available resources are greater because resources have not yet been used up.

4. Many coping options are still available as stressors are confronted before they are fully developed. (Ouwehand et al., 2006)

A proactive approach to coping is captured in the Proactive Coping Inventory, which consists of six scales that measure coping from a proactive perspective (Greenglass et al., 1999). For these theorists, proactive coping involves appraisal of demands as challenges, and consists of active coping, self-efficacy, anticipatory behaviour and planning, and utilising social resources (Greenglass et al., 1999). All these could be termed future-oriented coping and could be construed as building resilience.

What We Know from Research

Proactive coping integrates a positive and agentic approach to the management of future events. In a sample of 232 emerging adults, Social Wellbeing, Social Actualisation, such as, 'I think the world is becoming a better place for everyone'; Social Contribution 'I think we have something valuable to give to the world'; Goal Acceptance 'I believe that people are kind'; Social Integration 'I feel close to other people in the community'; Social Coherence 'The world is too complex for me' (reverse coded)—showed a positive relationship with proactive coping strategies such as 'after attaining a goal I look for another more challenging one'; reflective coping 'I think about every possible outcome to a problem before tackling it' and preventative coping 'I make plans for things to do before bad events happen' (Zambianchi & Bitti, 2014). Proactive coping was a partial mediator in the relationship between both optimism and self-esteem and trait anxiety. Findings have indicated that proactive coping enhances a perspective on life that involves positive attitude towards future events in the form of optimistic experiences and enhanced feelings of self-worth.

Two hundred and four undergraduate students using the proactive scale of the Proactive Coping Inventory (Greenglass et al., 1999) also confirmed that there is an association between optimism and proactive coping. The relationship between optimism and proactive coping is supported by other studies such as that of Aspinwall (2005). Optimists are more likely to be engaged in goal attainment (Griva & Anagnostopoulos, 2010).

Proactive coping competencies can be taught. It is suggested that introducing proactive coping skills can protect against anxieties about the future. Proactive coping skills can mitigate the lack of controllability about the future which is manifested in anxiety about the future. Applications for ageing, stigma and discrimination, organisational behaviour, and health, include genetic testing, health promotion, medical decision making, and management of chronic illness. As with coping in general, personal and social resources matter for proactive coping.

Concluding Remarks

Whilst coping in general has been widely reported, there are various more defined approaches to coping that have utility in research and practice. In this chapter communal dyadic and proactive coping are considered with a particular emphasis on social support as a key construct. Additionally there is a deliniation between proactive, anticipatory and preventative coping.

References

Aspinwall, L. G. (2005). The psychology of future-oriented thinking: From achievement to proactive coping, adaptation, and aging. *Motivation and Emotion, 29*(4), 203–235.

Aspinwall, L. G., & Taylor, S. E. (1997). A stitch in time: Self-regulation and proactive coping. *Psychological Bulletin, 121*(3), 417.

Bandura, A. (1997). *Self-efficacy : The exercise of control.* New York: Freeman.

Brandan, M. M., Goddard, N. A., Kabir, B., Lofton, S. S., Ruiz, J., & Hau, J. M. (2013). Resilience and retirement, coping self-efficacy and collective self-efficacy: Implementing positive psychology during times of economic hardship for late-career individuals. *Career Planning and Adult Development Journal, 29*(4), 25–36.

Carver, C. S., & Scheier, M. F. (1998). *On the self-regulation of behavior.* New York: Cambridge University Press.

Coyne, J. C., & Smith, D. A. (1991). Couples coping with a myocardial infarction: A contextual perspective on wives' distress. *Journal of Personality and Social Psychology, 61*(3), 404–412.

DeLongis, A., & O'Brien, T. B. (1990). An interpersonal framework for stress and coping: An application to the families of Alzheimer's patients. In M. A. P. Stephens, J. H. Crowther, S. E. Hobfoll, & D. L. Tennenbaum (Eds.), *Stress and coping in later life families* (pp. 221–239). Washington, DC: Hemisphere Publishers.

Englbrecht, M., Wendler, J., & Alten, R. (2012). Depression as a systemic feature of rheumatoid arthritis. *Zeitschrift für Rheumatologie, 71*(10), 859–863. doi:10.1007/s00393-011-0926-z.

Fiske, S. T., & Taylor, S. E. (1991). *Social cognition* (2nd ed.). New York: McGraw-Hill.

Folkman, S., & Lazarus, R. S. (1985). If it changes it must be a process: Study of emotion and coping during three stages of a college examination. *Journal of Personality and Social Psychology, 48*(1), 150–170.

Frese, M., Kring, W., Soose, A., & Zempel, J. (1996). PI at work: Differences between East and West Germany. *Academy of Management Journal, 39*, 37–63.

Greenglass, E. (2002). Chapter 3. Proactive coping. In E. Frydenberg (Ed.), *Beyond coping: Meeting goals, vision, and challenges* (pp. 37–62). London: Oxford University Press.

Greenglass, E. R., & Fiksenbaum, L. (2009). Proactive coping, positive affect, and well-being: Testing for mediation using path analysis. *European Psychologist, 14*(1), 29–39. doi:10.1027/1016-9040.14.1.29.

Greenglass, E. R., Schwarzer, R., & Taubert, S. (1999). *The Proactive Coping Inventory (PCI): A multidimensional research instrument.* [On-line publication]. Available at: http://userpage.fu-berlin.de/~health/greenpci.htm

Griva, F., & Anagnostopoulos, F. (2010). Positive psychological states and anxiety: The mediating effect of proactive coping. *Psychological Reports, 107*(3), 795–804.

Herzberg, P. Y. (2013). Coping in relationships: The interplay between individual and dyadic coping and their effects on relationship satisfaction. *Anxiety, Stress, and Coping, 26*(2), 136–153.

Hobfoll, S. E. (1989). Conservation of resources: A new attempt at conceptualizing stress. *The American Psychologist, 44*(3), 513–524.

Hobfoll, S. E. (1998). *Stress culture and community: The psychology and philosophy of stress.* New York: Plenum Press.

Hobfoll, S. E. (2002). Social and psychological resources and adaptation. *Review of General Psychology, 6*(4), 307–324. doi:10.1037/1089-2680.6.4.307.

Hobfoll, S. E. (2010). *Conservation of resources theory: Its implication for stress, health, and resilience.* New York: Oxford University Press.

Hobfoll, S. E., Johnson, R. J., Ennis, N., & Jackson, A. P. (2003). Resource loss, resource gain, and emotional outcomes among inner city women. *Journal of Personality and Social Psychology, 84*(3), 632–643.

King, D. B., & DeLongis, A. (2014). When couples disconnect: Rumination and withdrawal as maladaptive responses to everyday stress. *Journal of Family Psychology, 28*(4), 460–469.

Lazarus, R. S., & Folkman, S. (1984). *Stress, appraisal, and coping.* New York: Springer.

Lelorain, S., Tessier, P., Florin, A., & Bonnaud-Antignac, A. (2012). Posttraumatic growth in long term breast cancer survivors: Relation to coping, social support and cognitive processing. *Journal of Health Psychology, 17*(5), 627–639, 613p. doi:10.1177/1359105311427475.

O'Brien, T. B., DeLongis, A., Pomaki, G., Puterman, E., & Zwicker, A. (2009). Couples coping with stress: The role of empathic responding. *European Psychologist, 14*(1), 18–28. doi:10.1027/1016-9040.14.1.18.

Ouwehand, C., De Ridder, D. T. D., & Bensing, J. M. (2006). Situational aspects are more important in shaping proactive coping behaviour than individual characteristics: A vignette study among adults preparing for ageing. *Psychology & Health, 21*(6), 809–825.

Schwarzer, R. (2001). Social-cognitive factors in changing health-related behaviors. *Current Directions in Psychological Science, 10*(2), 47–51.

Schwarzer, R., & Knoll, N. (2003). Positive coping: Mastering demands and searching for meaning. In S. J. Lopez, C. R. Snyder, S. J. Lopez, & C. R. Snyder (Eds.), *Positive psychological assessment: A handbook of models and measures* (pp. 393–409). Washington, DC: American Psychological Association.

Schwarzer, R., & Taubert, S. (2002). Tenacious goal pursuits and striving toward personal growth: Proactive coping. In E. Fydenberg (Ed.), *Beyond coping: Meeting goals, visions and challenges* (pp. 19–35). London: Oxford University Press.

Taylor, S. E. (2010). *Health handbook of social psychology.* Hoboken: Wiley.

Taylor, S. E., Jarcho, J., Takagi, K., Dunagan, M. S., Sherman, D. K., & Kim, H. S. (2004). Culture and social support who seeks it and why? *Journal of Personality and Social Psychology, 87*(3), 354–362. doi: 10.103710022!3514.87.3.354.

Tedeschi, R. G., & Calhoun, L. G. (2004). Posttraumatic growth: Conceptual foundations and empirical evidence. *Psychological Inquiry, 15*, 1–18.

Thoits, P. A. (1986). Social support as coping assistance. *Journal of Consulting and Clinical Psychology, 54*(4), 416–423.

Thoits, P. A. (1995). Stress, coping, and social support processes: Where are we? What next? *Journal of Health and Social Behavior, 35*, 53–79.

Zambianchi, M., & Ricci Bitti, P. (2014). The role of proactive coping strategies, time perspective, perceived efficacy on affect regulation, divergent thinking and family communication in promoting social well-being in emerging adulthood. *Social Indicators Research, 116*(2), 493–507. doi:10.1007/s11205-013-0307-x.

7

Stress Resilience and Ageing

Stress, Coping, and Ageing

The experience of adversity has been considered to be critical to the development of resilience; and generally humans have the ability to adapt in the face of adversity. Older adults are likely to have experienced adversity throughout their life course, so their capacity to adapt has been well tested. Like coping 'resilience involves using behaviors, thoughts, and actions that individuals can learn and develop' (Resnick, 2014, p. 157).

As with coping, the capacity to adapt varies from individual to individual. Personality attributes play a part. That is, some people are likely to have a greater capacity to be resilient than others and moreover since life experiences are likely to vary from individual to individual, people's opportunities to benefit from their experience are likely to be varied. Instrumental resources such as money, that generally enables access to other resources, and provides access to supports, are likely to be available to differing extents under differing circumstances.

You learn to deal with negativity. You can't just 'put on dolphin music and be in la la land'. You have to confront setbacks and work through them. (Jackie, cancer survivor)

© The Author(s) 2017   **123**
E. Frydenberg, *Coping and the Challenge of Resilience*,
DOI 10.1057/978-1-137-56924-0_7

Additionally, there are different types of resilience such as general health resilience, psychological resilience (the opposite of hopelessness), emotional resilience (ability to separate between positive and negative emotions so as to remain positive), dispositional resilience and physical resilience, and cognitive resilience have been noted. These are all capacities that impact how an individual deals with life circumstances. Individual attributes of resilience in older adults are not that different from younger people. They are the things that are very much on the 'happiness register', that is, the things that are likely to make people happy. Numerous ways of dealing with life such as engaging in prosocial behaviour, strong self-efficacy, positive self-esteem, a sense of purpose, spirituality, ability to use humour, creativity, striving towards goal achievement, maintaining a positive attitude, flexibility, self-determination and optimism, are likely contributors to happiness.

Life expectancy is on the increase. For example, those born in 1900 were expected to live to 47.3 years; those born in 2004 are expected to live 77.8 years (NCHS, 2006); in Australia, male life expectancy at birth rose to 80.3 years in 2014 from 80.1 in 2013 and female life expectancy also increased to 84.4 years from 84.3 (ABS, 2015). It is acknowledged that there are increasing health-related conditions with age and people have differing health trajectories and the impact of stress on health is difficult to link causally (Aldwin & Werner, 2007). Nevertheless, stress is linked to elevated blood glucose and lipids (cholesterol) that can lead to chronic illness and suppression of the immune system, so some would say that chronic stress can contribute more to the development of chronic illness than life events per se (Friedman & McEwen, 2004). After reviewing the literature, Cohen, Janicki-Deverts, and Miller (2007) concluded there is considerable support for the link between stress and certain conditions such as depression, cardiovascular disease, and the progression of HIV AIDS. Stress may have more influence on the progression than the cause.

However, older adults report less stress despite poorer objective circumstances such as bereavement or illness. Older adults are likely to have survived changes in physical abilities, suffered losses of various sorts that include role-related losses such as career-related identity or become 'empty nesters' following children leaving home. Subsequently they are likely to have developed resilience in one or more areas such as, physical, emotional, and/or economic capacity.

There is an irony in that older adults are thought to experience more stress but they often report less stress than younger counterparts and appear to show greater resilience. Paradoxes are somewhat common in psychology. For example, when it comes to young people, those who are most successful at school and work may experience despair or depression whilst those who have the difficult role of caring for an ill or ageing relative remain positive and cheerful.

The two paradoxes of stress and ageing have been noted by Yancura and Aldwin (2009). They concluded that older adults learn to appraise and cope with stress differently and that protects them despite the increased physiological vulnerability. The second paradox is related to the positive aspects of stress in that under certain conditions stress can have positive or 'toughening' effects which can be construed as building resilience.

Aldwin investigated the paradoxes in two major longitudinal studies involving veterans who were screened in the mid-1960s and followed through from 22 to 80 years and who were college students from class of 1967 through to 2001. The types of problems experienced changed with age, but by the time the 80-year-olds were interviewed, nearly 20% of them could not come up with a single problem in the past week. There are multiple explanations such as those who survive in late life may be more resilient in that they are less vulnerable to stress. In younger adults chronic stress results in headaches, colds, or backaches whilst for older adults it is hypertension or high cholesterol (Gilmer & Aldwin, 2002). Older adults may be less likely to appraise things as problematic (Boeninger et al., 2009); they may have experienced the positive aspects of stress such as post-traumatic growth (Tedeschi & Calhoun, 2004) (see chapter on stress-related growth in Park & Fenster 2004); they may see the silver lining which may lead to turning points such as after a loss of a job or divorce. They often point to increases in mastery and coping skills, more positive values, closer relationships, and sometimes increased spirituality.

The mixed outcomes reported by 60% of subjects included problem-focused approaches to dealing with the problem, perspective taking and self-regulation whilst, as one would expect, escapism into taking drugs, blaming self or others resulted in poorer outcomes. Other studies with adult populations have shown that older adults (45–75 years) are less likely than their younger counterparts to worry or use tension reduction strategies such as eat, drink, or smoke to excess (Frydenberg & Lewis, 2002).

The conclusion that Aldwin and her colleagues reached was that for younger adults positive coping may be protective in older age and older adults who are ageing successfully may have learnt how to avoid becoming upset over problems that may be minor or chronic thus decreasing their negative responses to stress.

The paradox is further supported by other research. For example, Tomás, Sancho, Melendez, and Mayordomo (2012) using a sample of 225 noninstitutionalised older adults, were able to predict well-being using a latent variable of resilient coping with the Brief Resilient Coping Scale (BRCS; Sinclair & Wallston, 2004) which captures tendencies to cope with stress in a highly adaptive manner (Tomás et al., 2012). Golant (2015) reported that the assimilative or adaptive coping strategies of older persons depend on their secondary appraisal processes where they judge the availability, efficaciousness, and viability of their coping options.

There are key elements of coping in older adults that are relevant to consider. The first relates to the concept of appraisal and reappraisal. That is, how older adults see the situations that confront them. The second relates to how they make meaning of the circumstances that they encounter. The third is how they relate to the past, that is whether they ruminate or draw on the pleasures and learnings from past experience and be proactive so as to anticipate events and able to plan for management.

Appraisal and Reappraisal

The assimilative or accommodative coping strategies of older persons depend on their secondary appraisal processes whereby they judge the availability, efficaciousness, and viability of their coping options. Older persons with more enriched coping repertoires are theorised as being more resilient, making their own decisions and with access to more resource-rich (objectively defined) resilient environments (Golant, 2015; Nowlan, Wuthrich, & Rapee, 2015).

Nowlan et al. (2015) when considering positive reappraisal in older adults undertook a systematic review of the literature and concluded that the term 'reappraisal' originates from Lazarus and Folkman (1984) transactional model and is similar to 'positive reinterpretation and growth' (Carver, Scheier, & Weintraub, 1989) and positive reframing (Scheier & Carver, 1987). Also the literature on post-traumatic growth and benefit finding (Tedeschi & Calhoun, 2004) highlights the relevance of appraisal and reappraisal.

Meaning making is a cognitive based emotion regulation strategy that is frequently used by older adults to manage stresses. According to Nowlan et al. (2015) positive reappraisal is about first identifying positive value for oneself, second perceiving an event as personally meaningful, thirdly, acknowledging the gain from some negative experience and finally continuing to acknowledge the negativity of the situation.

When reviewing 22 studies that addressed positive reappraisal, Nowlan et al. (2015) considered mental and physical health benefits. Whilst the research evidence is relatively recent and based on a small number of studies, they were able to conclude that there is emerging evidence that positive reappraisal predicted better functional and physical health for old-old (80 years and older) than young old (less than 80 years old). Unsurprisingly positive reappraisal was related to improved psychological well-being for both community and residential dwelling adults. Positive reappraisal is negatively related to depressive symptoms with older adults: that is, the less positive reappraisal, the more likelihood of depression but no causality can be inferred. Those with physical health problems reported increased mental health if they used positive reappraisal suggesting that the strategy provides a psychological buffer. They were less likely to visit doctors, have medical interventions, and require other health-related assistance. They used reciprocal social support, such as husbands caring for wives, and they had a sense of fulfilment. Positive reappraisal increases with age provided that a person's cognitive ability remains intact. In short positive reappraisal is related to improvement in life satisfaction, self-acceptance, positive emotions, social relationships, and less depression. And in older adults it is associated with improvements in physical and psychological health.

Positive appraisal and positive reappraisal ('I have done my best and what can I learn from this experience') is a strategy that can be taught. It is used extensively in counselling and clinical contexts, where it is often referred to as positive reframing.

Another approach is that of Antonovsky's sense of coherence (SOC) model which has also been widely applied with adults and has been considered to have relevance for ageing. SOC comprises of three elements: comprehensibility, manageability, and meaningfulness (Antonovsky, 1987). According to Antonovsky, SOC is established by early adulthood and older people are likely to have a stronger SOC due to reinforcement through successful management of stress throughout their adult life.

In a review of eight studies (one qualitative and seven quantitative) using the SOC model, it was concluded that a sense of coherence among older people was correlated with better physical, social, and mental health. Appraisal and social support were correlated with their sense of coherence, perceived holistic health and quality of life (Tan et al., 2014).

Antonovsky (1987) also considered the relationship between SOC and resistance resources. He defined resistance resources as 'any phenomenon that is effective in combatting a wide variety of stressors' (Antonovsky, 1987, p. 12) and may be internal (physical and biochemical, valuative-attitudinal and cognitive-emotional) or external (artefactual-material, interpersonal-relational, and macro-sociocultural) (Antonovsky, 1979). Lewis (1997) used Antonovsky's self-administered SOC scale (Antonovsky, 1987) in six studies from Nordic countries (four from Sweden and one each from Norway and Finland). The health of older people was the key variable to be considered. Older people in care facilities reported lower SOC scores than those of community dwellers. Female community dwellers with at least one chronic health problem suggested that SOC mediated the effects of the limitations of physical health. Not surprisingly financial stature and physical activity was correlated with a stronger SOC (Nesbitt & Heidrich, 2000). Whilst improving a sense of coherence is one of the main recommendations, it was also clear that community dwellers were ageing in better health than those in the residential settings.

Proactive Coping and Ageing

Proactive coping (see Chap. 6) is deemed to be a strong contributor to resilience. It is also deemed to be helpful in leadership- and health-related domains. When it came to considering proactive coping in older adults, situational aspects were more important in shaping proactive coping behaviour than individual characteristics. The vignette study of 123 adults aged 50–70 years, described in Chap. 6, used proactive coping more in the health-related situation in contrast to focusing on finances and relationships when preparing for ageing (Ouwehand, De Ridder, & Bensing, 2006).

When it comes to resilient ageing it would seem that those who are proactive copers, that is, those who have something to plan for and anticipate in an active way, are likely to enjoy their ageing years more. Those who are proactive about their health are also likely to benefit with more resilient ageing. Thus both positive appraisal and proactive coping skills are likely to be helpful during the ageing process.

Reminiscing

Reminiscing can be both helpful and unhelpful when coping with life; reminiscing has to be clearly distinguished from rumination which is a persistent focus on the negative. When reminiscing is positive, it contributes to psychological well-being in part because it promotes assimilative and accommodative coping. A sample of 1100 positive reminiscences were found to relate to higher psychological well-being, through assimilative and accommodative coping, whilst negative reminiscences were associated with reduced psychological well-being (Cappeliez & Robitaille, 2010). The implications are that it is necessary to focus on positive reminiscing in everyday contexts.

Ellen Langer's landmark research on ageing which has been reported extensively on screen in a BBC series and her book titled *Counterclockwise: Mindful Health and the Power of Possibility* (2009) makes a strong case for the capacity of reflecting on the past to influence how we heal and how we age. In her landmark 1981 'counterclockwise' study she took two groups of men in their 70s and 80s to a monastery in New Hampshire, United States, and outfitted the environment to 1959 some 22 years earlier. The first group stayed for a week and were asked to pretend that they were young men living again in the 1950s whilst the second group were asked to stay in the present and reminisce about the era. At the end of their stay, both groups of men took a battery of cognitive and physical tests. Both groups improved in a range of markers that included strength, flexibility, memory, hearing, and vision, but the first group showed the greatest improvement. They had relived the past rather than just reminisced about it. These studies have been replicated by her team and that of others on multiple occasions including in the United Kingdom. Langer argues that it is possible to 'turn the clock back in time' through reimagining and having a positive mindset. Whilst there are critics of her work on 'counterclockwise' for not being published in peer-reviewed journals, there is growing evidence, particularly in the positive psychology literature, that having a positive mindset, not dwelling on the negative in the past or present, is helpful to well-being.

There are aspects of management and prevention that are relevant to specific health conditions. Generally, older adults exhibit more dyadic coping (see Chap. 6 for a discussion on dyadic coping), in situations such as illness where a supportive partnership is a key. Older adults are more focused on emotion regulation (Coats & Blanchard-Fields, 2008) and they use fewer escapist, hostile, and avoidant strategies, less wishful thinking, and more positive reappraisal (Wadsworth et al., 2004). They are also more reliant on religious coping (Krause, 2006), and they may learn to relinquish unattainable goals. When it comes to treatment and interventions there is generally a universal clinical approach. For example, Resnick's (2014) prescription for an intervention which is quite appropriate in any clinical context is highly relevant in the older age group.

The suggested intervention strategies are much like coping interventions:

1. Acknowledge loss and vulnerability experienced by the individual
2. Identify the source of stress
3. Attempt to stabilise or normalise the situation
4. Help the person take control

5. Provide resources for change
6. Promote self-efficacy
7. Collaborate…to encourage self-charge
8. Strengthen…problem-solving abilities
9. Address and encourage positive emotions
10. Listen to…stories and encourage past review of recovery from stressors
11. Help….make meaning of the stressors or challenging event
12. Help…make meaning of the adverse or challenging event.

Concluding Remarks

When it comes to building resilience, there is no single formula, prescription, or recipe. Whilst the capacity for older adults to have benefited from experience, utilise positive appraisals, call on their resources, and have an acceptance of their situation is of major benefit, there are periods of grief and loss that require clinical intervention. Teaching proactive coping skills may also be helpful in that being able to have age-appropriate goals gives meaning and purpose to everyday lives regardless of age.

References

Aldwin, C. M., & Werner, E. E. (2007). *Stress, coping, and development: An integrative perspective/Carolyn M. Aldwin; foreword by Emmy E. Werner.* New York: Guilford Press. 2.

Antonovsky, A. (1979). *Health, stress, and coping* (1st ed.). San Francisco: Jossey-Bass Publishers.

Antonovsky, A. (1987). *Unraveling the mystery of health : How people manage stress and stay well/Aaron Antonovsky* (1st ed.). San Francisco: Jossey-Bass.

Australian Bureau of Statistics. (2015). *Deaths, Australia, 2014 (cat. no. 3302.0).* Retrieved March 14, 2015, from www.abs.gov.au

Boeninger, D. K., Shiraishi, R. W., Aldwin, C. M., & Spiro III, A. (2009). Why do older men report low stress ratings? Findings from the veterans affairs normative aging study. *International Journal of Aging and Human Development, 68*(2), 149–170.

Cappeliez, P., & Robitaille, A. (2010). Coping mediates the relationships between reminiscence and psychological well-being among older adults. *Aging & Mental Health, 14*(7), 807–818. doi:10.1080/13607861003713307.

Carver, C. S., Scheier, M. F., & Weintraub, J. K. (1989). Assessing coping strategies: A theoretically based approach. *Journal of Personality and Social Psychology, 56*, 267–283.

Coats, A., & Blanchard-Fields, F. (2008). Emotion regulation in interpersonal problems: The role of cognitive-emotional complexity, emotion regulation goals, and expressivity. *Psychology and Aging, 23*(1), 39–51.

Cohen, S., Janicki-Deverts, D., & Miller, G. E. (2007). Psychological stress and disease. *Journal of the American Medical Association, 298*(14), 1685–1687. doi:10.1001/jama.298.14.1685.

Friedman, M. J., & McEwen, B. S. (2004). Posttraumatic stress disorder, allostatic load, and medical illness. In P. P. Schnurr & B. L. Green (Eds.), *Trauma and health: Physical health consequences of exposure to extreme stress* (pp. 157–188). Washington, DC: American Psychological Association.

Frydenberg, E., & Lewis, R. (2002). Do managers cope productively? A comparison between Australian middle level managers and adults in the general community. *Journal of Managerial Psychology, 17*, 640–654.

Gilmer, D. F., & Aldwin, C. M. (2002). Trajectories of health and social support in frail young-old and old-old patients after hospitalization. *Journal of the Aging Family System, 2*, 1–14.

Golant, S. M. (2015). Residential normalcy and the enriched coping repertoires of successfully aging older adults. *The Gerontologist, 55*(1), 70–82. doi:10.1093/geront/gnu036.

Krause, N. (2006). Twenty-two: Religion and health in late life. In *Handbook of the psychology of aging*, 499–518. doi:10.1016/B978-012101264-9/50025-2.

Langer, E. J. (2009). *Counter clockwise : Mindful health and the power of possibility/Ellen J. Langer.* New York: Ballantine Books, c2009.

Lazarus, R. S., & Folkman, S. (1984). *Stress, appraisal, and coping.* New York: Springer.

Lewis, J. S. (1997). Sense of coherence and the strengths perspective with older persons. *Journal of Gerontological Social Work, 26*(3/4), 99–112. doi:10.1300/J083V26N03_08.

National Center for Health Statistics (NCHS). (2006). *Health, United States, with chartbook on trends in the health of Americans.* Hyattsville, MD: National Center for Health Statistics (US); 2006 Nov. Report No.: 2006–1232. Health, United States

Nesbitt, B. J., & Heidrich, S. M. (2000). Sense of coherence and illness appraisal in older women's quality of life. *Research in Nursing and Health, 23*(1), 25–34, 10p.

Nowlan, J. S., Wuthrich, V. M., & Rapee, R. M. (2015). Positive reappraisal in older adults: A systematic literature review. *Aging & Mental Health, 19*(6), 475–484. doi:10.1080/13607863.2014.954528.

Ouwehand, C., De Ridder, D. T. D., & Bensing, J. M. (2006). Situational aspects are more important in shaping proactive coping behaviour than individual characteristics: A vignette study among adults preparing for ageing. *Psychology & Health, 21*(6), 809–825.

Park, C. L., & Fenster, J. R. (2004). Stress-related growth: Predictors of occurrence and correlates with psychological adjustment. *Journal of Social and Clinical Psychology, 23*(2), 195–215.

Resnick, B. (2014). Resilience in older adults. *Topics in Geriatric Rehabilitation, 30*(3), 155–163. doi:10.1097/TGR.0000000000000024.

Scheier, M. F., & Carver, C. S. (1987). Dispositional optimism an physical well-being: The influence of generalized outcome expectancies on health. *Journal of Personality, 55*(2), 169.

Sinclair, V. G., & Wallston, K. A. (2004). The development and psychometric evaluation of the brief resilient coping scale. *Assessment, 11*(1), 94–101.

Tan, K.-K., Vehviläinen-Julkunen, K., & Chan, S. W.-C. (2014). Integrative review: Salutogenesis and health in older people over 65 years old. *Journal of Advanced Nursing, 70*(3), 497–510. doi:10.1111/jan.12221.

Tedeschi, R. G., & Calhoun, L. G. (2004). Posttraumatic growth: Conceptual foundations and empirical evidence. *Psychological Inquiry, 15*, 1–18.

Tomás, J. M., Sancho, P., Melendez, J. C., & Mayordomo, T. (2012). Resilience and coping as predictors of general well-being in the elderly: A structural equation modeling approach. *Aging & Mental Health, 16*(3), 317–326. doi:1 0.1080/13607863.2011.615737.

Wadsworth, M. E., Gudmundsen, G. R., Raviv, T., Ahlkvist, J. A., McIntosh, D. N., Kline, G. H., et al. (2004). Coping with terrorism: Age and gender differences in effortful and involuntary responses to September 11th. *Applied Developmental Science, 8*(3), 143–157.

Yancura, L. A., & Aldwin, C. M. (2009). Stability and change in retrospective reports of childhood experiences over a 5-year period: Findings from the Davis longitudinal study. *Psychology and Aging, 24*(3), 715–721. doi:10.1037/ a0016203.

8

Development of Coping in the Formative Years: Building Resilience

Coping and development are interlinked in a bidirectional way, in that development determines coping but how an individual copes also impacts development. The relationship between coping and development provides a framework for understanding how coping can contribute to resilience. Ages and stages of development have an impact and the picture is compounded by the fact that at different stages of the lifecycle individuals are confronted by different stresses.

How we cope is also determined by how stress is defined, whether, for example, it is defined, in terms of hassles or traumas (Aldwin, 2010). There are individual differences and developmental trajectories of coping. For example, young children are reliant on parents for emotion regulation and become independent self-regulators at a later stage of development. Neurological development also comes into play in that children are likely to respond differently and utilise different coping resources than those in adolescence or adulthood. Individuals respond to their environments and they in turn influence their environments (Lazarus & Folkman,

---

Until I was 10 my mum and dad were people who said 'you can do whatever you want'. They were very encouraging and supportive. (Julian, accountant)

© The Author(s) 2017
E. Frydenberg, *Coping and the Challenge of Resilience*,
DOI 10.1057/978-1-137-56924-0_8

1984). Thus there are both normative changes and individual differences. Additionally, there is plasticity in developmental processes throughout the lifespan which is reflected in brain development and behavioural outcomes (Spear, 2000a, b).

Some Important Concepts

There is general debate as to whether or not infants start with a *tabula rasa* (a clear slate without knowledge), nevertheless there is agreement that throughout childhood they are active learners. Children develop theories about the world around them and the way it works from an early age. These theories are constantly modified. Parts of the brain are primed for language acquisition but this cannot take place without the catalyst of experience.

Emotional regulation is important for a number of social and relational reasons but particularly because anger and distress impede learning. Brain functioning, particularly in the amygdala, releases hormones that influence how information is transmitted along the nervous system. The frontal lobe of the brain is relatively late to mature and that is the location for the most rational part of our cognitions. Adults are expected to control their emotions, but aspects of emotion regulation begin developing through the early years of childhood (Centre for Research and Innovations, 2007). As Bruce Compas (2009) has pointed out, executive functioning continues developing through childhood, partly as a result of myelination of the prefrontal areas that lasts throughout an extended period. So, while coping and emotion regulation are an important part of early years' development, they continue to progress as children are required to manage increasingly complex situations and the accompanying emotions from early childhood through to adulthood.

Neuroscience and Development

In recent years there has been a keen interest in understanding the human brain and its relationship to lifelong learning and how deficits in one part of the brain can be compensated by developments in another. Knowledge of neuroscience is work in progress. But it is understood that brain development continues from infancy through to adulthood.

The human body has a bilateral symmetry running from the top of the head to the toes, that is, left arm and right arm and so on. The brain also has two hemispheres, left and right. The right hemisphere generally controls the activities on the left side of the body and is associated with spatial abilities and face recognition. The left hemisphere deals with language, mathematics, and logic, and is responsible for activities on the right side of the body. The brain's elements are complex. The hemispheres communicate through a set of up to 250 million fibres and the bundle of fibres is called the corpus callosum. There are two lobes in each hemisphere associated with particular functions. The frontal lobe is associated with planning and action, the temporal lobe is important for audition, memory, and object recognition, the parietal lobe is involved with sensation and spatial processing, and the occipital lobe is essential for vision. A complex set of interconnecting neurons joins each lobe. New neurons continue to generate throughout life. They communicate through interconnections or synapses and these are pruned or strengthened according to how often they are used. The two hemispheres work together for all cognitive tasks. That is, the brain is an integrated functioning system.

In addition to cognitive development, there is the important development in relation to the experience and regulation of emotions.

Humans are born with the ability to express six basic emotions, namely, fear, anger, sadness, joy, surprise, and disgust. These have been termed primary emotions. Secondary emotions develop from two years of age and they help children to evaluate their own behaviour and that of others. These emotions include self-consciousness, including shame, embarrassment, guilt, envy, and pride. These have been called the social emotions because they are seen as impacting on self-concept. As children approach two years of age, they are able to understand themselves and they start displaying empathy and a recognition of the feelings of others (Frydenberg, Deans, & O'Brien, 2012).

Overall emotional competence is about having well-developed emotional understandings and skills. It is about understanding one's own emotions and those of others. It is also about the capacity to cope with negative emotions, often termed self-regulation.

Positive social experiences play a role in the development of emotion regulation, which in turn can impact a child's ability to cope with stress and develop behavioural control (Wilmshurst, 2008). As children grow and gain more social experiences and cognitive sophistication, the social and emotional patterns set in early childhood continue to be refined.

Since the vast body of coping research has been drawn from adult theorising and there is a lack of integration of a comprehensive developmental component in the research, it is difficult to generalise the findings to children (Compas, Connor-Smith, Saltzman, Thomsen, & Wadsworth, 2001; Moreland & Dumas, 2008). Moreover, despite the consensus that development shapes every aspect of children's coping, little empirical progress has been made to produce an integrated and interpretable body of research on how coping changes across childhood, adolescence, and through to adulthood. Additionally, the stressors are diverse, ranging from daily difficulties to uncontrollable medical events and the degree to which developmental factors (e.g., age groups and gaps) are represented differ across studies. These limitations have led to difficulties in making comparisons across studies (see review by Compas et al., 2001; Zimmer-Gembeck & Skinner, 2011).

Despite the challenges of studying coping from a developmental perspective there are a number of longitudinal studies which affirm that patterns of coping become more differentiated with age (e.g., Compas, Worsham, & Ey, 1992; Omizo, Omizo, & Suzuki, 1988; Skinner & Zimmer-Gembeck, 2009a, b). The changes in neurophysiological, cognitive, emotional, attentional, and/or social resources and processes across the lifespan, could account for differences in the abilities and ways of coping in children and adults. Compared to adults, young children are more dependent on their environments and rely on direct help and participation of their social partners to reduce or prevent environmental causes of stress (Eisenberg et al., 2001; Frydenberg & Lewis, 2000; Yancura & Aldwin, 2009; Skinner & Zimmer-Gembeck, 2009a, b). For example, between the ages of two and five when it comes to self-regulation there is a shift from dependency on a parent for a form of co-regulation that subsequently becomes intrapersonal self-regulation (Compas, 2009). On the whole, longitudinal studies provide support for the stability of coping styles, that is, habitual ways of coping across the lifespan (Stone,

Greenberg, Kennedy-Moore, & Newman, 1991; Hewitt & Flett, 1996). Nevertheless, there are differences that are age- and gender dependent. For example, for girls there is a dip in their coping capacities in the mid-teens (Frydenberg & Lewis, 2000). Personality characteristics such as perfectionism are associated with vulnerability to depression over time (Hewitt & Flett, 1996). A matched-group design study of Amirkhan and Auyeung (2007) also supported the notion that coping remains somewhat stable over time with no age differences. In their examination of the coping responses of people in five demographically matched groups, with ages ranging from 9 to 70 years old, using both exploratory and confirmatory factor analyses, only preferential differences rather than absolute differences were found in the types of coping strategies. For instance, there was an increase in the use of problem-solving coping strategies and a decrease in the use of avoidant coping strategies with age.

Developmental Shifts in Coping

The introduction of the concept of 'developmental shifts' in coping by Skinner and Zimmer-Gembeck (2009a, b, Zimmer-Gembeck & Skinner, 2011) may provide an explanation for what appears to be conflicting findings about coping across the lifespan. Based on their reviews of theory and research on stress and coping, and on the conceptualisation of coping as regulation, Skinner and Zimmer-Gembeck identified age-related developmental shifts or changes in coping across ages. These developmental shifts occur at particular periods from infancy up to early adulthood during which structure, organisation, and flexibility in coping processes are likely to undergo significant qualitative and quantitative changes. Their presence suggests broad developmental phases that are characterised by different mechanisms of regulation and different involvement by social partners such as family and peers (Skinner & Zimmer-Gembeck, 2009a, b). The development story indicates that from two to five years the child engages in 'unitary direct actions' with an increase in executive functioning, motor skills and language (Skinner & Zimmer-Gembeck, 2009a, b). During middle childhood, ages six to nine, cognitive strategies such as cognitive distraction, self-reassuring, and cognitive reframing have been identified (Compas et al., 2001). Rumination is thought to arise in middle childhood (Broderick & Korteland, 2004).

There are numerous other age-related changes. For example, Eisenberg, Fabes, and Guthrie (1997) found that aggression decreases with age. Not surprisingly, those with externalising problems have been found to be more prone to anger and impulsivity and low regulation (Eisenberg et al., 2001). With neurological maturation in adolescence, a more sophisticated problem-focused coping approach is used, and there is an emergence of humour with boys using more sexual humour whilst girls cheer themselves up (Fuhr, 2002; Horton, 2002). Adolescents are more adept at self-regulation but parents are important (Seiffge-Krenke, 2000, 2006, 2011). Effective dyadic coping does not develop until late adolescence. Whilst adolescents are more adept and self-regulated, parents and culture also play an important part. How adolescents cope with stressors in romantic relationships (i.e., dyadic coping) are partly influenced or shaped by their attachment styles with parents (Seiffge-Krenke & Pakalniskiene, 2011). Over the course of romantic relationships from early adolescence to late adolescence, young adults learn to support each other in stressful situations, and their ways of dyadic coping also contribute to relationship functioning at different stages of their close relationships. For example, older adolescents (16–19 years old) were able to use compromising as a means of conflict resolution in romantic dyads more often than younger adolescents (14–15 years old) (Nieder & Seiffge-Krenke, 2001). Adolescence may also be a time for maladaptive coping strategies such as social withdrawal which is problematic and the use of external regulators of distress such as drugs or alcohol (Wills, Sandy, Yaeger, Cleary, & Shinar, 2001).

Since development is a continuous process throughout childhood it is expected that resilience can be fostered through the implementation of coping skills. Gains in coping are clearly identified post intervention, but it is difficult to separate the concurrent contribution of development, maturation, and learning. Nevertheless, universal interventions for adolescents in diverse settings provide evidence of efficacy for coping skills training during childhood and adolescence as a pathway to developing resilience. Universal programmes have been adapted for particular populations such as those with social, emotional, or health-related difficulties.

A number of studies that provide evidence of outcomes are reported in this chapter.

Coping Programmes

To date this volume has sought to demonstrate that coping theory is a good fit with the concepts and constructs relating to resilience. Following the development of tools to measure the coping construct it was possible to get a comprehensive understanding of how coping works in different contexts, at different stages of development, and in different circumstances (see Chap. 5). Tools such as the ACS (see Chap. 4 for details) were then used to develop universal and targeted intervention programmes to develop coping skills. The underlying principle and focus in coping skills development is that we can all do what we do better. There is no finite or perfect way to cope. Nevertheless, appraisal, taking the context, situation, and the resources into account, determines the best way to cope. Additionally, coping efficacy, that is, belief in one's capacity to cope also determines outcomes.

The ACS was used as a platform from which to develop coping skills programmes such as, *The Best of Coping* (BOC: Frydenberg & Brandon, 2002, 2007), *Think Positive: Developing Coping Skills in Adolescence* (Frydenberg, 2010) and a CD-ROM version called 'Coping for Success' (Frydenberg, 2007). The programmes are universal in that they are suitable for all students and young people rather than those with specific needs. The programmes are not prescriptive but rather utilise the concepts, constructs, and insights to teach young people to focus on coping skills. The message is always increase productive coping and decrease nonproductive coping. The revised coping modules are outlined in Table 8.1.

In a series of studies Frydenberg, Bugalski, Firth, Kamsner, and Poole (2007) set out to assess the utility of The Best of Coping (Frydenberg & Brandon, 2002, 2007) for young people 'at risk' on a range of criteria. Depression, learning problems, and anxiety are the most common mental health problems for adolescents. For example, 26% of young people aged 16–24 are suffering from a mental disorder with 15% of this population experiencing anxiety-related disorders, 13% substance abuse and 6% had

Table 8.1 The revised coping modules (Frydenberg, 2010)

1: The language of coping
Aim: To introduce the concept of coping, explore individual styles, and facilitate an understanding of the various coping strategies

2: Positive thinking
Aim: To facilitate an awareness of the connection between thoughts and feelings and to introduce basic skills in thought evaluation and change thinking

3: Strategies that don't help
Aim: To raise awareness of the ineffective coping strategies that people use and to explore some productive alternatives

4: Getting along with others
Aim: To explore and practise aspects of communicating and listening

5: Asking for help
Aim: To raise awareness of the importance of reaching out to others and to available networks and supports

6: Dealing with conflict
Aim: To explore conflict in your life and how to resolve conflicts

7: Problem solving
Aim: To learn and practise the six-step problem-solving model

8: Social problem solving
Aim: To deal with situations in relationships; handling and avoiding teasing, rejection, and so on

9: Decision making
Aim: To teach students how to make considered decisions through evaluating options

10: Coping in the cyber world
Aim: To create awareness of the risks and benefits of the cyber world and how to manage it

11: Goal-setting
Aim: To build awareness about the relationship between goals and achievement and to explore and set individual achievable goals

12: Time management
Aim: To evaluate how we spend our time and learn to manage it in an effective way

The 12 modules listed are an extension of those in the BOC programme (Frydenberg & Brandon, 2007) and are deemed to be useful in a wide range of contexts. Modules that cover these topic areas can be developed by practitioners for a range of different settings. Modules can be offered in different groupings. For example, modules 1–3 can be used to facilitate coping with a particular illness or a particular circumstance such as leaving school, entering the workforce, and so on an affective disorder such as depression (Australian Institute of Health and Welfare, 2014, p. 28) in Western communities. Additionally, students who show low academic achievement have an increased likelihood of encountering a number of problems and stressors (e.g., hyperactivity, social-behavioural, low self-esteem, depression, and the list goes on) (Gresham, Macmillan, & Bocian, 1996; Valas, 1999). The vulnerability of these groups makes resilience training highly relevant.

Three separate studies were conducted. The first study (Bugalski) with a sample of 115 students (57 males; 56 females) aged 15–17 years. Students were divided into three groups: at risk towards depression, not that vulnerable to depression, and resistant to depression. Students deemed to be at risk of depression were identified using the criteria determined by the Children's Attribution Styles Questionnaire (CASQ; Seligman et al., 1984) and the Perceived Control of Internal States Questionnaire (PCIS; Pallant, 2000). Using a pre-test–post-test design, students completed the Adolescent Coping Scale. All three groups completed the Best of Coping programme. There was a significant decrease in the level of nonproductive coping reportedly being used by the 'at risk' group post programme compared to the resilient group. The 'at risk' group reported a decrease in usage of worry and wishful thinking.

Study two (Firth) comprised a sample of 98 participants (age range 12–16 years) who had some form of a Specific Learning Disability. Participants were divided into four groups according to the nature of the intervention. Group 1 received an adapted coping programme; group 2 received the teacher feedback programme and the adapted coping programme; group 3 received teacher feedback only and group 4 was the control group. Additionally, there was a two-month follow-up of the programme.

The adapted coping programme group (Group 1) reported increased use of productive coping post programme, particularly the strategies of work hard and focus on solving the problem and a decrease in nonproductive coping such as 'giving up' or using tension reduction strategies such as taking drugs. These positive findings were maintained at a two-month follow-up. Whilst the other three groups made some gains in the use of working hard and solving the problem, these findings were not maintained at follow-up.

Study three (Kamsner) participants comprised 112 students (13–17 years) who were deemed to be performing poorly academically and were enrolled in a special literacy programme. These students subsequently participated in the BOC programme. In the pre-test analysis, female students showed a great use of tension reduction, not cope and self-blame. Following the ten-session programme that was modified for this group, post-test results for males showed a significant increase in invest in close friends and a significant decrease in use of wishful thinking. In contrast, females reported an increased usage of tension reduction. Whilst there was a trend for females to decrease their reliance on self-blame and not cope, these results were not significant in the analysis.

Overall, the implications of these findings are that it is possible to facilitate the development of coping skills in young people, particularly those at risk of depression or those who have learning disabilities. The findings are not always consistent and may be related to the particular needs and characteristics of a population of young people. However, we can help young people to appraise their circumstances differently and help to build up their coping resources. There are also resources over and above coping skills, such as teacher and parent support that remain important, particularly for certain populations. In addition to the availability of these resources, the coping skill of seeking social and or professional support would help in this regard. Moreover, the skills required to access support are an all important resource.

Two further studies evaluated the efficacy of the coping skills programme in different populations (Frydenberg, Eacott, & Clark, 2008). The first study (Clark) examined the impact of coping skills training on a population of senior secondary school students, ranging in age from 15 to 18 years, with a mean age of 16.8 years, who were deemed to have few resources. It had been established in previous studies that adolescents who have access to few resources are more likely to use nonproductive coping strategies and are particularly vulnerable to stress (McKenzie, Frydenberg, & Poole, 2004; Wojcik, McKenzie, Frydenberg, & Poole, 2004). This is all the more so for senior school students who face many stressors in their final years of high school such as high expectations by parents, teachers, and society whilst trying to complete their studies, and other factors including socio-economic status, trauma, or illness (physical or mental). Out of 206 (75 male; 131 female) students from year 11 ($n = 101$) and 12 ($n = 105$) from a senior secondary government school in Metropolitan Melbourne, Australia, students who scored in the lowest quartile on the modified version of the Conservation of Resources Evaluation (CORE: McKenzie et al., 2004) were classified to be in the lowest resourced group ($n = 52$). This select population ($n = 38$) was placed into either the 'Experimental' ($n = 16$) or the 'Wait List' ($n = 16$) Control Group. The Experimental group completed the Coping for Success CD-ROM.

The findings revealed that the Experimental group showed a significant increase in the reported use of solve the problem coping style and a significant reduction in nonproductive coping. The Experimental group indicated an increase in their knowledge and understanding of coping strategies. Students also reported that they would recommend the Coping for Success programme to other senior high school students. This study demonstrates that programmes such as Coping for Success are not skewed towards one particular age group of adolescents but can be used in most levels within a secondary school setting.

The second of these studies (Eacott) was conducted in a rural setting with two cohorts of students aged 15–16 years, 50 in 2006 and 60 in 2007. Again, of particular interest in that study were those students who were low in resources. The low-resource group made particular gains in being able to turn to others for professional help when required. Six months following the students' participation in the ten-session CD-ROM version of the coping skills programme, the at-risk group maintained their reduction in nonproductive coping but felt they would benefit from further intervention. Over 80% of the students indicated that it is helpful to be reminded of the coping skills that they had learned 12 months earlier.

The BOC programme was again adapted for a group of 13–16-year-olds who had Type 1 diabetes. Outcomes were evaluated in a randomised control trial (Serlachius et al., 2016). The therapeutic components added to the programme included: (1) conflict resolution as an adjunct to coping skills training, (2) health behaviour diaries to promote goal-setting, and (3) positive reinforcement and modelling to increase diabetes-related self-efficacy.

The CBT-based BOC programme was evaluated in a randomised control trial with 79 young people (13–16 years of age) being offered the BOC programme and 77 being offered standard care in a randomised controlled trial. The primary outcome measure was glycaemic control at 3 and 12 months post randomisation, and secondary measures were stress, self-efficacy, and quality of life at 3 and 12 months. Thirty participants attended all five two-hour weekly sessions of the adapted BOC, and whilst there was no change in glycaemic control, there was improvement in psychosocial well-being with the intervention group reporting greater self-efficacy than the control group at 3- and 12-month follow-up, as well as higher quality of life at the 3-month follow-up.

Participation in the intervention phase of the study was poor, with only 30 participants (38%) attending all five BOC sessions, showing little evidence of differences in glycaemic control between the intervention and control group at either time point. Nevertheless the programme showed promise for improving psychosocial well-being when all five sessions were attended (Serlachius et al., 2016). The challenge is how to engage participants and make targeted programmes attractive and relevant to a particular population's needs. For example, in this instance young people reported that they like to receive sophisticated information around topics of interest such as the mechanics of diabetes.

What We Have Learned

We know from our research and that of others that coping can be meaningfully measured across the lifespan. We have firmly established that both in the adult and adolescent area there are age, gender, and cultural differences in coping. Those who are high in resources are most likely to cope productively. There are some family patterns of coping, with some similarities but many differences. For example, mothers and fathers are more likely to use problem solving than their children, and daughters are more likely to use tension reduction than their parents. Whilst both problem- and emotion-focused coping are used simultaneously, the more emotion-focused coping that is used, the less successful the coping. Ultimately it is the belief in one's capacity, such as problem-solving efficacy (Frydenberg & Lewis, 2009) (see Chap. 5), which is important rather than the capacity itself. Well-being is associated with an increased use of productive coping and a reduced use of nonproductive coping, as is school connectedness. When it comes to aggression, reactively aggressive young people are more inclined to use nonproductive coping strategies than proactively aggressive young people. Cyber bullying is responded to differently by boys and girls, with boys more likely to ignore the problem and girls more likely to worry, blame themselves, and resort to tension reduction strategies.

Whilst there are no intrinsically right or wrong coping strategies, there are ways to review one's coping and change it to achieve the best outcomes. Generally, it is about reducing the use of nonproductive coping strategies and increasing the use of productive ones. Whether this is done in a self-help format or through a universal or targeted programme for a group or for an individual, there are benefits to be gained. The benefits can be the build-up of a pool of coping resources for occasions when the individual is challenged and needs to draw upon coping strategies which they have in store, that is, resilience. Universal and targeted programmes provide the opportunity to be proactive. Parenting programmes that incorporate coping skills have been demonstrated to be a helpful way of enhancing parents' confidence, well-being, and their relationship with their children (Gulliford, Deans, Frydenberg, & Liang, 2015). It is an ideal way to strengthen parent-child relationships and to be a tool for prevention and scaffolding against difficulties in the later years.

References

Aldwin, C. (2010). Stress and coping across the lifespan. In *The Oxford handbook of stress, health, and coping* (pp. 15–34). Oxford, UK: Oxford University Press. doi:10.1093/oxfordhb/9780195375343.013.0002.

Amirkhan, J., & Auyeung, B. (2007). Coping with stress across the lifespan: Absolute versus relative changes in strategy. *Journal of Applied Developmental Psychology, 28*(4), 298–317.

Australian Institute of Health and Welfare. (2014). *Australia's health 2014*. Australia's health series no. 14. *(Cat. no. AUS 178)*. Canberra: AIHW.

Broderick, P. C., & Korteland, C. (2004). A prospective study of rumination and depression in early adolescence. *Clinical Child Psychology and Psychiatry,* *9*(3), 383–394.

Centre for Research and Innovations. (2007). *Understanding the brain: The birth of a learning science.* Paris: OECD.

Compas, B. E. (2009). Coping, regulation, and development during childhood and adolescence. *New Directions for Child and Adolescent Development, 2009*(124), 87–99. doi:10.1002/cd.245.

Compas, B. E., Connor-Smith, J. K., Saltzman, H., Thomsen, A. H., & Wadsworth, M. E. (2001). Coping with stress during childhood and adolescence: Problems, progress, and potential in theory and research. *Psychological Bulletin, 127*(1), 87–127.

Compas, B. E., Worsham, N. L., & Ey, S. (1992). Conceptual and developmental issues in children's coping with stress. In A. M. La Greca, L. J. Siegel, J. L. Wallander, & C. E. Walker (Eds.), *Stress and coping in child health* (pp. 7–24). New York: Guilford Press.

Eacott, C., & Clark, N. (2008). From distress to success: Developing a coping language and programs for adolescents. *Prevention Researcher, 15*(4), 8–12.

Eisenberg, N., Cumberland, A., Spinrad, T. L., Fabes, R. A., Shepard, S. A., Reiser, M., et al. (2001). The relations of regulation and emotionality to children's externalizing and internalizing problem behavior. *Child Development, 72*(4), 1112–1134.

Eisenberg, N., Fabes, R. A., & Guthrie, I. K. (1997). Coping with stress: The roles of regulation and development. In S. A. Wolchik & I. Sandler (Eds.), *Handbook of children's coping: Linking theory and intervention* (pp. 41–70). New York: Plenum.

Frydenberg, E. (2007). *Coping for success.* ISBN 978-0-7340-2741-2. University of Melbourne's eShowcase web site: http://eshowcase.unimelb.edu.au/eshowcase/

Frydenberg, E. (2010). *Thinking positively!: A course for developing coping skills in adolescents.* London/New York: Continuum.

Frydenberg, E., & Brandon, C. (2002). *The best of coping: Developing coping skills for adolescents.* South Melbourne, VIC: Oz Child, Children Australia, c2002.

Frydenberg, E., & Brandon, C. (2007). *The best of coping: Developing coping skills for adolescents.* Camberwell, VIC: ACER Press.

Frydenberg, E., Bugalski, K., Firth, N., Kamsner, S., & Poole, C. (2007). Teaching young people to cope: Benefits and gains for at risk students. *Australian Educational and Developmental Psychologist, 23*(1), 91–110.

Frydenberg, E., Deans, J., & O'Brien, K. (2012). *Developing everyday coping skills in the early years.* London: Continuum.

Frydenberg, E., & Lewis, R. (2000). Teaching coping to adolescents: When and to whom? *American Educational Research Journal, 37,* 727–745.

Frydenberg, E., & Lewis, R. (2009). The Relationship between problem-solving efficacy and coping amongst Australian adolescents. *British Journal of Guidance and Counselling, 37*(1), 51–64.

Fuhr, M. (2002). Coping humor in early adolescence. *Humor- International Journal of Humor Research, 15*(3), 283–304.

Gresham, F. M., MacMillan, D. L., & Bocian, K. M. (1996). Learning disabilities, low achievement, and mild mental retardation: More alike than different? *Journal of Learning Disabilities, 29,* 570–581.

Gulliford, H., Deans, J., Frydenberg, E., & Liang, R. (2015). Teaching coping skills in the context of positive parenting within a preschool setting. *Australian Psychologist, 50*(3), 219–231. doi:10.1111/ap.12121.

Hewitt, P. L., & Flett, G. L. (1996). *The multidimensional perfectionism scale.* Toronto, ON: Multi-Health Systems Inc.

Horton, P. C. (2002). Self-comforting strategies used by adolescents. *Bulletin of the Menninger Clinic, 66*(3), 259–272.

Lazarus, R. S., & Folkman, S. (1984). *Stress, appraisal, and coping.* New York: Springer.

McKenzie, V., Frydenberg, E., & Poole, C. (2004). What resources matter to young people: The relationship between resources and coping style. *The Australian Educational and Developmental Psychologist, 19*(2), 78–96.

Moreland, A. D., & Dumas, J. E. (2008). Evaluating child coping competence: Theory and measurement. *Journal of Child and Family Studies, 17*(3), 437–454.

Nieder, T., & Seiffge-Krenke, I. (2001). Coping with stress in different phases of romantic development. *Journal of Adolescence, 24*(3), 297–311.

Omizo, M. M., Omizo, S. A., & Suzuki, L. A. (1988). Children and stress: An exploratory study of stressors and symptoms. *School Counselor, 35,* 267–274.

Pallant, J. F. (2000). Development and validation of a scale to measure perceived control of internal states. *Journal of Personality Assessment, 75*(2), 308–337.

Seiffge-Krenke, I. (2000). Causal links between stressful events, coping style, and adolescent symptomatology. *Journal of Adolescence, 23*(6), 675–691. doi:10.1006/jado.2000.0352.

Seiffge-Krenke, I. (2006). Leaving home or still in the nest? Parent – Child relationships and psychological health as predictors of different leaving home patterns. *Developmental Psychology, 42*(5), 864–876.

Seiffge-Krenke, I. (2011). Coping with relationship stressors: A decade review. *Journal of Research on Adolescence, 21*(1), 196–210. doi:10.1111/j.1532-7795.2010.00723.x.

Seiffge-Krenke, I., & Pakalniskiene, V. (2011). Who shapes whom in the family: Reciprocal links between autonomy support in the family and parents' and adolescents' coping behaviors. *Journal of Youth and Adolescence, 40*(8), 983–995.

Seligman, M. E. P., Peterson, C., Kaslow, N. J., Tanenbaum, R. L., Alloy, L. B., & Abramson, L. Y. (1984). Attributional style and depressive symptoms among children. *Journal of Abnormal Psychology, 93*, 235–238.

Serlachius, A. S., Scratch, S. E., Northam, E. A., Frydenberg, E., Lee, K. J., & Cameron, F. J. (2016). A randomized controlled trial of cognitive behaviour therapy to improve glycaemic control and psychosocial wellbeing in adolescents with type 1 diabetes. *Journal of Health Psychology, 21*(6), 1157–1169. doi:10.1177/1359105314547940.

Skinner, E. A., & Zimmer-Gembeck, M. (2009a). Challenges to the developmental study of coping. *New Directions for Child and Adolescent Development, 2009a*(124), 5–17. doi:10.1002/cd.239.

Skinner, E. A., & Zimmer-Gembeck, M. J. (Eds.) (2009b). Introduction: Challenges to the developmental study of coping,*Perspective on children's coping with stress as regulation of emotion, cognition and behavior. New directions in child and adolescent development series* (Issue 124, pp. 5–17). New York: Wiley.

Spear, L. P. (2000a). Neurobehavioral changes in adolescence. *Current Directions in Psychological Science, 9*(4), 111–114.

Spear, L. P. (2000b). The adolescent brain and age-related behavioral manifestations. *Neuroscience and Biobehavioral Reviews, 24*(4), 417–463.

Stone, A. A., Greenberg, M. A., Kennedy-Moore, E., & Newman, M. G. (1991). Self-report, situation-specific coping questionnaires: What are they measuring? *Journal of Personality and Social Psychology, 61*, 648–658.

Valas, H. (1999). Students with learning disabilities and low achieving students: Peer acceptance, loneliness, self-esteem, and depression. *Social Psychology of Education, 3*, 173–192.

Wills, T. A., Sandy, J. M., Yaeger, A. M., Cleary, S. D., & Shinar, O. (2001). Coping dimensions, life stress, and adolescent substance use: A latent growth analysis. *Journal of Abnormal Psychology, 110*, 309–323.

Wilmshurst, L. (2008). *Abnormal child psychology: A developmental perspective.* New York: Routledge.

Wojcik, Z., McKenzie, V., Frydenberg, E., & Poole, C. (2004). Resources loss, gain, investment, and coping in adolescents. *Australian Educational and Developmental Psychologist, 19/20*(2/1), 52–77.

Yancura, L. A., & Aldwin, C. M. (2009). Stability and change in retrospective reports of childhood experiences over a 5-year period: Findings from the Davis longitudinal study. *Psychology and Aging, 24*(3), 715–721. doi:10.1037/a0016203.

Zimmer-Gembeck, M. J., & Skinner, E. A. (2011). The development of coping across childhood and adolescence: An integrative review and critique of research. *International Journal of Behavioral Development, 35*, 1–17. Supplementary material.

9

Building Resilience Through Coping in the Early Years

There are many ways to develop resilience, particularly through the building of resources, personal and interpersonal, to minimise the impact of stress. Personal qualities such as Dweck's concept of mindset (See Chap. 2) or coping skills and interpersonal characteristics, such as relational skills, are strong contributors to resilience. What is clear is that to deal with situational factors or circumstances that occur throughout the life course, it is helpful to acquire the requisite life skills at an early age so that they can become part of one's coping repertoire and be augmented during the different phases of development. To that end, a team of researchers at the University of Melbourne have embarked on the journey of developing coping skills in the early years in a systematic step by step fashion. It is never too early to teach coping skills.

Having identified the constructs of coping and reported on a range of correlates in the adolescent, adult, and children's domains (see Chap. 5) and extensively utilised interventions in the adolescent domain (see Chap. 8), we set about to examine ways in which we could develop coping skills in children and ways to incorporate coping skills into a parenting programme. Firstly, we identified preschool children's coping responses and matched these with parent understandings of their children's coping responses. We then developed visual images of challenging situations and the age-appropriate coping strategies that might be used by children. The visual representations of young people's concerns and coping strategies

My mother gave me belief in my self, by treating me as **special** every day of my life. I got from her a real belief in myself. (Martin, property developer)

© The Author(s) 2017   **153**
E. Frydenberg, _Coping and the Challenge of Resilience,_
DOI 10.1057/978-1-137-56924-0_9

were used with children, parents, and teachers. We then incorporated the coping concepts into an early years parenting programme and more recently we have incorporated the concepts and tools into a programme designed to develop young children's empathy and prosocial skills.

The 'early years' is generally defined as children from three- to eight-year-olds who are in the early stages of group care or starting formal schooling. Young children entering school with 'more positive profiles of social-emotional competence have not only more success in developing positive attitudes about school and successful early adjustments to school but also improved grades and achievement' (Denham, 2006, p. 59). Conversely, it has been found that children who display deficits in this developmental area are at risk of experiencing multiple problems including dislike of school, inability to manage routines, academic difficulties, victimisation by peers, and less acceptance by teachers (Raver & Knitzer, 2002). Thus developing coping skills early has to be considered as a significant contributor to building resilience.

There is little debate about the fact that children experience emotions from the earliest stages of infancy and that these emotions are reflected in their behaviour. Whether it is joy, fear, or displeasure the signals are made evident to an adult. It is also becoming clear that children can identify emotions, provide labels or descriptions for them, and learn to regulate their emotions (Chalmers, Frydenberg, & Deans, 2011). Just as adolescents and adults utilise skills to cope with everyday life and manage their circumstances, so do children exercise their curiosity, explore, make decisions, ask for help, avoid difficulties, or tackle new situations head-on. They show discomfort, physical and emotional distress, such as when they are embarrassed, and satisfaction when they have success. Like adults, they also see difficult situations as those involving stress, often expressed as fear, harm, loss, or challenge.

The Concerns of Four- to Eight-Year-Old Children

It is now readily acknowledged that children have uncertainties and concerns that are often represented as fears that are expressed in numerous ways, such as tantrums, hiding from an adult, stomach aches, headaches, or eczema. These fears are often not articulated but can be observed through children's play, storytelling or drawing. From the literature it is apparent that, as children move through the early years, they may experience a range of concerns or fears in response to regularly experienced life events. These have been categorised into the following age groups:

Children aged between four and six years may experience:

- Feelings of uncertainty in new situations
- Fear of being abandoned by a significant adult
- Sadness about not having a friend
- Fear of wetting themselves
- Fear of being reprimanded or punished by parents or teachers.

Children aged between six and seven years may experience:

- Sadness about not having a friend
- Fear of wetting in class
- Fear of teacher disapproval
- Fear of being ridiculed by peers and older students in the school setting
- Fear of receiving a first report card and not passing on to the next year level.

Children aged between seven and eight years may experience:

- Feelings of sadness or insecurity associated with frequently missing a parent who is not around or while the child is away at school
- Sadness about not having a friend
- Fear of not being able to understand a given lesson (e.g., won't be able to pass a test)
- Feelings of uncertainty about not being selected to be a 'teacher helper' or not getting attention from the teacher
- Fear of being disciplined by the teacher
- Fear of being different from other children in dress and appearance. (See Youngs, 1985)

Whilst these groupings have been made according to age and stage, it is clear that there is an obvious overlap, with children aged between four and eight years experiencing many of the same fears and uncertainties.

How children manage these concerns is coping.

The question could be asked: When is it too early to discuss coping and teach coping skills so as to build resilience?

The Early Years Coping Project

This chapter focuses on the insights that have been obtained through the Early Years Coping Project at the University of Melbourne. The findings validate and expand on research reported in the previous chapters. For example, in Chap. 5 the measurement of young children's coping was outlined followed by insights, particularly as they relate to anxiety in young children. In this chapter interventions that utilise the Early Years Coping Cards as tools of intervention are described, followed by a discussion of the parenting programme, *Families Coping* and the more recent empathy with caring and sharing *COPE-R* programme. The eight phases of the Early Years Coping research is sequenced below:

- **Phase 1–2008:** Identifying preschool children's coping responses and matching these with parents' understandings of their children's coping responses (Deans, Frydenberg, & Tsurutani, 2010; Chalmers et al., 2011).
- **Phase 2–2009:** Development of the *Early Years Coping Cards*, a teaching and learning tool, depicts a range of visual representations of challenging situations to be used to stimulate children's verbal responses about their coping strategies (Frydenberg & Deans, 2011b).
- **Phase 3–2010:** Application of the *Early Years Coping Cards* in multiple settings (early childhood centres and homes) with teachers and parents (Deans, Frydenberg, & Liang, 2012).
- **Phase 4–2011:** Investigation of parents' use of the *Early Years Coping Cards* (Phases 1–5: Frydenberg, Deans, & Liang, 2014).
- **Phase 5–2012:** *Families Can Do Coping (FCDC) parenting programme* (Frydenberg et al., 2014).

- **Phase 6–2013:** Families Coping (FC—adapted version of FCDC) parenting programme for families from CALD backgrounds and disadvantaged communities—the *Early Years Productive Parenting Programme (EYPPP)* (Deans, Liang, & Frydenberg, 2016).
- **Phase 7–2014:** Exploring the relationship between anxiety and coping (Pang, Frydenberg, & Deans, 2015; Yeo, Frydenberg, Northam, & Deans, 2014).
- **Phase 8–2015:** *COPE-R Programme for Preschoolers: Teaching empathy and prosocial skills through the Early Years Coping Cards* (Cornell, Dobee, Kaufman, Kiernan Frydenberg, & Deans, in press); the process of socialisation and embodiment of a Social Emotional Learning programme in an early years setting: COPE-R (Deans, Liang, Zapper, & Frydenberg, in press).

Over the past eight years, researchers have investigated the ability of young children (specifically those aged between four and five years), their parents, and their teachers to articulate their understanding of coping. Children aged between four and five years were able to articulate up to 36 different coping responses, some of which had not been identified previously (Deans et al., 2010; Chalmers et al., 2011). The children were asked to describe how they would manage seven typical situations that included saying goodbye to a parent, fear of the dark, fear of trying something new, being in trouble with a teacher or parent, being bullied, losing something special, and being hurt. Parents were also surveyed with the aim of identifying the ways in which they described their children's coping, and to identify whether or not a correlation existed between the children's understandings of coping and their parents' views. Results from this study indicated that the children articulated 36 active and passive coping strategies such as play, work hard, go to bedroom, seek comfort, have happy thoughts or feelings, cry, feel sad, do nothing, keep feeling to self, get angry with self, complain of illness, or get angry with others. Active strategies describe what children do proactively and passive strategies typically involve withdrawing from or avoiding difficult situations. Parents on the other hand reported fewer coping strategies with a larger number of passive strategies being reported. The children were found to have a comprehensive range of coping strategies available beyond those recognised in the current literature. These strategies were grouped into:

- Productive coping—self-reliant—seek comfort, play/do something else, solve the problem, think positively, calm down, ignore the problem
- Productive coping—reference to others—seek comfort, seek help
- Nonproductive coping—seek comfort, do nothing/don't know, cry/ can't feel better, get angry/tantrum.

When 112 parents and teachers were surveyed with the aim of identifying and exploring differences between cross-informant understandings of children's coping, it was found that in relation to problems in general, parents indicated that their children were more likely to cry/ feel sad, complain of illness, seek help from grown-ups, or blame others. Teachers, on the other hand, indicated that children were more likely to do nothing, keep their feelings to themselves, or seek help from others. More fathers than mothers considered that their children worked hard at solving problems. Importantly, all the situations that were presented to the children were also recognised by both teachers and parents to relate frequently to the children's experiences; the one exception was choosing between two groups of friends for play as this was more frequently identified by the teachers because of its relevance in the school situation. The overall conclusions drawn from these studies is that young children do relate to challenging situations, that they can articulate and utilise a wide range of coping strategies that are not generally recognised in the current literature, and that parents' perceptions of their children's coping strategies vary from that of the teachers' and the children themselves (Deans et al., 2010).

In general, what we know about coping in the early years are as follows:

- Young children can identify a range of coping strategies.
- Boys and girls cope differently.
- Coping capacity varies with age.
- Coping can be learnt.

- There is no right or wrong coping (much as for older children or adults). It is the circumstances that make the difference.
- Coping strategies fall into three broad categories: productive coping self-reliance, productive coping relating to others, and nonproductive coping.

The aim for those involved with young children, such as clinicians, educators, and parents is to help reduce the number of nonproductive strategies used by children and increase the number of productive strategies used. See Chap. 8 or Frydenberg (2008) for a comprehensive coverage of insights on adolescent and children's coping.

To support the development of resilience, clinicians and educators are encouraged to engage with children to develop a 'language of coping' and a belief in their own capacity to deal with life circumstances. Having the language enables the awareness to be put to use. Conversations can be about challenging situations, the feelings that arise from the situation, and how to manage both the situation and the resulting emotion. The development of a language of coping supports the enhancement of self-esteem, critical reflection and the exploration of shared values, and codes of behaviour.

The *Early Years Coping Cards* (Frydenberg & Deans, 2011a, b) are a useful extension of existing measurement and clinical tools that have already been published for use with adolescents and adults. They provide clinicians and educators with a **visual tool** to help focus the attention of either individual children or groups of children on a range of challenging everyday situations that may cause uncertainty or fear and strategies for coping with these situations. They have been designed to support effective learning outcomes and include children learning about:

- How to respect self and others
- Relationships and the importance of friendship
- How to communicate feelings appropriately
- Who they are and their place in the world
- Cultural diversity and difference
- Empathy and care for others and the environment.

The cards are primarily a tool to stimulate conversation about coping with various situations. It is made up of 9 Situation Cards, 2 blank Situation Cards, and 22 Coping Cards. The Situation Cards represent 'real-life' events that are generally experienced by young children, and they offer a starting point for conversations between adults and children about how to consider these events and how to cope when faced with the challenges these events present. For most children, the cards stimulate questions about the situations depicted in the images that can be discussed either individually or in groups and it is up to the creativity and imagination of the clinician, educator, or parent as to how the questioning is developed and explored.

The situations and coping images are available commercially but they can also be drawn or cut out from magazines or downloaded from the Internet as required.

The Situation Cards depict the following events that are commonly encountered by young children:

- A change (in food)/Try new things
- Choosing a group to play with
- Saying goodbye
- Scared of the dark
- Being told off by the teacher
- Wanting to play with others
- Bullied
- Get hurt.

The Coping Cards provide visual cues about the different ways in which children may respond to the situations presented. They include:

- Think happy thoughts
- Hug a toy
- Blame others
- Blame self
- Scream/Cry/Tantrum
- Talk to an adult/someone
- Worry/Scared
- Keep feelings to self/Stay quiet
- Run away (leave home)

- Stop and think
- Hide
- Help others • Cry • Broken Toy • Get Angry • Work hard (play)
- Complain of Pain.

The 'I See, I Think, I Feel' Approach

Situation or Coping Cards can be presented one at a time to either individuals or groups of children and users can ask questions such as:

- What do you **see?**
- What do you **think** is happening?
- How does the child in the picture **feel?**
- What do you think this child would do?
- Has this happened to you?
- How would you feel if that was you?
- What would you do when you feel like this?
- What would you do to make yourself feel better?

The description on the back of each card can be used as a guide but essentially the pictures denote whatever the child or children see, and these can be elaborated in the children's own language.

The 'See and Tell' Approach

This approach provides a stimulus to describe coping with a particular situation. That is, the user displays the situation card and then asks the child or children to indicate which of the coping cards would best describe how the child depicted in the card is coping. The user can encourage the child or children to think more deeply about the situation and the coping response by asking the question: Is there anything else you would like to do to deal with the situation? This approach can also be used with a random choice approach, where the child or children are asked to select a card from the stack and begin a conversation that supports the interpretation of the situation and the coping response.

The 'Scatter and Select' Approach

The Situation and Coping Cards can be used to help stimulate conversations with individuals or groups of children. It is recommended that the user place the cards on the floor or table and invites the child or children to firstly select one card from the Situation Cards. It is then suggested that, as a form of problem solving, the child or children can select a way of coping with the situation from the range of Coping Cards provided. Whilst each card depicts a way of coping and there is a description on the back of each card, the children may see something different that they want to describe as coping. Theoretically, there are an infinite number of ways to cope and there is no right or wrong way of coping. This approach is designed to open the conversation and prompt ongoing and deeper discussion.

The 'Sort and Group' Approach

The user can make a place for three piles of Coping Cards on the floor or the table and can show the child or children three groups which are labelled:

- The 'a lot or often' group,
- The 'a little or sometimes' group
- The 'not at all or never' group.

The child or children can pick up the Coping Cards and see which pile they would put a particular card into, for example, when you say goodbye to your parent do you worry 'a lot', 'a little', or 'not at all'.

The 'Display and Discuss' Approach

The user can stimulate conversation by displaying the Situation and Coping Cards either on a screen, notice board or table top. It is helpful to be able to visually refer to both the Situation Cards and the Coping

Cards over the course of a day or a few weeks. Acknowledging challenging situations and coping responses in this way affirms that all children experience difficulties at some time or other and that there is a positive outcome if thoughts and feelings are shared with others. Coping together, sometimes called communal coping, is considered a form of stress reduction. With collaborative planning and discussion, children develop social and emotional confidence. Users can ask children:

- 'How would you do it next time?'
- 'Who would you like to get help from or work with next time?'

The 'Display and Play' Approach

The user can integrate the Situation and Coping Cards into a range of play experiences. For example, if cooperative and inclusive play between children is an objective, the Coping Cards that depict positive interactions can be placed alongside some play blocks and the children can be asked to brainstorm how they would work together to achieve a positive outcome.

Theoretically there are an infinite range of situations that children find themselves in and likewise an infinite range of coping strategies that can be called upon. The range of situations and coping strategies are often determined by the context and the person using the cards is encouraged to augment the list of what is considered appropriate to meet the needs of individuals or groups of children.

Building Family Resilience

One key factor that contributes to both parents' and children's healthy adaptation to everyday experiences is their capacity to cope (Armstrong, Birnie-Lefcovitch, & Ungar, 2005; Cappa, Begle, Conger, Dumas, & Conger, 2011; Cooklin, Giallo, & Rose, 2011). In addition to the universal communication skills of active listening, assertiveness, and managing conflict, parent coping skills are key approaches emphasised in the *Families Coping* programme. The ability of parents to manage the demands associated with raising a child, as well as to show willingness to engage in a process of self-enquiry so as to improve their parenting practice and learn new skills, inherently calls on the use of everyday coping skills.

Historically, early parenting programmes such as *Parent Effectiveness Training* (Gordon, 1970) and *Systematic Training for Effective Parenting* (Dinkmeyer, McKay, & Dinkmeyer, 1989) were underscored by core principles of good communication skills and the notion that all children's behaviour is intentional (Dreikurs, 1958), with the aim of enhancing parenting skills, knowledge, and positive attitudes towards parenting. Since that time, research and community-based projects have produced a range of programmes that include the *Triple P Positive Parenting Programme* (Sanders, Markie-Dadds, Tully, & Bor, 2000), *The Incredible Years* (Webster-Stratton, Reid, & Stoolmiller, 2008) and *Parent Management Training* (Pearl, 2009). There is an abundance of parenting programmes available. However, since we know the relationship between anxiety and negative coping has been recognised (Yeo et al., 2014), it is recommended that parenting programmes incorporate coping skills for children, as well as for parents in order to develop resilience in the early years. *Families Coping: Effective Strategies for you and your Child* (Frydenberg, 2015) incorporates the elements of the early programmes, that is, good communication skills, positive psychology principles, coping skills, and mindfulness. The elements are underscored by a guiding principle, that it is important to have adults and children share an understanding of the language of coping so that social learning and modelling can take place both in the home and in the school setting.

The Programme

The five sessions of *Families Coping* introduces parents to information associated with positive parenting principles, family communication, and use of a visual resource to help parents stimulate coping conversations with their children. The twin aim is to teach parents communication skills while receiving practical psycho-education and training on how their own productive coping skills can be developed and their use of nonproductive strategies minimised. Learning mediums include direct facilitator instruction, a self-directed workbook, and participation in role plays and group discussions. The intended outcome is to contribute to early years' well-being through enhancing the application of positive parenting skills in addition to the development of adaptive coping in both parent and child.

Table 9.1 describes the content of five sessions of the parenting programme.

The evaluation of the programme showed significant changes in parents' coping skills. Specifically, parents reported greater use of productive coping such as improving relationships, physical recreation, and relaxing diversions and a concurrent reduction in nonproductive coping skills, namely, worry, tension reduction, self-blame, and keep to self. Overall, there is benefit in incorporating parent and child coping skills into a universal positive parenting programme for preschool-aged children. Most parents perceived a trend towards the development of more positive parenting practices and use of productive coping by their child, as well as some aspect of improvement in both parent and child well-being (Gulliford, Deans, Frydenberg, & Liang, 2015). Families Coping is considered to be a useful addition to the pool of programmes currently available to parents.

Coping skills are helpful for parenting. The conversational exposure and modelling of coping skills that is provided by parents is instrumental to the development of healthy coping and well-being in children. Although coping skills can be learned, parenting programmes do not generally have a comprehensive component on articulated coping skills. Through the teaching of communication and coping skills in a positive parenting context, the *Families Coping* programme supports the parent's capacity to deal with the circumstances they encounter as part of their lives in a productive and proactive way.

Having developed tools for children, parents, and teachers, the extension of this work involved the development of additional resources for teachers in the early childhood setting.

Table 9.1 Overview of the five sessions comprising the *Families Coping* parenting programme

Session 1	
Positive psychology of parenting	History and core principles of positive psychology and positive parenting
	Family health and well-being
	Parents review subjective well-being and personal strengths
Coping with stress in the family	Everyday stresses associated with family life
	Social learning theory and the transactional model of stress and coping
	Parenting styles and the building blocks of healthy and happy families
Session 2	
Parents dealing with difficult situations	How adult coping can be operationalised
	Productive and nonproductive coping
	Social learning and what it means to cope as a parent
	Parents examine their own styles of coping specific to the parenting role
Everyday worries and anxieties of children	Ages and stages of social-emotional development
	Children's worries and how they cope
	How to help children identify stressors and the physical symptoms of stress in the body
Session 3	
Listening to children: the neuroscience of communication	Neuroscience of communication
	Reflective listening and barriers to communication
	How to respond to children's concerns and worries in a helpful way
Purposeful behaviour of children: when assertiveness helps	Self-reflection of own parenting style as parents explore the skill of assertiveness
	Understanding children's behaviour, needs, and wants
Session 4	
How children deal with their worries and talking about challenging situations with children	Open questioning and reflective listening as helpful communication tools
	The early years coping cards

Table 9.1 (continued)

Collaborative problem solving	Problem solving—a core skill that can be drawn on in diverse contexts
	Apply the skill to their own problems and children's problems
	How problem solving can be used with children as a collaborative process
Session 5	
Mindfulness as a way of achieving well-being	Origins of mindfulness and contemporary evidence-based applications in relation to well-being
	Mindfulness activities and resources to benefit both the child and the parents
Putting it together	Core messages from the five sessions are drawn together
	Parents reflect on their personal experiences from during programme in relation to parenting, coping, and well-being for both themselves and their child
	Parents share highlights and areas they will continue to focus on to improve family life

The COPE-R Program

There are numerous programmes that are recommended for clinicians and/or teachers to enhance resilience in young children. The emphasis is generally through the building of skills, attitudes, and behaviours that are known to be linked to resilience, such as gratitude and empathy (see Alba, Justicia-Arraez, Pichardo, & Justicia-Justicia, 2013; Domitrovich, Greenberg, Kusche, & Cortes, 2004; Webster-Stratton, 2002)

The COPE-R Programme comprises activities on Caring for Others (C); Open communication (O); Polite/Respectful behaviours (P); Empathise/Sharing behaviours (E), and a Review (R) incorporated the Early Years Coping Cards along with explicit empathy and prosocial skills. It has been developed to incorporate coping skills and utilise them to teach empathy and prosocial skills to children aged four to eight years. The topics are taught through the use of discussions and activities and are designed to be implemented in the classroom or in small groups. There are core activities along with additional resources and activities.

Core themes for each session of the COPE-R programme:

- **Session 1: C**are for others—caring behaviours, how to show others you care, recognising caring acts
- **Session 2: O**pen communication—importance of communicating with others, listening skills, verbal/nonverbal communication, expressing concerns for others
- **Session 3: P**oliteness—respectful behaviours, appreciating individual differences, understanding the outcomes of polite and impolite behaviours, how to identify and display polite behaviours such as gratitude
- **Session 4: E**mpathic Sharing—understanding the value of sharing with others, emotions elicited by sharing, appropriate ways to ask to share, benefits of sharing
- **Session 5: R**eview—review and consolidation of the concepts taught throughout the programme

During the session, the Coping Cards are used to help children explore their feelings, that of others, and what they might do in the different situations presented. Children are asked to become a 'Feelings Detective'. There is use of drawings, puppetry, and role plays.

An early evaluation of the programme was delivered by classroom teachers at the Melbourne University Early Learning Centre (ELC) (Cornell, Kiernan, Kaufman, Dobee, Frydenberg, & Deans, in press). A total of 31 parents (24 mothers, 7 fathers) of 20 boys and 11 girls, completed questionnaires before and after the implementation of the programme, providing quantitative and qualitative data for the purposes of evaluating the programme. Qualitative data, in the form of drawings and comments made by preschool participants were also collected during the programme to facilitate evaluation. There were significant reductions in emotional problems post programme. Qualitative responses from parents indicated they noticed positive differences in their children post programme. A thematic analysis of parents' responses was conducted, revealing two major themes in the differences parents noticed, 'an increase in prosocial behaviour' and 'enhanced communication skills'. Drawings and comments made by preschool participants provided further support for the efficacy of the programme (Cornell, Kiernan, Kaufman, Dobee, Frydenberg, & Deans, in press).

Caring

Parents noticed difference in their child's caring post programme. Differences described include *'She appears to be more aware of being caring towards family members'* and *'Moments of being thoughtful about her brother, for example, drawing him a picture of a friend at school.'*

Open Communication

For differences in Open Communication, 12 parents noticed a change in their child. One parent noted their child is *'getting better at talking about things that are troubling him rather than yelling or crying'*, while another parent noted their child *'can express he is sad or upset'*.

Politeness

Nine parents noticed differences in their child's politeness, with one parent stating their child is *'asking nicely for things more often'* while another parent noticed their child has a *'big focus on "manner" words'*.

Empathic Sharing

Seven parents noticed a difference in Empathic Sharing with one parent acknowledging *'he's been talking more about other people's feelings'* and another parent noting that their child *'gives some food/toys to his brother or friends'*.

Other

When asked if they noticed any other differences in their child, four parents answered *yes*. One parent reported their child's *'interpersonal skills have gone from strength to strength'* while another parent expressed that their child *'now will say sorry or give you a pat if he hits you and hurts you by accident'.*

Thematic Analysis

A series of thematic clusters were obtained from the written responses provided by parents in the post-programme questionnaire, Two major themes were identified, 'Increase in Prosocial Behaviour' and 'Increase in Communication Skills'. For 'Increase in Communication Skills', two subthemes were identified, being 'Increase in Expression of Feelings' and 'Enhanced Vocabulary'. The analyses highlight that post COPE-R programme, parents noticed an increase in open communication, politeness, and general prosocial behaviour in their children.

Increase in Prosocial Behaviour

'Increase in Prosocial Behaviour' was identified by 38.1% of parents. Examples include *'more caring towards her younger brother', 'moments of being thoughtful about her brother, for example, drawing him a picture of a friend at school'* and *'now will say sorry or give you a pat if he hits you and hurts you by accident'.* The majority of comments included examples of prosocial behaviour towards family members, particularly siblings.

Increase in Communication Skills

Ninety per cent of parents mentioned an increase in their child's communication skills. The first subtheme, 'Increase in Expression of Feelings' was endorsed by 57.1% of parents. Examples include *'he's a bit better at talking when he's upset sometimes', 'getting better at talking about things that are troubling him rather than yelling or crying',* and *'he can express he is sad and upset'.* While these are general examples of expressing feelings, more specific comments made by parents include *'uses phrases like "that makes me angry" when his little brother annoyed him', 'he talks about missing his friends'* and *'trying to use his words when upset/angry'.* The second subtheme, 'Enhanced Vocabulary' was endorsed by 33.3% of parents. Examples such as '*more "excuse me" when asking questions/interrupting*', '*using words like "I feel…" more in self-initiated conversation*' and '*big focus on "manner" words*'.

Concluding Remarks

Promoting social and emotional skills early in a child's schooling life can lead to successful interactions and experiences at school, both socially and academically. Enhancing prosocial skills in preschool-aged children can promote positive developmental outcomes such as positive peer relationships, reduction in externalising and internalising problems, and enhanced emotional regulation. The presented study aimed to evaluate a pilot five-week programme targeting the development of empathy and prosocial skills in preschool-aged children. Qualitative responses from parents indicated they noticed positive differences in their children post programme. A thematic analysis of parents' responses was conducted, revealing two major themes in the differences parents noticed, 'an increase in prosocial behaviour', and 'enhanced communication skills'. All these skills contribute to the building of resilience in the early years.

References

Alba, G., Justicia-Arráez, A., Pichardo, M. C., & Justicia, F. (2013). Aprender a Convivir. A program for improving social competence in preschool and elementary school children. *Electronic Journal of Research in Educational Psychology, 11*(3), 843–904. doi:10.14204/ejrep.31.13105.

Armstrong, M. A., Birnie-Lefcovitch, S., & Ungar, M. T. (2005). Pathways between social support, family wellbeing, quality of parenting, and child resilience: What we know. *Journal of Child and Family Studies, 14*, 269–281. doi:10.1007/s10826-005-5054-4.

Cappa, K., Begle, A., Conger, J., Dumas, J., & Conger, A. (2011). Bidirectional relationships between parenting stress and child coping competence: Findings from the pace study. *Journal of Child and Family Studies, 20*(3), 334–342. doi:10.1007/s10826-010-9397-0.

Chalmers, K., Frydenberg, E., & Deans, J. (2011). An exploration into the coping strategies of preschoolers: Implications for professional practice. *Children Australia, 36*(3), 120–127. doi:10.1375/jcas.36.3.120.

Cooklin, A. R., Giallo, R., & Rose, N. (2011). Parental fatigue and parenting practices during early childhood: An Australian community survey. *Child: Care, Health and Development, 38*, 654–664. doi:10.1111/j.1365-2214.2011.01333.x.

Cornell, C., Kiernan, N., Kaufman, D., Dobee, P., Frydenberg, E., & Deans, J. (in press). Developing social emotional competence in the early years. In E. Frydenberg, A. Martin, & R. Collie (Eds.), *Social and emotional learning in Australia and the Asia Pacific*. Melbourne, VIC: Springer.

Deans, J., Frydenberg, E., & Liang, R. (2012). Building a shared language of coping: Dynamics of communication between parents and preschool children. *New Zealand Research into Early Childhood Research Journal, 15*, 67–89.

Deans, J., Frydenberg, E., & Tsurutani, H. (2010). Operationalising social and emotional coping competencies in kindergarten children. *New Zealand Research in Early Childhood Education Journal, 13*, 113–124.

Deans, J., Liang, R., & Frydenberg, E. (2016). Giving voices and providing skills to families in culturally and linguistically diverse communities through a productive parenting program. *Australasian Journal of Early Childhood, 41*(1), 13–18.

Deans, J., Liang, R., Zapper, S., & Frydenberg, E. (in press). *The process of socialisation and embodiment of a social emotional learning program in an early years setting: COPE-R.* Unpublished manuscript, University of Melbourne.

Denham, S. A. (2006). Social-emotional competence as support for school readiness: What is it and how do we assess it? *Early Education and Development, Special Issue: Measurement of School Readiness, 17*, 57–89. doi:10.1207/s15566935eed1701_4.

Dinkmeyer, D. C., McKay, G. D., & Dinkmeyer, J. S. (1989). *Parenting young children: Helpful strategies based on systematic training for effective parenting (STEP) for parents of children under six*. Circle Pines, MN: AGS.

Domitrovich, C., Greenberg, M., Kusche, C., & Cortes, R. (2004). *PATHS preschool program*. South Deerfield, MA: Channing Bete Company.

Dreikurs, R. (1958). *The challenge of parenthood*. New York: Duell, Soan and Pearce.

Frydenberg, E. (2008). *Adolescent coping: Advances in theory, research and practice*. Hoboken, NJ: Taylor and Francis.

Frydenberg, E. (2015). *Families coping: Effective strategies for you and your child.* Camberwell, VIC: ACER Press.

Frydenberg, E., & Deans, J. (2011a). Coping competencies in the early years: Identifying the strategies that preschoolers use. In P. Buchwald, K. A. Moore, & T. Ringeisen (Eds.), *Stress and anxiety: Application to education and health* (pp. 17–26). Berlin, Germany: Logos.

Frydenberg, E., & Deans, J. (2011b). *The early years coping cards.* Melbourne, VIC: Australian Council for Educational Research.

Frydenberg, E., Deans, J., & Liang, R. (2014). Families can do coping: Parenting skills in the early years. *Children Australia, 39,* 99–106. doi:10.1017/cha.2014.7.

Gordon, T. (1970). *Parent effectiveness training: The tested new way to raise responsible children.* New York: David McKay.

Gulliford, H., Deans, J., Frydenberg, E., & Liang, R. (2015). Teaching coping skills in the context of positive parenting within a preschool setting. *Australian Psychologist, 50*(3), 219–231. doi:10.1111/ap.12121.

Pang, I., Frydenberg, E., & Deans, E. (2015). The relationship between anxiety and coping in preschoolers. In P. Buchenwald & K. Moore (Eds.), *Stress anxiety* (pp. 27–36). Berlin, Germany: Verlag.

Pearl, E. S. (2009). Parent management training for reducing oppositional and aggressive behavior in preschoolers. *Aggression and Violent Behavior, 14,* 295–305. doi:10.1016/j.avb.2009.03.007.

Raver, C. C., & Knitzer, J. (2002). *Ready to enter: What research tells policy makers about strategies to promote social and emotional school readiness among three- and four- year olds.* New York: National Centre for Children in Poverty.

Sanders, M., Markie-Dadds, C., Tully, L., & Bor, W. (2000). The Triple P—Positive Parenting Program: A comparison of enhanced, standard, and self-directed behavioral family intervention for parents of children with early onset conduct problems. *Journal of Consulting and Clinical Psychology, 68,* 624–640. doi:10.1037//022-006X.68.4.624.

Webster-Stratton, C. (2002). *Basic parent training program – School age.* Seattle, WA: Incredible Years.

Webster-Stratton, C., Reid, M. J., & Stoolmiller, M. (2008). Preventing conduct problems and improving school readiness: Evaluation of the incredible years teacher and child training programs in high-risk schools. *Journal of Child Psychology and Psychiatry, 49*(5), 471–488.

Yeo, K., Frydenberg, E., Northam, E., & Deans, J. (2014). Coping with stress among preschool children and associations with anxiety level and controllability of situations. *Australian Journal of Psychology*, 66(2), 93–101. doi:10.1111/ajpy.12047.

Youngs, B. B. (1985). *Stress in children: How to recognise, avoid, and overcome it.* New York: Arbor House.

10

Spiritual Approaches to Coping and Mindfulness

In the post-transactional coping era founded by Richards Lazarus, religious coping and meaning making have emerged as responses to trauma. At times of trauma and major life stresses that are less amenable to problem solving, 'implicit religiousness' is often incorporated into a religious meaning-making model where spirituality plays a part. There are many 'faces' of religious coping as researchers consider the challenges of later life when the majority of adults claim that they incorporate religion and/ or spirituality into their coping repertoire. Mindfulness has also emerged as a strong contributor to an individual's capacity to deal with stress and thus has become a personal coping resource within many people's contemporary pattern of coping.

On November 3, 2015, Michelle Payne was the first female jockey to win Australia's most celebrated horse race, the Melbourne Cup, on Prince of Penzance, a horse that she had ridden 22 times but was considered an unlikely winner with betting odds of 100:1. The story was a reality fairy tale. Payne, the youngest of ten children, whose mother had died

---

It is helpful to spend time with people that I love; tribal connections are valuable. ... People make me feel better about life. (Celine, surgeon)

© The Author(s) 2017   **175**
E. Frydenberg, *Coping and the Challenge of Resilience*,
DOI 10.1057/978-1-137-56924-0_10

in a car crash when she was six months old, came from a racing family with four female jockeys, one who had died following a racing accident and a brother, Stevie, with Down's syndrome, who was the strapper for Michelle's horse. Payne herself had suffered numerous riding-related injuries including having broken eight or nine vertebrae in the 1 year and having a fractured skull and 'bruised brain' injuries when she fell off a horse some 12 years earlier. In her victory speech she described the chauvinistic industry of horse racing and the reluctance of some of the owners to let her ride in the Melbourne Cup. She showed determination, resilience, and a belief in her own capacity and that of her horse. She declared after the success:

> I always feel my mum and sister are with me when I ride. My dad is religious, he always says his prayers and you can't help but take after your parents. I always say a little prayer to myself in the barriers, and hope mum is looking after me. (Payne, 2015)

In the last decade, a growing body of research has begun to explore the relationship between religion, coping, stress, and mental health (Pargament, Falb, Ano, & Wachholtz, 2005). Religion and spirituality provide a resource for some people as they cope with the stresses of everyday life. However, there are circumstances where these resources come to the fore, such as in situations of trauma, loss, and ageing. Annual Gallup polls in the United States consistently show that '90% of the population report a "belief in God" and approximately 70% report affiliation with a faith community and "attend religious services"' (Foy, Drescher, & Watson, 2011, p. 90). Around seven out of ten Australians (69%) believe in the existence of God or some kind of higher power. In contrast, a survey in 2009 that asked about church attendance found that 15% of Australians go to church at least once per month (Stetzer, 2013). The recent picture in the United Kingdom regarding religious belief is slightly different. The YouGov/the Times survey (Jordan, 2015) results show a third (33%) of British adults do not believe in God or in a greater spiritual power of any kind, roughly the same number as those who believe in 'a God' (32%). The findings also show that 42% of British adults don't have any religion, while about half of those who do (49%) identify as Christians.

For many, spirituality offers a positive meaning-making framework (Park, 2011). When discussing spirituality and coping it is helpful to have a wide-ranging definition that incorporates beliefs, values, and practices that are shared in common with a community. Additional factors associated with resilience identified by the positive psychology movement include hope (Snyder, 2000), morality, self-control (Baumeister & Exline, 2000), and forgiveness (McCullough, 2000). These characteristics are often linked to the spiritual-religious domain. Additionally, when it comes to ageing, spiritual coping has been seen as a resilience resource when navigating the hardships in later life (Manning, 2013). In 30 interviews with women in their 80s and 90s that Manning conducted with octogenarians, she established that spirituality is a tool to promote and maintain resilience in later life (Manning, 2013).

To some, religion is interpreted as a language of spirituality (Sandage & Morgan, 2014). Whilst religion and spirituality are not the same phenomena they are construed as related. That is, there is an interface between religion and spirituality. Spirituality and religion have been seen as a resiliency factor. They are considered to provide attachment relationships, sources of support, moral values, and opportunities for personal growth, and a mechanism for dealing with adversity. The development of these capacities occurs in the context of the community, school, and the family (Kim & Esquivel, 2011). It needs to be pointed out that appraisals and strategies are part of the coping process and for many, religion informs coping behaviours that individuals use. The strategies that people use emerge from their meaning-making systems; religion and culture influence their coping processes.

Culture and Context

Spirituality and culture are important aspects of individuals' meaning-making systems (Cruz-Ortega, Gutierrez, & Waite, 2015; Pargament, 1997). Pargament (1997) who defines religion as 'a search for meaning in ways related to the sacred' (p. 3) used spirituality and religion interchangeably. Individuals who report spirituality as an important part of their lives are more likely to use spiritual coping when facing stressful events. Bereavement and loss are commonly linked to studies of spirituality and coping. That is, those with high religious engagement are more likely to report positive religious coping strategies to cope with bereavement. In a study of 319 bereaved adults, individuals who had experienced the death of a loved one in the past 36 months and who engage in traditional spiritual practices (74.6% of whom were female) were more likely to engage in positive religious coping. Similarly, those with high ethnic identity development were also more likely to engage in positive religious coping strategies (Cruz-Ortega et al., 2015). Culture selectively encourages some religious expression and how the individual deals with grief. Additionally, those with clear sense of identity report greater self-esteem and well-being. For example, undergraduates who had lost a close friend and who engaged in positive religious appraisals and spiritual support were more likely to report personal growth (Park & Cohen, 1993).

Several studies with college students illustrate the ways in which young people utilise spiritual ways of coping. One cross-cultural and cross-denominational study of 610 college students aged between 18 and 30 years completed a creative coping scale and a spiritual coping scale and found that participants used both constructs when dealing with acute and chronic stress. There was a small correlation between the two constructs (0.3). Whilst the health benefits of creativity and spirituality have been well documented, both religion and nationality influenced the results (Corry, Mallett, Lewis, & Abdel-Khalek, 2013).

In a study of 84 volunteers aged 19–63 years, Christian College students (using the Anxiety Stress Scales of DASS [Lovibond & Lovibond, 1995]) somewhat unsurprisingly, there was an overall strong positive relationship between faith maturity and religious coping. And those who practised negative religious coping (questioning God's power in adversity) were inclined to use experiential avoidance, that is, a tendency to avoid negative internal experiences, depression, anxiety, and stress (Knabb & Grigorian-Routon, 2014).

In the Coping Scale for Adults (Frydenberg & Lewis, 1997, 2014) and the Adolescent Coping Scale (Frydenberg & Lewis, 1993, 2011) the strategy of seeking spiritual support appears and is represented by three items that were frequently nominated by respondents as coping strategies: pray for help guidance so that everything will be all right, pray for

God to look after me, and let the Lord take care of my worries. In reality, some people use these coping actions a great deal and some people use them very little. As noted in numerous studies, the cultural context determines the approach to spirituality and the frequency of use. When populations were compared on their use of coping strategies on the ACS what was evident was that culturally similar groups, such as Palestinian and Columbian adolescents, were more likely to use spiritual coping strategies in contrast to populations such as the German and Australian young people (Frydenberg et al., 2003). Culture and context are all important. However, there is a great deal of diversity within each community, in terms of spiritual and religious coping as there is in the ways that religious coping or spirituality are expressed.

There has been a great deal of research on people who meditate having better physical and mental health (Oman, Hedberg, & Thoresen, 2006) but not all people who see themselves as spiritual meditate. People who see themselves as high on spirituality rate themselves as high on personality traits that are protective such as agreeableness, conscientiousness, extraversion and low on health-risk factors such as neuroticism (Simpson, Newman, & Fuqua, 2007). Labbé and Fobes (2010) used a racially diverse US college sample of 80 students grouped according to high, medium and low on spirituality and reported similar results. The term 'spirituality' is used in different ways and sometimes those who are meditators have a more spiritual approach to life.

A meta-analytic study of 49 studies (Ano & Vasconcelles, 2005) utilised Pargament's 1997 model of religious coping which identified positive strategies, ranging from forgiveness and seeking spiritual direction to finding spiritual connection and benevolent religious reappraisal, and negative strategies including spiritual discontent, demonic reappraisal, passive deferral, interpersonal religious discontent and reappraisal of God's powers. Psychological adjustment was also dichotomised into positive and negative categories. Positive indicators included acceptance, emotional well-being, hope, happiness, self-esteem, and quality of life. Measures for negative adjustment ranged from anxiety, depression, and symptoms of post-traumatic stress disorder (PTSD) to social dysfunction, suicidality, and trait anger.

It should be pointed at that whilse ACS and ACS-2 measure spirituality as one of the coping strategies, despite it not being used frequently used by many young people, spirituality is gaining interest as a resource (Kim & Esquivel, 2011) and those who use it often use it a great deal. Just as coping research, in general, has been led by a focus on adults, the literature on adolescent spirituality mirrors that in the adult domain. When the research is conducted in religion-affiliated school settings perhaps the outcomes are more predictable, as with the college student studies reported earlier. In the adolescent arena, Terreri and Glenwick (2013) reported that 587 students from 9th to 12th grade attending Catholic schools reported that perceived stress, negative religious coping, and avoidant coping were significantly associated with psychological distress. A longitudinal study considered the moderating effects of religious coping between life stress and substance abuse in adolescents. For those young people turning to religion in the form of prayer and beliefs when faced with negative life events buffered the impact of initial substance use and the increase in substance use (Wills, Yaeger, & Sandy, 2003). In a study of spiritual coping in adolescents with the chronic illness of cystic fibrosis with measures taken at two time points two years apart, positive spiritual coping predicted fewer symptoms of depression and less negative spiritual coping over time (Reynolds, Mrug, Hensler, Guion, & Madan-Swain, 2014).

Overall culture and context do determine the use of spirituality as a coping resource. Nevertheless there are sufficient indications in the research literature to show the links between well-being and spirituality.

Meaning-Focused Coping

According to the transactional theory of stress, appraisal is shaped by the person's beliefs, values, and goals. When it comes to coping, the original Lazarus and Folkman model proposed two approaches, problem-focused such as dealing with the problem through information gathering and decision making and emotion-focused coping which highlighted the ways that individuals managed negative emotions. Following her extensive work with caregivers of HIV/AIDS patients, Folkman (1997) identified a third type of coping which she labelled 'meaning-focused' coping when she reported that positive emotions could coexist with negative ones during intensely stressful situations. She argues that this is consistent with Fredrickson's (2004) 'Broaden and Build' theory of positive emotions that highlights the fact that positive emotions can serve a beneficial purpose by reviewing a stressful situation as one of challenge and so can lead to a revision of goals. There is a highly interactive system at play when the various types of coping can act in tandem (in ways that, for example, regulate anxiety, that is, emotions) to address a problem and which can them lead to revised goals after meaning and relevance are assessed. Being hopeful allows us to have conflicting views of a situation.

Disasters have provided researchers with many opportunities to explore meaning making. Numerous studies have investigated the relationship between religious coping and disasters such as Hurricane Katrina that struck the Gulf Coast of the United States on August 29, 2005. Questions asked relate to how individuals dealt with the traumatic experience and whether there was post-traumatic growth following the experience. One thousand eight hundred and thirty-three people died in the hurricane and the flooding that followed.

One Hurricane Katrina study of 810 adults in Mississippi (21 % interviews conducted in person and 79 % by telephone) (Henslee et al., 2015) was conducted between February 2007 and July 2007. If participants indicated that they believed in God or a higher power they were asked the positive and negative religious coping questions. Ninety-eight per cent of respondents affirmed the existence of God or a higher power.

Negative religious coping (measured by the item 'I feel God is punishing me for my sins or lack of spirituality') was positively associated with major depression and poorer quality of life, and positive religious coping (measured by the item 'I look to God for strength, support and guidance') was negatively associated with PTSD, depression, poorer quality of life, and increased alcohol use (Henslee et al., 2015). Positive religious coping was also associated with post-traumatic growth among Katrina survivors (Chan & Rhodes, 2013). This study suggests that positive religious coping may serve as a protective factor against PTSD, major depression, and poor quality of life. A limitation of this study was that a more comprehensive measure of religious coping was not used. However, the implication for clinical services is that religious coping should be assessed for post-disaster clinical services.

Whilst there is a vast literature on coping with disasters and how individuals and communities are judged to be resilient, the literature has extended into domains that relate to meaning making, a form of spiritual explanation, and growth through the experience of post-traumatic growth (Guo, Gan, & Tong, 2013).

A study by Guo et al. (2013) was conducted three years following the 2008 Sichuan earthquake on May 12 when 70,000 people were killed (347,000 injured and 18,000 listed as missing), to examine the impact of whether a group of senior high schoolers used problem-, emotion-, or meaning-focused coping on post-traumatic growth. Park and Folkman (1997) proposed that the concept of meaning-focused coping (MFC) had a significant incremental value in predicting positive affect and well-being above and beyond problem- and emotion-focused coping (Park & Folkman, 1997). In contrast, the incremental effects were not there for negative affect and depression. That is, strong MFC was associated with more post-traumatic growth, fewer depression symptoms, and higher well-being and positive affect. MFC has the impact of improving positive outcomes whereas problem-focused coping has the effect of decreasing negative outcomes. Emotion-focused coping failed to improve the adolescents' well-being in their study.

Others studies have shown that MFC and adaptation are related. For example, the study by Holahan, Moos, Holahan, and Brennan (1995) using the construct of MFC with 400 questionnaires sent to senior high school students and using Tedeschi and Calhoun's (2004) post-traumatic growth scale; Carver's Brief COPE (Carver, Scheier, & Weintraub, 1989) of 28 items with 14 subscales used to deal with stressful situations, namely, self-distraction, denial, emotional support, positive reframing, instrumental support, substance use, active coping, behavioural disengagement, venting acceptance, religion, humour, planning, and self-blame (with the religion scale deleted because of Chinese cultural background), self-rating depression scale, positive and negative affect schedule, index of well-being, and MFC with 26 items, relating to perspectives, beliefs, and acceptance. They found that post-traumatic growth (PTG) mediated the path from MFC to well-being and positive affect. The authors point out that the study illustrates how even without a religion subscale being included, MFC is relevant.

Post-traumatic Growth (PTG)

The notion that individuals can experience positive effects following highly stressful or traumatic events is discussed in the literature under a number of different labels, for example, 'benefit finding', 'post-traumatic growth', and 'stress-related growth' (Park & Helgeson, 2006). The relationship between religious coping, post-traumatic growth, and health was explored with a sample of 85 women. That study identified a mechanism, namely, a deliberate cognitive process of rumination, as a mediator between religious coping and post-traumatic growth.

For Tedeschi and Calhoun (1996), PTG encompasses three categories of change: perceived change of self, changed sense of relations with others, and a changed philosophy of life. The broad categories have five specific areas: relation with others, new possibilities, personal strength, appreciation of life, and spirituality. People report increased awareness of support, change in career, self-reliance, valuing of life, and ability to empathise with others (Tedeschi & Calhoun, 2004). Pargament, Smith, Koenig, and Perez (1998) distinguish between positive and negative religious coping, that is the belief in a spiritual deity in contrast to an active disbelief. Cognitive rumination in this study is not negative (Tedeschi & Calhoun, 2004) but rather deliberate cognitive thoughts (rather than the intrusive ones) and are associated with finding meaning, that is, making the experience manageable and comprehensible. Religious beliefs can provide the scaffolding to deal with grief and loss.

In the past decade, positive psychology has focused on empowering and skilling individuals to enhance their well-being and mental health. Two constructs which have a 'spiritual dimension' (albeit in a secular sense), namely, hope and mindfulness, have been widely applied in the pursuit of well-being and resilience building.

Hope

Hope has different definitions but is about remaining positive in the face of possible negative outcomes. For many, it has a basis in religion and spirituality. It is a cognitive process that, in the case of illness, is about coping with uncertainty. In many situations hope is helpful in the face of uncertainty and could be considered an emotion or an influence on emotions.

One of the most widely cited definitions of hope is based on goals in that a case could be made that all those who have hope have purpose or goals in a general sense.

> Hope is a positive motivational state that is based on interactively derived sense of successful a) agency (goal directed energy), and b) pathways (planning to meet goals). (Snyder, Irving, & Anderson, 1991, p. 287)

Hope is a trait-like capacity for pursuing goals. Hope involves two main components: agency cognitions and pathway cognitions. Agency cognition is the belief that one can reach desired goals, and pathway cognitions are the perceived capacity to find workable routes towards those goals. Hope correlates with well-being, goal achievement, self-regulation, healthy moral emotion, and positive mental health functioning and negatively with depression and distress (Snyder, 1995).

Hope has been discussed widely from different perspectives but in the stress and coping literature it has often been considered from a viewpoint of its absence, that is the sense of helplessness and despair which indicates a lack of hope. Hopelessness gives rise to despair and depression. Like psychological stress it is contextual, meaning based, and dynamic. Folkman considers hope from the perspective of serious illness where there is an exposure to prolonged stress such as in the case of those with HIV/AIDS and their carers, who nevertheless experience hope and positive emotions.

For Folkman (2010) hope is more than about goals; it is about exploring existential issues. When it comes to resilience it is about having a capacity to reframe, reappraise, deal with both positive and negative emotions, and have hope.

Mindfulness

Mindfulness and self-compassion are two approaches that have received increased attention to the point that it has reached our common vernacular, as individuals are encouraged to be mindful in various aspects of their everyday lives, such as in eating or leisuring, where the emphasis is on having a full experience and being able to stay in the moment. Whilst meditation has had clear associations with well-being in the literature, the more recent dominant expression of meditational practice is through mindfulness.

Mindfulness has become of increasing interest in the last decade as evidence is emerging regarding the benefits for both adults and children. In simple terms, it is the conscious awareness and focus on the present moment, and nonjudgementally focusing on the unfolding of the event, moment by moment. It is about observing one's experiences, sometimes the internal thoughts and emotions, without evaluating or judging each experience. In short, it is about staying in the present rather than dwelling on the past or thinking about future events. Many of the specific techniques and practices derive from the Asian contemplative tradition, generally Buddhist meditation practices. Mindfulness is generally attributed to Gautama Siddhartha, the Buddha, about 2600 years ago. Jon Kabat-Zinn (2005) is one of the pioneers of mindfulness in North America. However, mindfulness is now being adopted globally across the lifespan without any reference to its spiritual origins. Whilst there are some like the social psychologist Ellen Langer, who has published extensively in the field of mindfulness (2009), who see a sharp contrast between the meditative, introspective approaches to mindfulness that originated as a part of the Buddhist philosophy, and an approach which is more akin to the contemporary positive psychology movement, where mindfulness is a state of mind.

Like others, Langer emphasises the importance of staying in the moment, being attentive, looking and appreciating the detail in one's experiences and surroundings and having wonderment and curiosity in everyday events. But in contrast to others, Langer cautions against continual evaluation of oneself and being hyperanalytical about what is happening and why. Self-analysis is often associated with self-criticism and self-blame which is associated with less well-being and should be avoided for maximum well-being. Excessive self-analysis and self-blame provide the potential for rumination which is akin to having a depressive mindset. In her book *Counter Clockwise: Mindful Health and the Power of Possibility* (2009) Langer writes about mindfulness being a search for 'novelty' rather than being introspective and searching for certainty (see Chap. 7).

She also contrasts 'mindlessness' with mindfulness in that the former is about passively experiencing everyday life (Langer, 1992).

The widespread uptake of mindfulness reflects the recognition that is a contributor to well-being and resilience. The principles can be learnt and put into practice. The elements of mindfulness are as follows:

1. Observing one's experiences
2. Describing them
3. Acting with awareness
4. Not judging the inner experience
5. Not reacting to the experience.

These five elements require attention and reflection.

Cultivating Mindfulness Attitudes

The following attitudes can be found in the mindfulness literature, and they represent an orientation for healthy interpersonal relationships in all settings, be it family, friendship, or workplace.

- Nonjudging—do no harm, curiosity, acceptance
- Patience—let yourself allow things to unfold as they need to
- Beginner's mind—curiosity about exploring the nature of your mind, seeing, and thinking
- Trust—faith in your own deepest experience, not what your mind thinks but in that deeper nonverbal, nonconceptual place of knowing, trust in yourself, your intuition, and your abilities
- Nonstriving—the state of not doing anything, just simply accepting that things are happening in the moment just as they are supposed to (Chinese word for busy equals heart-killing)
- Acceptance—completely accepting your thoughts, feelings, sensations, and beliefs, and understanding that they are only simply those things; remember, life is a way of being, being awake to the actual experience of your life on a moment-by-moment basis.

Numerous studies have attested to the benefits of the teaching and practice of mindfulness. For example, Fredrickson, Cohn, Coffey, Pek, and Finkel (2008) found that after teaching loving kindness meditation, those who practised increased their positive emotions towards themselves and others. Self-compassion is also associated with increased mental health (Neff, Rude, & Kirkpatrick, 2007).

In a study of children, researchers found that using a mindfulness-based cognitive therapy designed to help children reduce anxiety, increased the children's ability to attend, and a reduction in behavioural problems (Semple, Lee, Rosa, & Miller, 2010). In a study of adults, using police recruits, those who demonstrated relatively high levels of mindfulness were less likely after a year of service to experience depressive symptoms (Williams, Ciarrochi, & Patrick Deane, 2010).

Experiencing harmony between the physical, emotional, spiritual, and intellectual is a salient aspect of our lives. Increased mindfulness is considered to reduce the impact of stress and de-centering from the negative cognitions (Rybak, 2013). Characteristics that include having a sense of awareness of the present with acceptance, a sense of vitality, combined with mindfulness-based stress reduction techniques contribute to having a sense of coherence. Additionally, given that well-being is associated with a sense of coherence, having these characteristics enables individuals to resonate with others and have greater empathy. Interpersonal coherence is linked to mirror neurons. The mirror neuron system seems to fire as a person makes an empathic connection with another, as if the observer has had the same experience. There is a significance of a sense of connectedness and evolutionary processes. Throughout the process connections are formed and strengthened through continued use thus contributing to neuroplasticity (see Chap. 11).

Concluding Remarks

While transactional and dyadic coping has emerged as a response to health and relational issues, religious coping and meaning making have emerged as a response to trauma. For some researchers such as Ross,

Handal, Clark, and Wal (2009), religiousness and nonself-directedness are predictive of psychological adjustment. Others, like Park (2011), highlight that at times of trauma and major life stress that are less amenable to problem solving, 'implicit religiousness' is incorporated into a religious meaning-making model where spirituality plays a part. There are many 'faces' of religious coping and Emery and Pargament (2004) consider the challenges of later life where the majority of adults claim that they incorporate religion and spirituality into their coping repertoire. In the contemporary context, hope and mindfulness can both be considered as elements or approaches to spiritual coping, albeit in a secular nonreligion-affilitated sense.

References

Ano, G. G., & Vasconcelles, E. B. (2005). Religious coping and psychological adjustment to stress: A meta-analysis. *Journal of Clinical Psychology, 61*, 461–480.

Baumeister, R. F., & Exline, J. J. (2000). Self-control, morality, and human strength. *Journal of Social and Clinical Psychology, 19*(1), 29–42.

Carver, C. S., Scheier, M. F., & Weintraub, J. K. (1989). Assessing coping strategies: A theoretically based approach. *Journal of Personality and Social Psychology, 56*, 267–283.

Chan, C. S., & Rhodes, J. E. (2013). Religious coping, posttraumatic stress, psychological distress, and posttraumatic growth among female survivors four years after Hurricane Katrina. *Journal of Traumatic Stress, 26*(2), 257–265. doi:10.1002/jts.21801.

Corry, D. A. S., Mallett, J., Lewis, C. A., & Abdel-Khalek, A. M. (2013). The creativity-spirituality construct and its role in transformative coping. *Mental Health, Religion and Culture, 16*(10), 979–990. doi:10.1080/13674676.2013.834492.

Cruz-Ortega, L. G., Gutierrez, D., & Waite, D. (2015). Religious orientation and ethnic identity as predictors of religious coping among bereaved individuals. *Counseling and Values, 60*(1), 67–83.

Emery, E. E., & Pargament, K. I. (2004). The many faces of religious coping in late life: Conceptualization, measurement, and links to well-being. *Ageing International, 29*, 3–27.

Folkman, S. (1997). Positive psychological states and coping with severe stress. *Social Science & Medicine, 45*(8), 1207–1221, 1215.

Folkman, S. (2010). Stress, coping, and hope. *Psycho-Oncology, 19*(9), 901–908. doi:10.1002/pon.1836.

Foy, D. W., Drescher, K. D., & Watson, P. J. (2011). Religious and spiritual factors in resilience. In S. M. Southwick, B. T. Litu, D. Charney, & M. J. Friedman (Eds.), *Resilience and mental health: Challenges across the lifespan* (pp. 90–101). Cambridge, UK: Cambridge University Press.

Fredrickson, B. L. (2004). The Broaden-and-Build theory of positive emotions. *Philosophical Transactions of the Royal Society of London, 359,* 1367–1377.

Fredrickson, B. L., Cohn, M. A., Coffey, K. A., Pek, J., & Finkel, S. M. (2008). Open hearts build lives: Positive emotions, induced through loving-kindness meditation, build consequential personal resources. *Journal of Personality and Social Psychology, 95*(5), 1045–1062.

Frydenberg, E., & Lewis, R. (1993). *Manual, The adolescent coping scale.* Melbourne, VIC: Australian Council for Educational Research.

Frydenberg, E., & Lewis, R. (1997). *Coping scale for adults.* Melbourne, VIC: Australian Council for Educational Research.

Frydenberg, E., & Lewis, R. (2011). *Adolescent coping scale – Second Edition (ACS-2).* Melbourne, VIC: Australian Council for Educational Research (ACER Press).

Frydenberg, E., & Lewis, R. (2014). *Coping scale for adults – Second Edition (CSA-2).* Melbourne, VIC: Australian Council for Educational Research. (ACER Press).

Frydenberg, E., Lewis, R., Kennedy, G., Ardila, R., Frindte, W., & Hannoun, R. (2003). Coping with concerns: An exploratory comparison of Australian, Colombian, German and Palestinian adolescents. *Journal of Youth and Adolescence, 32*(1), 59–66.

Guo, M., Gan, Y., & Tong, J. (2013). The role of meaning-focused coping in significant loss. *Anxiety, Stress, and Coping, 26*(1), 87–102.

Henslee, A. M., Coffey, S. F., Schumacher, J. A., Tracy, M., Norris, F. H., & Galea, S. (2015). Religious coping and psychological and behavioral adjustment after hurricane katrina. *Journal of Psychology, 149*(6), 630–642.

Holahan, C. J., Moos, R. H., Holahan, C. K., & Brennan, P. L. (1995). Social support, coping, and depressive symptoms in a late-middle-aged sample of patients reporting cardiac illness. *Health Psychology, 14,* 152–163.

Jordan, W. (2015, February 12). A third of British adults don't believe in a higher power. Retrieved from https://yougov.co.uk/news/2015/02/12/third-british-adults-dont-believe-higher-power/

Kabat-Zinn, J. (2005). *Wherever you go, there you are: Mindfulness meditation in everyday life/Jon Kabat-Zinn.* New York: Hyperion, c2005.

Kim, S., & Esquivel, G. B. (2011). Adolescent spirituality and resilience: Theory, research, and educational practices. *Psychology in the Schools, 48*(7), 755–765. doi:10.1002/pits.20582.

Knabb, J. J., & Grigorian-Routon, A. (2014). The role of experiential avoidance in the relationship between faith maturity, religious coping, and psychological adjustment among Christian university students. *Mental Health, Religion and Culture, 17*(5), 458–469. doi:10.1080/13674676.2013.846310.

Labbé, E. E., & Fobes, A. (2010). Evaluating the interplay between spirituality, personality and stress. *Applied Psychophysiology and Biofeedback, 35*(2), 141–146.

Langer, E. J. (1992). Matters of mind: Mindfulness/mindlessness in perspective. *Consciousness and Cognition, 1*(3), 289–305. doi:10.1016/1053-8100(92)90066-J.

Langer, E. J. (2009). *Counter clockwise : Mindful health and the power of possibility/Ellen J. Langer.* New York: Ballantine Books, c2009.

Lovibond, S. H., & Lovibond, P. F. (1995). *Manual for the depression anxiety stress scales.* (2nd ed.) Sydney, NSW: Psychology Foundation. ISBN 7334-1423-0.

Manning, L. K. (2013). Navigating hardships in old age: Exploring the relationship between spirituality and resilience in later life. *Qualitative Health Research, 23*(4), 568–575. doi:10.1177/1049732312471730.

McCullough, M. E. (2000). Forgiveness as a human strength: Theory, measurement, and links to well-being. *Journal of Social and Clinical Psychology, 19*(1), 43–55.

Neff, K. D., Rude, S. S., & Kirkpatrick, K. L. (2007). An examination of self-compassion in relation to positive psychological functioning and personality traits. *Journal of Research in Personality, 41*(4), 908–916.

Oman, D., Hedberg, J., & Thoresen, C. E. (2006). Passage meditation reduces perceived stress in health professionals: A randomized, controlled trial. *Journal of Consulting and Clinical Psychology, 74*, 714–719.

Pargament, K. I. (1997). *The psychology of religion and coping: Theory, research, practice.* New York: The Guilford Press.

Pargament, K. I., Falb, K., Ano, G., & Wachholtz, A. B. (2005). The religious dimension of coping: Advances in theory, research, and practice. In R. Paloutzian & C. Park (Eds.), *The handbook of the psychology of religion* (pp. 479–495). The Guilford Press: New York.

Pargament, K. I., Smith, B. W., Koenig, H. G., & Perez, L. (1998). Patterns of positive and negative religious coping with major life stressors. *Journal for the Scientific Study of Religion, 37*(4), 710.

Park, C. L. (2011). Implicit religion and the meaning making model. *Implicit Religion, 14*(4), 405–419. doi:10.1558/imre.v14i4.405.

Park, C. L., & Cohen, L. H. (1993). Religious and nonreligioius coping with the death of a friend. *Cognitive Therapy and Research, 17*, 561–577. doi:10.1007/BF01176079.

Park, C. L., & Folkman, S. (1997). Meaning in the context of stress and coping. *General Review of Psychology, 1*, 115–144.

Park, C. L., & Helgeson, V. S. (2006). Introduction to the special section: Growth following highly stressful life events – Current status and future directions. *Journal of Consulting and Clinical Psychology, 74*(5), 791–796.

Payne, M. (2015, November 4). Michelle Payne looks to future after achieving lifelong dream of winning Melbourne Cup. *Herald Sun*. Retrieved from http://www.heraldsun.com.au/

Reynolds, N., Mrug, S., Hensler, M., Guion, K., & Madan-Swain, A. (2014). Spiritual coping and adjustment in adolescents with chronic illness: A 2-year prospective study. *Journal of Pediatric Psychology, 39*(5), 542–551.

Ross, K., Handal, P. J., Clark, E. M., & Wal, J. S. V. (2009). The relationship between religion and religious coping: Religious coping as a moderator between religion and adjustment. *Journal of Religion and Health, 48*, 454–467. doi:10.1007/s10943-008- 9199-5.

Rybak, C. (2013). Nurturing positive mental health: Mindfulness for wellbeing in counseling. *International Journal for the Advancement of Counselling, 35*(2), 110–119.

Sandage, S. J., & Morgan, J. (2014). Hope and positive religious coping as predictors of social justice commitment. *Mental Health, Religion and Culture, 17*(6), 557–567. doi:10.1080/13674676.2013.864266.

Semple, R. J., Lee, J., Rosa, D., & Miller, L. F. (2010). A randomized trial of mindfulness-based cognitive therapy for children: Promoting mindful attention to enhance social-emotional resiliency in children. *Journal of Child and Family Studies, 19*(2), 218–229.

Simpson, D. B., Newman, J. L., & Fuqua, D. R. (2007). Spirituality and personality: Accumulating evidence. *Journal of Psychology and Christianity, 26*(1), 33–44.

Snyder, C. R. (1995). Conceptualising, measuring and nurturing hope. *Journal of Counseling and Development, 73*, 355–360.

Snyder, C. R. (2000). The past and possible futures of hope. *Journal of Social and Clinical Psychology, 19*(1), 11–28.

Snyder, C. R., Irving, L., & Anderson, J. R. (1991). Hope and health: Measuring the will and the ways. In C. R. Snyder & D. R. Forsyth (Eds.), *Handbook of social and clinical psychology: The health perspective* (pp. 285–305). Elmsford, NY: Pergamon Press.

Stetzer, E. (2013, December 2). How Religious are Australians? Retrieved from http://www.christianitytoday.com/edstetzer/2013/december/how-religious-are-australians.html

Tedeschi, R. G., & Calhoun, L. G. (1996). The posttraumatic growth inventory: Measuring the positive legacy of trauma. *Journal of Traumatic Stress, 9*(3), 455–471.

Tedeschi, R. G., & Calhoun, L. G. (2004). Posttraumatic growth: Conceptual foundations and empirical evidence. *Psychological Inquiry, 15*, 1–18.

Terreri, C., & Glenwick, D. (2013). The relationship of religious and general coping to psychological adjustment and distress in urban adolescents. *Journal of Religion and Health, 52*(4), 1188–1202. doi:10.1007/s10943-011-9555-8.

Williams, V., Ciarrochi, J., & Patrick Deane, F. (2010). On being mindful, emotionally aware, and more resilient: Longitudinal pilot study of police recruits. *Australian Psychologist, 45*(4), 274–282. doi:10.1080/00050060903573197.

Wills, T. A., Yaeger, A. M., & Sandy, J. M. (2003). Buffering effect of religiosity for adolescent substance use. *Psychology of Addictive Behaviors: Journal of the Society of Psychologists in Addictive Behaviors, 17*(1), 24–31.

11

The Resilient Coper

The resilient coper knows that there is no right or wrong coping, just what works and what does not work in a particular context. Resilient adults, be they teachers, managers, administrators, and parents are able to assess their own coping and develop the skills that are required to enhance their performance. Following an event they are likely to ask the question: What can I learn from the experience? What would I do differently next time?

Whilst resilience is generally about assessment of an individual or community's performance post an event, it is also about prediction. That is, how well an individual or group is likely to recover from setbacks or adversity. To some resilience is akin to adaptation, and adaptation is akin to coping. It is considered to be a state rather than a trait (Brandan et al., 2013) However to have predictive power it is more likely to have elements of a trait or inherent capacity. Thus, like coping, it is both situation specific and a general predisposition. It has both state and trait-like qualities, depending on which elements best fit a given circumstance. For

---

I think everyone is born with a range of predispositions, a number of developing abilities. Neuroplasticity is underrated. We need to be more plastic in how we adapt. Our genes adapt so why not everything else! (Celine, medical specialist)

© The Author(s) 2017   **193**
E. Frydenberg, *Coping and the Challenge of Resilience*,
DOI 10.1057/978-1-137-56924-0_11

example, different characteristics comprise resilience such as a positive attitude, maintaining healthy relationships, having interests, spirituality/ religion, coping self-efficacy, and collective self-efficacy (Bandura, 1997).

Whether it is dealing with a career choice, a life transition such as marriage or having a first child, leaving a workplace or entering retirement the question or appraisal remains relevant: 'Is the situation one of threat, harm, loss, or challenge?' and 'Do I have the resources or strategies to cope?'

Revisiting High Achievers

In the year 2000 the author interviewed a diverse range of people who were known to me and who had achieved exceptionally, despite setbacks. At that time my key interest was to determine what over-and-above ability and opportunity made the difference in terms of the achievements of those interviewed. A comprehensive report of the interviews was published in a volume titled *Beyond Coping: Meeting Goals Visions and Challenges* (Frydenberg, 2002). Each of the interviewed subjects had losses and setbacks but demonstrated a capacity to be resilient and bounce back from adversity. Each had core resources in the form of supports such as parents, coaches, or someone who encouraged them and believed in their capacity to succeed. In 2015 I revisited the interviews to see how the interviewees were faring and with what outcomes.

The purpose of this chapter is to see how the high achievers interviewed in 2000 were faring 15 years later, and to see how five additional interviewees from a different range of settings dealt with setbacks in 2015. The interest was in resilience in a broad sense, that is, what coping strategies were used to meet challenges; how mindset, emotional intelligence, hardiness, and grit contributed to their resilience. The core interest was to identify elements that contribute to successful achievements despite setbacks.

My initial interest in the interviews that were conducted 2000 was sparked by a chance meeting with Atti,[1] a surgeon who was a distinguished medical professor and international philanthropist. He was the keynote speaker at a conference that I was attending as an accompanying

---

[1] All names have been changed.

spouse. Having been a researcher in the field of coping, I was fascinated by his story. Born in Ethiopia, in 1942 in Chevo, Atti came from an isolated traditional village, 150 kilometres from Addis Ababa, where there was no electricity or tap water. This village has a 'religious culture' with monasteries and churches in abundance. Atti stayed there until the age of seven, when he was sent to Addis Ababa to live with his uncle and to attend the French school for a few hours each day. When his mother came to visit some months later, he begged to return to be with his brothers and sisters. Back home he took care of sheep and cattle, travelling for two to three days at a time to tend the herds. At the age of 11, he returned to Addis Ababa, to recommence his schooling and moved through two grades each year until he completed his Baccalaureate. When he was 20 his older brother died after a 6-month illness. Not knowing why he died Atti decided to study medicine 'to help people escape death'. In Europe, he became an internationally eminent professor of surgery. He is guided by his father's philosophy 'don't try to move the mountain', that is, do something that you can really do.

In the intervening years (2001–2015) Atti had lost his son, a medical student, to suicide, and his marriage fell apart. One of the ways he dealt with the loss of his son was through forging ahead further in medicine by producing a new medical invention in his field of specialisation. He lives in Paris with his Ethiopian wife and travels regularly to Ethiopia to teach surgery and to support a local hospital.

Atti's story stimulated my interest to interview others who had succeeded in the world of arts, sports, and commerce. The participants, ranging from early adulthood to midlife, were generally known to the author, and were recruited to represent a range of endeavours. The interviews centred around the subjects' life experiences and the coping strategies they had used. Additionally the aim was to understand how these achievers set goals and met challenges. Questions centred around their life histories, including their journey to success, their family and school life, the ways in which they coped, and how they dealt with obstacles and setbacks that came their way.

Andrew graduated as an indigenous medical practitioner when there were only 50 in the country. Now in his mid-40s he has continued to work in indigenous health, and more recently has been elevated to a professorship at an early age as a highly successful researcher. He had confronted covert racism in his early years but was considered to have good people skills. He had never been in a fight in his life, something completely 'unheard of' in the rough and tumble of the working-class environment in which he grew up. He used his advanced language skills to respond when challenged. Andrew, along with Martin, a successful property developer, along with each of those interviewed in the two cohorts, demonstrated emotional intelligence and a determination to succeed.

Martin grew up in a rural community and attended boarding school. His brother, who was six years older, succeeded at school and subsequently became an academic. At school, Martin was neither successful academically nor was he successful at sport. He left school at 16 but never saw himself as a failure. 'My mother gave me belief in myself, by treating me as *special* every day of my life. I got from her a real belief in myself.' He has had financial and industry setbacks when his giant building empire collapsed. Today, having scaled down his operations he continues to run a successful property company.

Support, often spiritual and generally social, can be construed as a key protective factor. For example, Martin describes his mother as 'incredibly Christian'. She would leave soup for poor people in the neighbourhood. Church and Sunday school were part of his childhood.

Robyn, an Australian born concert pianist, was acclaimed as a child prodigy at the age of three. She has personality characteristics that are conducive to talent development such as grit and hardiness, along with having the support of her family and teachers. After performing for Arthur Rubenstein at the age of five, Rubenstein proposed that an American philanthropist sponsor her American and European education. Robyn made her American debut with the Detroit symphony at age ten and performed with the Philadelphia Orchestra at 11. She has since performed with many of the leading orchestras and conductors and given recitals across Europe, United States, Canada, South America, China, and Australia. She has twice performed for presidents of the United States.

Her parents separated before she went to the United States, where she studied at the Juliard School; her entire family is musical with a brother who is a conductor and a violinist, and her sister a pianist. Music was constant in the home and it was regarded as 'normal'.

She described the music culture in the United States as a highly pressured 'hot house' environment which was both competitive and demanding. Students felt that they were on probation from the day they were accepted into the Juliard School until the day they left. They could be expelled any day before graduation if it wasn't thought that they were up to the standard. Of the 160 applicants who were chosen to audition, 2 were accepted. While she felt both 'privileged', she also felt 'pressured'. One of her mother's sayings helped her to cope, 'How do you eat an elephant? One bite at a time.' She learnt to tackle each new score bit by bit. Her mother gave her the message that she should enjoy her music. 'Play was a four-letter word', according to her mother who was her piano teacher in her early years. There was an emphasis on taking responsibility for one's own life and work but at the same time enjoying it.

Robyn has two children who are now adult and successful in their own right. She contracted a virus from her daughter soon after giving birth that left her with rheumatoid arthritis. 'It just cut me flat for nine months.' She used the same approach to get through performances, 'this virus, or IVF, I focus on positive outcomes. It's the projection of how it's going to feel when you've succeeded.' She continued to perform and became a director of a music academy. When that closed due to loss of funding, she overcame the disappointment and continued to run Master Classes and perform in her own right.

Tania, a marathon swimmer now in her 40s, has had many successes, including swimming Manhattan, Loch Ness, and the English Channel. She talked about knowing when to give up and not seeing oneself as a loser. There were failures and disappointments such as when the tide was just not helpful during a swim. 'There are no failures. You just go back and give it your best.' She construes these variations in the environment as 'nature throwing up challenges'. After a loss or setback there is no self-discrimination or self-blame.

Learning to deal with failure was a gradual process. The swimmers had to keep a logbook in which they recorded and gave a rating of their own performance in the training session. They would record how they felt and what they wanted to improve. There were swimming competitions and the swimmers would write down their comments to the coach and the coach would write a response. Setting goals was a feature of training.

When there were losses, parents were waiting with open arms to say, 'You gave it your best, let's look at what you're going to do next.' Today Tania is a trainer and motivational speaker. For an athlete to be able to change track once his or her high-performance days have passed, is also an indicator of adaptability and resilience.

The impact of mindset on achievement is demonstrated by Dweck and her associates. Dweck (1990, 2006) gives clear guidelines as to the experiences that develop helplessness rather than a sense of mastery and believes that abilities are changeable (see Chap. 2). She points out that it is the rewarding of effort rather than labelling of talents or abilities that determines motivation and how goals are achieved. Perception of the self is determined by feedback after completing tasks. Rather than praise for speed and perfection, there needs to be acknowledgement of effort. This is illustrated by the experiences of the high achievers who were interviewed in 2000 and again those who were interviewed in 2015.

Doug, a successful businessman described how responding to challenges requires a positive mindset. When the 'gauntlet is down', there is a keenness to take up the challenge. Doug did that when he accepted the presidency of an ailing football club, which was then at the bottom of the league but during the time of his leadership subsequently rose to the top three in the competition. He continued as president for 16 years during which time he supported his wife through a protracted illness. He remarried sometime after she died. Doug relied on the family's input, saying that 'two heads are better than one'. The support network amongst the family was evident when the family sat down and talked about issues and achieved solutions 'even when not setting out to do that'.

An additional source of support for Doug was the Forum group which emerged from the Young Presidents organisation.[2] The group was made up of seven men who had been together for nearly 12 years. They meet every six weeks and there is complete confidentiality. It provides an opportunity to 'take your mask off, to take off the veil, to talk about your

---

[2] An international organisation of business and corporate achievers who reach heights of success at an early age.

own issues, your own self, and talk about your real feelings and thoughts'. He went on to explain that at first they would meet 'just to talk' and that it was invigorating without being threatening.

> With men there's a lot of frustration built up simply because we can't sit down and talk about the issues. I draw on the values I've been brought up with and then go and talk to the Forum group. I might say 'it's not my problem; it's the organisation's [problem] and I'm learning. Don't take it on yourself, share the issues around.'

> I believe in the glass table. If you have an issue and you keep it under the table you can't see it or touch it so it can't be deal with. I say at every meeting 'put the issue on the table because then we can all see it and deal with it and move it. You're not going to get rid of it by ignoring it.'

Tania, the long distance swimmer, had to deal with many setbacks out of the water. Her mother and sister were involved in a car accident which placed her mother in hospital for several months 'with her knee cap smashed in 20 pieces and her ankle obliterated'. Her father was critically ill while she was training to swim around Manhattan Island, but he encouraged her to do the swim. After her father's death, which came shortly after her swim, she reflected on all the things she should or shouldn't have done, but tried to stop herself by thinking, 'Well you can't change anything, it's over and it's gone.' Rather, she focuses on the positive. There is a general reframing of events to produce helpful outcomes.

> The two things I look at are: we had that time together, and that I was able to get my brother and sister on the phone and get them to the hospital, and Dad acknowledged the fact that we were all there. Generally, I try and look at things and see that there are always people in worse situations than myself. We tend to get caught up in our own problems. There are always inspirational people around us and I try and draw on people around me and look at different things, watching TV, reading and seeing people who have overcome difficulties.

Justin, a tennis player, also used the strategy of comparing himself to others who are worse off. Comparing oneself 'downwards' rather than 'upwards' with those who are better off, is more helpful in retaining a positive outlook. Justin's parents divorced whilst he was in his teens and focusing on his tennis career. He learned to deal with losses early in his career.

> As a tennis player you are guaranteed to lose every week of the year. You always look to the tournament next week. You learn how to handle pressure. In tennis you get into many situations when you just don't think you can do it and at the end of the day you can. When you're doing something you really love you give it 100 percent.

Justin married another successful tennis player, became a father and took a leadership role at the age of 40 in the tennis community.

Jason landed at his first job as a producer of a commercial radio show, after finishing a bachelor's degree. He describes himself as not having setbacks but rather as having 'opportunities'. As a burgeoning writer, however, there were always rejections of submitted work. To him a setback is 'just an opportunity to take a different path to maybe the same destination'. In recent years he has lived in the United States and works in media.

Doug, the businessman, describes seeing his glass as being half full rather than half empty. Justin, the tennis player, describes himself as learning to lose every day of his life and still going out to play the next match. Robyn, the concert pianist, who had been in and out of hospital with a back injury for several years, having received various treatments and epidurals, describes IVF (in vitro fertilisation) which went on for nine years, as the most difficult to endure but was able to reframe it by focusing on positive outcomes. 'It's the projection of how it's going to feel when you've succeeded.' She uses the same approach to get through performances as she did to manage her virus or IVF.

Livia was in her mid-40s when interviewed and at the height of her career as a court[3] judge. She described herself as being regarded as 'bright but not exceptional'. She describes herself as organised and approached her university studies much like a nine-to-five working day. Her mother

---

[3] The type of court is removed for confidentiality reasons.

died of cancer at age 47. Although the youngest in the family, she felt a responsibility to look after everybody else. 'When I have a goal, I just do it.' Family life is where her coping resources were most challenged. While no one is invincible, there is generally a resilience or capacity to cope effectively, albeit differently, under different circumstances.

> There can be crises at work and it can upset me or agitate me or annoy me but I cope with it. If there is a minor crisis like that at home, I actually don't cope well. That's my soft spot. That's my vulnerable spot. Minor crises at work remain minor crises, minor crises at home become major in my mind.

Livia continued in the law for a decade more and then took on leadership roles in the arts and sporting arenas until more recently when she took up a significant government appointment.

Numerous high achievers call upon a guiding principle or 'mantra'. These are messages imprinted in their minds, often from parents or significant others, and used as reminders of what is possible and what is not. These sayings are a support, and a comfort, to which they return with regularity, especially when the going gets difficult. They may in some ways act as the invisible permanent presence of a support person. Each has a mentor, a coach, or a supportive parent who was with them through setbacks and victories, at least during the development years. It is not IQ that sets these people apart but rather each can be construed as possessing the elements of emotional intelligence; they have insight into their own lives and that of others. They generally rely on the support of trainers, crew, or workplace teams.

Many of the high achievers have been exposed to risk factors such as divorce in the family (Robyn, Justin), illness or loss of a parent (Tania, Livia) and experienced setbacks such as failed enterprises (Martin, Doug), sporting losses (Tania, Justin), or illness (Robyn) which prevented them from pursuing their passions. Sports people learnt to cope with losses early in their careers, as have business people who have generally recovered from substantial losses. However, it is not the losses that dominate the present. There appears to be a capacity to recover and strengthen the resolve to amass additional resources to see them through the next challenge. Like others in different walks of life, they have enthusiasm and passion in the pursuit of their main endeavours. Their pursuits are generally in their areas of interest, such as sport, music, writing, or commerce. Awareness of time disappears in the pursuit of their goals. All their pursuits are valued in their community. They do not use the self-denigrating strategies of self-blame or excessive release of tension. Instead they have enough drive to reframe events in a positive way, acknowledge the part that circumstances play, and then they move on in pursuit of their goals.

Risk and Resilience

The question as to why some people cope despite adversity and others do not, is explained in part by the way the risk factors and protective factors work together to facilitate or inhibit adaptation. There are both risk and protective factors inherent in adaptation. Risk factors are those things that threaten well-being and the capacity for continuing adaptive development. Risk factors include parental conflict, separation and divorce, chronic illness in child or parent, poverty and social disadvantage, and race. It is clear from the stories of successful achievers that each had been subject to some risk factors. However, it is the protective factors that appear to play a significant part in achieving success. Two classes of protective factors have been studied. There are the intrinsic or intrapersonal factors, believed to be constitutional in large part, such as personality, temperament and intelligence, and extrinsic or environmental influences such as having a caring family, the availability of social supports, or caring mentors, positive school experiences, and strong attachments. The interaction of these factors has been demonstrated as an important element of coping and resilience (Rutter, 1985, 2012). Each of the high achievers has both intrinsic and extrinsic resources to help them deal with setbacks.

The 2015 Cohort

In 2015 the original set of interviews was complemented by five additional interviews, with a more explicit focus on resilience rather than achievement per se. This second set of interviews provided an opportunity to determine whether there were both additional and similar insights that emerged to extend our understanding of resilience.

To complement the most widely cited theories of coping such as the transactional model of Richard Lazarus, and the Conservation of Resources Model of Stevan Hobfoll (see Chap. 3), there are a range of theories identified in Chap. 2, that help us to understand how people achieve resilience. Firstly, there is the concept of emotional intelligence (Goleman, 2005; Salovey & Mayer, 1990). Secondly, there is the work of Dweck and her colleagues (Dweck, 2006) on mindset which explains how people become mastery-oriented, seeing their abilities as malleable rather than becoming helpless and defeated. Thirdly, there is the concept of hardiness (e.g., Maddi, 2002), the capacity to persevere despite adversity. And finally the concepts of grit and determination that have been expounded by Duckworth and colleagues (2014). The five recent interviews focused specifically on how individuals dealt with adversity or setbacks. The setbacks varied and included family divorce, job loss, multiple experiences with cancer, loss of a friend or friends through a drug overdose or murder, harassment in the workplace, and having a child with developmental delay.

It has been established that personality plays an important part in coping and resilience. For example, an agreeable temperament at an early age is a predictor of successful coping in adulthood (Prior, 1999). Indeed each of the five interviewees could be described as having an agreeable personality and despite having experienced setbacks, demonstrated resilience. They were willing subjects and had enjoyed opportunities to give back to their communities in the form of community service and leadership. As with the subjects interviewed in 2000, they had had support from family and/or professional colleagues and utilised helpful coping skills. In addition to the questioning around resilience and coping, the interviewees were asked about qualities that are associated with resilience, namely, emotional intelligence, mindset, grit, and hardiness. Table 11.1 highlights the qualities that these five interviewees shared. Some gave excellent examples of these characteristics from their own life stories.

Jacki, now 63, grew up in a working-class suburb of Melbourne, Australia. There she felt different to everyone else as her family strongly supported and actively assisted with her education and that of her sister.

Table 11.1 Resilience 2000 and 2015 interviews

Highflyer	Resources						
	Success at school	Emotional savvy	Support from coach/ teacher/professional	Reframe losses	Hardiness	Mindset	Grit
Doug (Business)		✓		✓			
Martin (developer)		✓		✓			
Atti (doctor)	✓✓	✓✓	✓✓				
Livia (judge)	✓✓	✓✓	✓✓				
Jason (script writer)	✓	✓✓		✓			
Tania (swimmer)	✓	✓✓	✓✓	✓✓			
Justin (Tennis player)		✓✓	✓✓	✓✓			
Robyn (pianist)	✓	✓✓	✓✓	✓✓			
Jacki (pharmacist)		✓		✓	✓	✓	✓
Julian (accountant)		✓		✓	✓	✓	✓
Carlie (company director)		✓	✓	✓	✓	✓	✓
Henry (Vietnam veteran)		✓		✓	✓	✓	✓
Celine (surgeon)		✓		✓	✓	✓	✓

Her mother took care of the humanities and her father the sciences. Her father was five years older than her mother when they married on her mother's 18th birthday. Her mother was an only child, whilst her father was one of four brothers. They were seen as an ideal family of four with a close extended family in which the sisters often stayed with their grandparents on weekends.

Jacki completed high school and went onto pharmacy college. She married soon after graduating from pharmacy and not long after her husband finished his medical training. The newly weds set out for an eight-month trip overseas but returned to Australia when her father[4] took his own life. At that time she was in her early 20s. Subsequently she started a family. She wanted to fill a void for her mother, who found herself a widow in her mid-40s. However, her mother died of an overdose three years after her father's death.

As a 25-year-old, one month after her father's death, she was pregnant with her daughter, followed by a miscarriage and another pregnancy. 'I had to make a choice. Do I fall apart, go into my shell or make a life?'

Her resilience had been tested in her mid-20s with the death of her parents, then again at the age of 38 (1991) when she was diagnosed with breast cancer. She has had breast cancer two additional times at 47 and 54 years of age.

At 38 she had an 8-year-old and a 10-year-old whom she wanted to 'protect' from her stresses. She received tangible help from her mother-in-law. Emotionally she drew from the experience of the loss of her parents. She remembers how angry she was after that experience, so she did not want her children to be angry with her. She was ready to accept whatever was on offer medically. At that time she thought, 'If I get it a second time that will be the undoing of me.' Nine years later, in 2000, when she was at the same age as when her mother died, she had the recurrence. She realised then that she needed to look at her illness differently.

---

[4] Several years earlier the family home had a fire that started with a faulty water heater and much of the home and possessions were lost. Some years later, after the house was rebuilt, it was burgled and the family lost a considerable amount of cash that were the takings from the family business. The losses were compounded by her father's sense of failure as a strong supporter of his own and extended family.

I had a daughter of 21. It was easier in one way because I was able to be more open with my children. Now I have knowledge I will use that. My daughter is my left hand (she is left-handed).

The third bout came when she was in her 50s. That changed things to the point that she considered, 'What are the most extreme measures that were needed to survive?'

She was given some coping strategies between the first and second bout, in 1997, when an accident at a sporting complex prompted her to visit a psychologist with her son. She continued to meet with the professional over a six-month period. There she learnt that she hadn't dealt with the death of her parents. She was given skills that have become her 'mantras' for life.

> The healing can't start till the treatment is finished.
> I will be a new person.
> Little 't' is time out. I need to give myself permission to take time out.
> The disease does not have to define me.

She coped by making her focus to be the support or 'mainframe' for her family. She measures success on how the family functions. 'When things have to be done I make a list, have a program, get my head in the right space. When there is no structure I am not coping.'

She drew on the mantras to cope with cancer episodes two and three.

> Episode two was the scariest. You don't prepare yourself. You are in the euphoria. You have beaten it. I am 6 months, 12 months, 5 years etc. It is all numerical. You have to reach these milestones. You are not in the present. The next time it has destroyed all you have worked on.

She saw her parents as 'not coping' with their setbacks, so she was determined to deal with her circumstances in 'the opposite way'. At one point she was selling property insurance and learnt that when you have a rejection in sales, you should not take it personally.

> You learn to deal with negativity. You can't just 'put on dolphin music and be in la la land'. You have to confront setbacks and work through them.

She wanted to give back into medicine, so having found her love in art for the last 15 years, she has developed the arts space in a major cancer hospital.

She sees IQ as changeable, as just one building block. She sees that overall one needs more grit and determination than ability. When it comes to emotional intelligence the more vulnerable you are, the more you have to bring in resources. She and her sister recognise the 'shut down' in each other.

Jacki considers that her hardiness has been tested. She describes how she was trusting on a medical front. For example, when she had surgery that went very wrong she went back to the surgeon who commented, 'You are walking in and smiling and we nearly killed you', and she replied that she wanted to tough it out. 'I am smiling because I am here.' 'The path of life is fraught with obstacles. You must have to want to be here. My parents didn't want to be here.'

Julian, a 43-year-old accountant, started life in the western suburbs of Melbourne. He has been married for 16 years and has two children, a 10-year-old daughter and an 8-year-old son. His own mother was 17 when he was born and subsequently married the man he knew as dad. He did not see his biological father. His mother and step-father separated when he was 11, but he remains and lives close to his mother. At the time of his parents' separation, he felt his world had turned upside down. He was full of anger and frustration and got into fights. He studied business and accounting at a regional university. In his late 20s, he moved to the United States for six to seven years before returning to Melbourne seven years prior to the interview.

In the working-class suburb of Melbourne where Julian grew up, aggressive behaviour was the norm. His mother was always there and someone he could talk to, but his family didn't have skills to support him through the aggressive norms in his neighbourhood.

When at 13 he learnt that the man he had called 'dad' was not his biological father, his resilience was tested. His parents were already separated, but it affected his sense of identity. His resilience was again challenged at 19 when a female friend died of a drug overdose. Several weeks earlier, she had asked for his help by letting him know that she was involved with people that she didn't want to be around. Two weeks later, she was dead.

This precipitated feelings of guilt and became his impetus to improve things. 'I felt that the slope that I was on was so slippery, that if I didn't change things, I would head down the same path.'

The change occurred when he became aware that he had control over his own behaviour. He gained insights about personal development through reading. He no longer thought that there was a fixed path of who you are and who your parents are. At 17 years of age, he was a high school dropout but returned to school followed by university in his early 20s. Sport, particularly cricket, was where he was most successful. He took up golf, felt he was good at it, and went on to work at a golf club as a trainee golf professional. The General Manager at the golf club was a big supporter who took an interest in him and helped to make him calmer.

> Until I was ten my mum and dad were people who said 'you can do whatever you want'. They were very encouraging and supportive. In late primary years all friends smoked cigarettes. I was the only person who didn't despite pressure. I was never enticed that strongly. I went my own way. When I said I wanted to be a 'golfpro' [professional] there were a lot who said you can't. 'Do you think you are cleverer than us.?' Same with going to university and living in the US, some would say, 'Why would you want to do that?'

Despite others having doubts about his capacity to succeed he had a healthy dose of self-belief and could be described as a self-starter. His teenage years were particularly challenging as were his school years. He went from being the smartest in class and smartest in school to being constantly in trouble and performing poorly. He put that down to the separation of his parents.

Rather than having any significant individual play a role in his gaining insight and understanding, he credits the books that he has read, particularly the work of Carolyn Dweck on mindset (see Chap. 2), as having helped him most.

Whilst he was in the United States during his 30s with two young children and having recently bought a house, Julian had a major test of resilience, and a 'big knock to self-esteem'. Following a series of errors in his work that led to the loss of his job with a major US company, he completed a battery of psychological tests that led to a diagnosis of

ADHD. During that time friends assisted him to obtain a 'speedy visa' review so that he could stay in the United States. Prior to being diagnosed with ADHD he had felt that the condition was overdiagnosed. Given that ADHD is a 'lifelong condition' some of the challenges were not only about his parents' separation, but were compounded by the undiagnosed ADHD. This gave him the impetus to work in the not-for-profit sector with people with specific learning difficulties.

> I wanted to contribute to change a systematic way; I wanted to contribute to the non-profit sector in education and particularly to policy. Having to overcome those things has given me strength; I have benefitted from the challenges.

His daughter had minor brain injury, at the age of three, following a stroke and that is when he learnt of Carol Dweck's work in relation to a growth mindset. That has highlighted for him that IQ is changeable, 'within boundaries'. In the workplace he sees elements of EI such as how you relate to people and how you get the best out of people as very important. As for grit, if he has well-defined goals, he is as determined as anyone. Personalities such as Richard Branson and Steven Spielberg have been role models in terms of resilience and coping.

For him the question remains, 'How can we provide children with opportunity to overcome obstacles in a safe way so it is not just left to chance?'

Carlie, a 52-year-old company director, has held directorships in diverse areas such as crisis refuge and housing services. She spent half of her life in small country towns in regional Australia where her father was involved in banking. She describes her father as an 'average bloke' and her mother, a nursing sister who managed a small country town hospital as 'polished'. She and her sister grew up with horses. She loved school, where she was House captain, and a sports leader with a good circle of friends. The second half of her adult years has involved extensive travel. Her parents divorced when she was 12 years old, which impacted her sister negatively but not her. Her father played a key role in keeping things together. She contrasts her own approach of 'analyse not agonise' to her sister's 'emotional approach'.

The challenges came when she was ready to leave the country town. She was encouraged by senior colleagues to apply for a senior executive assistant role with a progressive CEO in the city. She moved to Melbourne within two weeks, stayed with friends, bought a bean bag and small television and found somewhere to live. The workplace was a taxing environment, and she wanted to walk out after four days. The Deputy Chairwoman talked her into staying. I said to myself, 'Get over this. You have to help sort it out.' She stayed for nine years. She overcame self-doubt through external endorsement and encouragement when someone believed in her.

She describes herself as having been fortunate to have had opportunities that enabled her to shine. Three days after finishing high school she accepted a position in hospital administration where she worked in a highly professional environment with the CEO and the Director of the Board. She was given numerous opportunities but when she felt that the workload was excessive she raised the issue with the CEO who 'got onto his knees and begged' her to stay. The Chairman asked her to be on his Board and when she refused he asked her to reconsider and offered her support of a female lawyer as a mentor. He described Carlie as 'his youngest and best Board member'. That support crystallised what she has wanted to do in her career, that is, work in corporate directorship roles.

For Carlie it has been a combination of good experiences and external endorsement. However, her most recent career experience tested her resilience. Having accepted a university position that did not prove to be a good fit, she decided not to look back but 'cut her losses'.

She did some thinking without agonising. She went to Fiji and 'looked at the turquoise water'. She approached the search for the next job methodically with energy and enthusiasm. She focused on outcomes and sat at her computer each day at 8.00 a.m., as if she was in a workplace. She did not allow herself to be dragged back into a vortex thinking 'poor me'. She tried to turn the experience into a positive one, having overcome the feeling of 'devastation' when it first happened.

> IQ is changeable with the benefit of experience and exposure. If I had stayed in a small country town with a dad who was a bank manager and never been to a university I would probably not be where I am today, in the way I think and the level at which I think.

When she did an emotional intelligence assessment she was rated as high. She has had to adjust to working with a range of CEOs. 'If it comes to the crunch I will trust my head rather than my heart.'

One example of how she dealt with disappointment was as a 12-year-old in a country town when she was to model children's clothing. She had sport on the afternoon of the event so she went home to have a shower, but when she came back she was told that clothes had been given to other children. She had no regrets because she had done what she thought was right.

At times of particular difficulty, 'I have got dressed, got organised and put a face on.' For example, in one particular role, when five fire-fighters died, faxes with messages from people all around the world came for two days. She stopped reading them to keep her emotions under control whilst working for the Chairman. Her sister and brother-in-law refer to her as 'tenacious'. She sees herself as not dogged but committed and willing to change course if she hears logic.

Even if she is 'caving in internally' she will put on a front and withstand pressure so displaying hardiness. For example, at a time when she was working in a male-dominated emergency service area, and was told that staff were too busy to do what was required, she sent an email to the Chief Officer who yelled at her. She kept up the front, but when he walked out of the office 'I was in a mess, in tears'.

Recently, following an extensive selection interview process, she landed a top leadership management role with an organisation involving company directors.

Henry, a veteran of the Vietnam War, was born in 1948 as the eldest of five children. He has worked in local government finance as an accountant for 20 years before becoming a university academic.

He was conscripted by ballot to serve in the Vietnam War as a 20-year-old. He readily accepted the call to military service as both his parents and grandfather had served in the armed forces. He was married within 12 months of returning from Vietnam and had four children (two boys and two girls). He remarried in 2000 and has a 13-year-old from his second marriage.

In the military he did not see combat but was a stores clerk and then an air traffic controller. However, he was traumatised when two men, one with whom he had shared a tent, and the other with whom he had worked, were murdered. That was difficult to deal with. His way of coping was initially withdrawal and subsequently seeking medical help.

His resilience was challenged again when his mother died at the age of 53. It was at that time that his marriage started to disintegrate. It was also the time when his wife had a series of miscarriages.

In 2007 he completed a post-traumatic stress disorder course which he found really helpful. More recently his second wife has been undergoing chemotherapy and has had 'one of her lungs' removed. That has made his other health issues 'pale into insignificance'. He relies heavily on the veteran community for support where he leans on a few strong people.

Celine, a 40-year-old medical specialist surgeon was first married at 19 and divorced when 30 during the final year of her medical specialisation training and residency. She was highly challenged during her divorce whilst living away from family and completing the final year of her medical training. She saw the divorce as an opportunity to build 'self-sufficiency'. She moved back to Melbourne and has subsequently remarried at the age of 35. She married a medical physician with whom she has two daughters. She is fiercely independent and wanted to finance and support her own household, which she has done.

Celine's father taught her to meditate when she was five years old, and she continues to practice it in some form. One of her coping strategies is 'putting one foot in front of the other and tackling one task at a time'. She uses mindfulness and often thinks of the 'worst case scenario'. She can focus on a task and finds that strategy to be productive at times of stress. She is also conscious of an 'internal mechanism' when coping, so can work on a crowded bus or in a noisy household by drowning out extraneous noise and distraction.

She describes herself as having anxious Obsessive Compulsive Disorder (OCD) tendencies which she uses to channel energy. Her house is in immaculate order to the extent that you can do the 'white glove test' on her cupboards with 'all shoes lined up'. She is sufficiently aware to concede that one can clean things too much.

Additionally, mindfulness has helped to channel her OCD. Her father reminded her that there are lots of benefits and skills associated with her OCD tendencies. Her child is similar in that she can go to kinder in white and return in white, that is, 'pristine clean'. Her grandfather was much the same, so the tendencies can be considered to be generational. She does not like 'loss of control' so does not do drugs or drink.

When active, she has a sense of power that provides her with physical and emotional resilience whilst walking and yoga give her calm and 'physical flow'. She finds it helpful to spend time with people that she loves. 'Tribal connections' are valuable in that it helps her to gain perspective. Being with people helps her anxieties to melt away; people make her feel better about life. She enjoys meeting people from different backgrounds through doctoring.

When her children were born, there were lots of medical issues which turned into opportunities. She had complicated miscarriages with adhesions and has had numerous surgical procedures post pregnancy with the surviving twin.[5]

> There were recurrent adhesions which led to surgery and miscarriage, and then I fell pregnant. Altogether I had 10 operations. They made me a better doctor. I understand what is important for a patient. My husband was traumatised by the operations.

She was told about her own twin when she was three. Father is also one of a twin. For eight weeks perinatal she continued to work whilst carrying a dead foetus and having a ten-month toddler to look after.

> I had work to keep me occupied. It helped to be doing something that was helpful to others. There was something constant in my life. It provides a framework. It helps me to know what to do next.

She can control emotions and has empathy for others as she has grown up in a privileged household. She sees setbacks as opportunities to move forward.

The second big challenge that tested her resilience was the surgical training programme. There are 30 men in the partnership. She had children and was breastfeeding in that environment. She felt emotionally dis-

---

[5] She was also one of a twin and her mother lost her brother prior to her birth.

criminated; she had many arguments and fights and saw those times as an opportunity to educate people at the same time as looking after herself.

> It was an opportunity to learn how to respond to people who behave badly, rather than feeling victimised. I have determination. I don't believe that things are too hard. I seem to be hardy to people who don't know me well.

She is conscious of wearing her stress anatomically such as in her neck and back. She has an ability to break down and considers herself to be a soft person. She considers that like females and mothers she has a different emotional response that makes her feel emotionally vulnerable. Nevertheless she doesn't want to be defined by having 'male detachment'.

When it comes to mindset she sees everyone as being born with a range of predispositions, a number of developing abilities. 'Neuroplasticity is underrated. We need to be more plastic in how we adapt. Our genes adapt so why not everything else!'

Each of the group interviewed in 2015 had experienced setbacks. Jackie had experienced the suicide of both parents and major illnesses during her adult life, Carlie and Julian had both experienced job loss. Both Celine and Henry had experienced divorce, with Celine having multiple miscarriages and operations whilst having a career in a male-dominated environment. Henry was traumatised by the murder of two of his army mates during his military experience and has had to deal with serious illness in his family.

In 2015 the interviewees demonstrated resilience in many ways that were similar to that of the 2000 cohort in that they had personal resources, social support resources, and personal histories that both challenged them and tested their resilience. However, by 2015 the social environment had transformed in that individuals seemed to recognise and label their vulnerabilities as they utilised professional resources in the form of counsellors or related professionals. Self-help tools such as widely available books like *Mindset* (Dweck, 2006) and *Emotional Intelligence* (Goleman, 2005), along with meditation or mindfulness were practised. Many of those interviewed had spontaneously disclosed how they had utilised professional counselling to help them deal with trauma or crises. They each displayed grit and hardiness along with a disciplined approach to managing stressful events. Emotional intelligence along with a belief in one's capacity to change seemed to be a hallmark of their resilience. Table 11.1 highlights the various areas such as school, emotional intelligence (EI), support, capacity to reframe losses, hardiness, mindset, and grit that were displayed by the 2000 and 2015 interviewees.

In the main, all of the interviewees displayed the characteristics described throughout this volume as contributing to resilience. The 2000 cohort talked about supportive family and/or mentors or coaches. Not one spontaneously disclosed that they had sought professional help in the form of medical or psychological assistance. Fifteen years later, the landscape had changed. Three out of the five interviewees had or were seeing a psychologist.

Both cohorts demonstrated that they had a healthy collection of intrapersonal and interpersonal resources which they used to deal with setbacks.

References

Bandura, A. (1997). *Self-efficacy : The exercise of control*. New York: Freeman.

Brandan, M. M., Goddard, N. A., Kabir, B., Lofton, S. S., Ruiz, J., & Hau, J. M. (2013). Resilience and retirement, coping self-efficacy and collective self-efficacy: Implementing positive psychology during times of economic hardship for late-career individuals. *Career Planning and Adult Development Journal, 29*(4), 25–36.

Dweck, C. S. (1990). Self-theories and goals: Their role in motivation, personality, and development. *Nebraska Symposium on Motivation. Nebraska Symposium on Motivation, 38*, 199–235.

Dweck, C. S. (2006). *Mindset: The new psychology of success* (1st ed.). Carol S. Dweck. New York: Random House, c2006.

Frydenberg, E. (2002). *Beyond coping : Meeting goals, visions, and challenges*. Oxford, UK: Oxford University Press.

Goleman, D. (2005). *Emotional intelligence*. New York: Bantam Books.

Maddi, S. R. (2002). The story of hardiness: Twenty years of theorizing, research, and practice. *Consulting Psychology Journal: Practice and Research, 54*(3), 173–185. doi:10.1037/1061-4087.54.3.

Prior, M. (1999). Resilience and coping: The role of individual temperament. In E. Frydenberg (Ed.), *Learning to cope: Developing as a person in complex societies* (pp. 33–52). Oxford, UK: Oxford University Press. vii + 360. ISBN 0-19-850318-0.

Rutter, M. (1985). Resilience in the face of adversity: Protective factors and resistance to psychiatric disorder. *British Journal of Psychiatry, 147*, 598–611.

Rutter, M. (2012). Resilience as a dynamic concept. *Development and Psychopathology, 24*(2), 335–344. doi:10.1017/S0954579412000028.

Salovey, P., & Mayer, J. D. (1990). Emotional intelligence. *Imagination, Cognition, and Personality, 9*, 185–211 .doi: 0.2190/DUGG-P24E-52WK-6CDG.

12

Concluding Thoughts

The literature is replete with varying definitions of resilience, a selection of which were presented in Chap. 1 of this volume. Some definitions ascribe resilience as a feature of an individual's adaptation growth and development whilst others emphasise collective and communal resilience, taking into account ecology and biology. The benefit of considering resilience through the lens of coping has been noted, and that is the approach that underscores this volume.

Coping is a positive psychological tool, consistent with the developments in positive psychology, with its emphasis on what people can do rather than what they can't do, and it can be integrated into coping research and practice. Resilience is best captured by the construct of coping. Coping can be operationalised and measured. It can be used to augment development across the lifespan. Resilience as an adaptive response is relatively recent; it is goal directed, intentional, prospective and includes future-oriented actions. Approach behaviours are a contrast to withdrawal and avoidance and also challenge the 'fight or flight' response that has been a hallmark of stress and coping research for many decades. Resilience is a return to homeostasis and sustainability whilst in

© The Author(s) 2017
E. Frydenberg, *Coping and the Challenge of Resilience*,
DOI 10.1057/978-1-137-56924-0_12

some situations it goes beyond sustainability to growth and flourishing. Coping literature provides the tools with which to understand resilience.

Two major theories underpin coping research, namely, the transactional appraisal theory of Richard Lazarus and his colleagues and the resource theory which has most clearly been articulated by Stevan Hobfoll. The identified constructs are used to develop intervention and prevention programmes for children, adolescents, and adults so that both short-term and long-term benefits can be achieved. The concepts can be used in organisational, educational, and clinical settings as well as in a self-initiated change format.

As psychological literature continues to progress, global coping theory and research can incorporate and integrate a range of constructs and philosophical orientations. Chapter 2 illustrated how, in addition to the underpinnings of positive psychology, constructs such as emotional intelligence, hardiness, mindset, and grit can be readily accommodated into coping research and practice. Additional insights that relate to hope, meaning making, and post-traumatic growth can also be readily accommodated.

Coping is best seen as a useful heuristic device once operationalised in that it is possible to identify elements that are helpful and those that are unhelpful. The language that represents the constructs can be used to teach people what to do and what not to do so as to achieve the best outcomes. The constructs of coping have been extended to develop tools to assess coping in children, adolescents, and adults with an explicit purpose of assisting self-reflection and helping to identify elements that can be changed to develop an individual's resources. There is substantial research that provides evidence for correlates of coping such as age, gender, ethnicity, and culture. In addition to developmental factors, there are the situational factors that impact how individuals cope. All these need to be taken into account in the context of resilience.

Coping has traditionally been defined in terms of reaction, that is, how people respond after or during a stressful event. But more recently coping is being defined more broadly to include anticipatory coping, preventive coping, and proactive coping. Proactive coping is future oriented, has the main features of planning, goal attainment, and the use of resources to obtain goals. The proactive coper takes initiative, uses others, and takes the credit for successes, but does not blame himself or herself for failures. The proactive coper chooses actions according to how they imagine the future. In that sense proactive coping it is closely aligned to resilience. This approach is particularly useful in leadership contexts.

Social support has been a key index of successful coping and an interest of many researchers. An extension of the focus on community and the notion of support from individuals and collectives is dyadic coping. Much of the research in this field has addressed couples in the context of married life. Issues of spousal support in the context of marital or stepparenting, conflict, chronic pain, illnesses such as rheumatoid arthritis and cancer have been reported extensively. Overall, there is strong evidence of empathic coping contributing to relationship building and personal success.

Universal interventions for adolescents in diverse school settings have been developed with evidence of utility. Such generic programmes can be adapted for particular populations such as those with social-emotional, learning, or health-related difficulties. Recently developed coping interventions for children that focus on social-emotional skills such as self-regulation and empathy show promising results.

Building resilience through a universal parenting programme that incorporates coping skills along with contemporary principles of positive psychology, effective communication, and problem solving in a family context contributes to good parenting practices. Generic parenting programmes can be readily adapted to culturally and linguistically diverse populations.

In the post-transactional coping era founded by Richards Lazarus, religious coping and meaning making have emerged as responses to trauma. At times of trauma and major life stress that are less amenable to problem solving, 'implicit religiousness' is incorporated into a religious meaning-making model where spirituality plays a part. There are many 'faces' of religious coping and researchers are now considering the challenges of later life where the majority of adults claim that they incorporate religion and spirituality into their coping repertoire. Mindfulness has also emerged as a strong contributor to an individual's capacity to deal with stress and thus has become a personal coping resource within individuals' contemporary coping practice.

The resilient coper knows that there is no right or wrong coping strategy, just what works and what does not work in a particular context. The question has to be asked: What would I do differently next time? Resilient adults, be they teachers, managers, administrators, and parents, are able to assess their own coping and develop the coping skills that are required. Case studies of resilient adults in a range of settings highlight how coping resources have helped them to overcome adversity and deal with circumstances in a productive way that contributes to growth and personal success.

Whilst research is a dynamic process that continues and will continue to provide new insights into our understanding of resilience, the scaffolding and contribution that coping theory and practice provide in the ongoing pursuit of well-being and resilience could be considered to be beyond comparison.

References

Alba, G., Justicia-Arráez, A., Pichardo, M. C., & Justicia, F. (2013). Aprender a Convivir. A program for improving social competence in preschool and elementary school children. *Electronic Journal of Research in Educational Psychology, 11*(3), 843–904. doi:10.14204/ejrep.31.13105.

Aldwin, C. (2010). Stress and coping across the lifespan. In *The Oxford handbook of stress, health, and coping* (pp. 15–34). Oxford, UK: Oxford University Press. doi:10.1093/oxfordhb/9780195375343.013.0002.

Aldwin, C. M., Sutton, K. J., & Lachman, M. (1996). The development of coping resources in adulthood. *Journal of Personality, 64*(4), 837.

Aldwin, C. M., & Werner, E. E. (2007). *Stress, coping, and development: An integrative perspective/Carolyn M. Aldwin; foreword by Emmy E. Werner.* New York: Guilford Press. 2.

Ames, C., & Archer, J. (1988). Achievement goals in the classroom: Students' learning strategies and motivation processes. *Journal of Educational Psychology, 80*(3), 260.

Amirkhan, J., & Auyeung, B. (2007). Coping with stress across the lifespan: Absolute versus relative changes in strategy. *Journal of Applied Developmental Psychology, 28*(4), 298–317.

Andrews, M., Ainley, M., & Frydenberg, E. (2011). Adolescent coping styles and task-specific responses: Does style foreshadow action? In G. Reevy &

© The Author(s) 2017
E. Frydenberg, *Coping and the Challenge of Resilience,*
DOI 10.1057/978-1-137-56924-0

E. Frydenberg (Eds.), *Research on stress and coping in education Volume VI: Personality, stress, and coping: Implications for education* (pp. 3–23).*Charlotte, N.C. : Information Age Pub., c2011.*

Ano, G. G., & Vasconcelles, E. B. (2005). Religious coping and psychological adjustment to stress: A meta-analysis. *Journal of Clinical Psychology, 61,* 461–480.

Anshel, M. H., & Si, G. (2008). Coping styles following acute stress in sport among elite Chinese athletes: A test of trait and transactional coping theories. *Journal of Sport Behavior, 31*(1), 3.

Anson, K., & Ponsford, J. (2006). Evaluation of a coping skills group following traumatic brain injury. *Brain Injury, 20*(2), 167–178.

Antonovsky, A. (1979). *Health, stress, and coping* (1st ed.). San Francisco: Jossey-Bass Publishers.

Antonovsky, A. (1987). *Unraveling the mystery of health : How people manage stress and stay well/Aaron Antonovsky* (1st ed.). San Francisco: Jossey-Bass.

Armstrong, M. A., Birnie-Lefcovitch, S., & Ungar, M. T. (2005). Pathways between social support, family wellbeing, quality of parenting, and child resilience: What we know. *Journal of Child and Family Studies, 14,* 269–281. doi:10.1007/s10826-005-5054-4.

Aspinwall, L. G. (2005). The psychology of future-oriented thinking: From achievement to proactive coping, adaptation, and aging. *Motivation and Emotion, 29*(4), 203–235.

Aspinwall, L. G., & Taylor, S. E. (1997). A stitch in time: Self-regulation and proactive coping. *Psychological Bulletin, 121*(3), 417.

Australian Bureau of Statistics. (2015). *Deaths, Australia, 2014 (cat. no. 3302.0).* Retrieved March 14, 2015, from www.abs.gov.au

Australian Institute of Health and Welfare. (2014). *Australia's health 2014.* Australia's health series no. 14. *(Cat. no. AUS 178).* Canberra: AIHW.

Averill, J. R., & Thomas-Knowles, C. (1991). Emotional creativity. In K. T. Strongman (Ed.), *International review of studies on emotion* (Vol. 1, pp. 269–299). New York: Wiley.

Ayers, T. S., Sandier, I. N., West, S. G., & Roosa, M. W. (1996). A dispositional and situational assessment of children's coping: Testing alternative models of coping. *Journal of Personality, 64*(4), 923–958.

Baldwin, J. S., & Dadds, M. R. (2007). Reliability and validity of parent and child versions of the multidimensional anxiety scale for children in community samples. *Journal of the American Academy of Child and Adolescent Psychiatry, 46*(2), 252–260.

Band, E. B., & Weisz, J. R. (1988). How to feel better when it feels bad: Children's perspectives on coping with everyday stress. *Developmental Psychology, 24*(2), 247–253.

Bandura, A. (1997). *Self-efficacy : The exercise of control.* New York: Freeman.

Bandura, A. (2012). Guest editorial: On the functional properties of perceived self-efficacy revisited. *Journal of Management: JOM, 38*(1), 9–44.

Barrett, P. M., Rapee, R. M., Dadds, M. M., & Ryan, S. M. (1996). Family enhancement of cognitive style in anxious and aggressive children. *Journal of Abnormal Child Psychology, 24*(2), 187–203.

Barron, R. G., Castilla, I. M., Casullo, M. M., & Verdu, J. B. (2002). Relationship between coping strategies and psychological wellbeing in adolescents. *Psicothema-Oviedo, 14*(2), 363–368.

Baumeister, R. F., & Exline, J. J. (2000). Self-control, morality, and human strength. *Journal of Social and Clinical Psychology, 19*(1), 29–42.

Beck, J. S., Beck, A. T., Jolly, J. B., & Steer, R. A. (2005). *Beck youth inventories-second edition for children and adolescents manual.* San Antonio, TX: PsychCorp.

Beesdo, K., Knappe, S., & Pine, D. S. (2009). Anxiety and anxiety disorders in children and adolescents: Developmental issues and implications for DSM-V. *The Psychiatric Clinics of North America, 32*(3), 483–524.

Biederman, J., Hirshfeld-Becker, D. R., Rosenbaum, J. F., Herot, C., Friedman, D., Snidman, N., et al. (2001). Further evidence of association between behavioral inhibition and social anxiety in children. *The American Journal of Psychiatry, 158*(10), 1673–1979.

Billings, A. G., & Moos, R. H. (1984). Coping, stress, and social resources among adults with unipolar depression. *Journal of Personality and Social Psychology, 46*(4), 877–891.

Blair, K. A., Denham, S. A., Kochanoff, A., & Whipple, B. (2004). Playing it cool: Temperament, emotion regulation, and social behavior in preschoolers. *Journal of School Psychology, 42*(6), 419–443.

Blount, R. L., Simons, L. E., Devine, K. A., Jaaniste, T., Cohen, L. L., Chambers, C. T., & Hayutin, L. G. (2008). Evidence-based assessment of coping and stress in pediatric psychology. *Journal of Pediatric Psychology, 33*(9), 1021–1045.

Boeninger, D. K., Shiraishi, R. W., Aldwin, C. M., & Spiro III, A. (2009). Why do older men report low stress ratings? Findings from the veterans affairs normative aging study. *International Journal of Aging and Human Development, 68*(2), 149–170.

Boldero, J., Frydenberg, E., & Fallon, B. (1993, September–October). Adolescents' view of themselves as predictors of their coping strategies. Paper presented at the *28th Annual Conference of the Australian Psychological Society*, Gold Coast, QLD.

Bonanno, G. A. (2004). Loss, trauma, and human resilience: Have we underestimated the human capacity to thrive after extremely aversive events? *The American Psychologist, 59*(1), 20–28.

Brandan, M. M., Goddard, N. A., Kabir, B., Lofton, S. S., Ruiz, J., & Hau, J. M. (2013). Resilience and retirement, coping self-efficacy and collective self-efficacy: Implementing positive psychology during times of economic hardship for late-career individuals. *Career Planning and Adult Development Journal, 29*(4), 25–36.

Broderick, P. C., & Korteland, C. (2004). A prospective study of rumination and depression in early adolescence. *Clinical Child Psychology and Psychiatry, 9*(3), 383–394.

Bronfenbrenner, U. (1978). The social role of the child in ecological perspective. *Diesoziale Rolle des Kindes in ökologischer Perspektive, 7*(1), 4–20.

Cain, K., & Dweck, C. S. (1995). The development of children's achievement motivation patterns and conceptions of intelligence. *Merrill-Palmer Quarterly, 41*, 24–52.

Cannon, W. B. (1989). *Wisdom of the body* (Special ed.). Birmingham, AL: Classics of Medicine Library.

Cappa, K., Begle, A., Conger, J., Dumas, J., & Conger, A. (2011). Bidirectional relationships between parenting stress and child coping competence: Findings from the pace study. *Journal of Child and Family Studies, 20*(3), 334–342. doi:10.1007/s10826-010-9397-0.

Cappeliez, P., & Robitaille, A. (2010). Coping mediates the relationships between reminiscence and psychological well-being among older adults. *Aging & Mental Health, 14*(7), 807–818. doi:10.1080/13607861003713307.

Carver, C. S., & Scheier, M. F. (1998). *On the self-regulation of behavior.* New York: Cambridge University Press.

Carver, C. S., Scheier, M. F., & Weintraub, J. K. (1989). Assessing coping strategies: A theoretically based approach. *Journal of Personality and Social Psychology, 56*, 267–283.

Centre for Research and Innovations. (2007). *Understanding the brain: The birth of a learning science.* Paris: OECD.

Chalmers, K., Frydenberg, E., & Deans, J. (2011). An exploration into the coping strategies of preschoolers: Implications for professional practice. *Children Australia, 36*(3), 120–127. doi:10.1375/jcas.36.3.120.

Chan, C. S., & Rhodes, J. E. (2013). Religious coping, posttraumatic stress, psychological distress, and posttraumatic growth among female survivors four years after Hurricane Katrina. *Journal of Traumatic Stress, 26*(2), 257–265. doi:10.1002/jts.21801.

Cheshire, G., & Campbell, M. (1997). Adolescent coping: Differences in the styles and strategies used by learning disabled students compared to non-learning disabled students. *Australian Journal of Guidance and Counselling, 7*(1), 65–73.

Coats, A., & Blanchard-Fields, F. (2008). Emotion regulation in interpersonal problems: The role of cognitive-emotional complexity, emotion regulation goals, and expressivity. *Psychology and Aging, 23*(1), 39–51.

Cogan, N., & Schwannauer, M. (2011). Understanding adolescent risk-taking behaviour: Exploring the motivations, personalities and coping styles of young people in a school-based population. In *Personality and coping, Series on stress and coping in education* (pp. 91–110). Greenwich, CT: Information Age Publishing.

Cohen, S., Janicki-Deverts, D., & Miller, G. E. (2007). Psychological stress and disease. *Journal of the American Medical Association, 298*(14), 1685–1687. doi:10.1001/jama.298.14.1685.

Compas, B. E. (1987). Coping with stress during childhood and adolescence. *Psychological Bulletin, 101*(3), 393–403.

Compas, B. E. (1998). An agenda for coping research and theory: Basic and applied developmental issues. *International Journal of Behavioral Development, 22*, 231–237.

Compas, B. E. (2009). Coping, regulation, and development during childhood and adolescence. *New Directions for Child and Adolescent Development, 2009*(124), 87–99. doi:10.1002/cd.245.

Compas, B. E., Connor-Smith, J. K., Saltzman, H., Thomsen, A. H., & Wadsworth, M. E. (2001). Coping with stress during childhood and adolescence: Problems, progress, and potential in theory and research. *Psychological Bulletin, 127*(1), 87–127.

Compas, B. E., Hinden, B. R., & Gerhardt, C. A. (1995). Adolescent development: Pathways and processes of risk and resilience. *Annual Review of Psychology, 46*, 265–293.

Compas, B. E., Worsham, N. L., & Ey, S. (1992). Conceptual and developmental issues in children's coping with stress. In A. M. La Greca, L. J. Siegel, J. L. Wallander, & C. E. Walker (Eds.), *Stress and coping in child health* (pp. 7–24). New York: Guilford Press.

Connor, K. M., & Davidson, J. R. T. (2003). Development of a new resilience scale: The Connor-Davidson Resilience Scale (CD-RISC). *Depression and Anxiety, 18*(2), 76–82.

Cooklin, A. R., Giallo, R., & Rose, N. (2011). Parental fatigue and parenting practices during early childhood: An Australian community survey. *Child: Care, Health and Development, 38*, 654–664. doi:10.1111/j.1365-2214.2011.01333.x.

Cornell, C. (2015). *The relationship between coping and anxiety in preschoolers: Does situation and anxiety types make a difference?* Unpublished Masters manuscript. Graduate School of Education, University of Melbourne, Melbourne, VIC.

Cornell, C., Dobee, P., Kaufman, D., Kiernan, N, & Frydenberg, E. (2015). *COPE-R program for preschoolers: Teaching empathy and pro-social skills through the early years coping cards.* Unpublished manuscript, University of Melbourne.

Cornell, C., Kiernan, N., Kaufman, D., Dobee, P., Frydenberg, E., & Deans, J. (in press). Developing social emotional competence in the early years. In E. Frydenberg, A. Martin, & R. Collie (Eds.), *Social and emotional learning in Australia and the Asia Pacific.* Melbourne, VIC: Springer.

Corry, D. A. S., Mallett, J., Lewis, C. A., & Abdel-Khalek, A. M. (2013). The creativity-spirituality construct and its role in transformative coping. *Mental Health, Religion and Culture, 16*(10), 979–990. doi:10.1080/13674676.201 3.834492.

Coyne, J. C., & Smith, D. A. (1991). Couples coping with a myocardial infarction: A contextual perspective on wives' distress. *Journal of Personality and Social Psychology, 61*(3), 404–412.

Cruz-Ortega, L. G., Gutierrez, D., & Waite, D. (2015). Religious orientation and ethnic identity as predictors of religious coping among bereaved individuals. *Counseling and Values, 60*(1), 67–83.

Csikszentmihalyi, M. (2008). *Flow : The psychology of optimal experience.* New York: Harper Perennial, c1990. 1st Harper Perennial Modern Classics ed.

Cunningham, E. (1997). *A model of predicting adolescent depressive syndromes using teacher and self-evaluations.* Unpublished Bachelor of Science (Honours), Department of Psychology, Monash University, Melbourne, VIC.

Dadds, M. R., & Barrett, P. M. (2001). Practitioner review: Psychological management of anxiety disorders in childhood. *Journal of Child Psychology and Psychiatry, 42*(8), 999–1011.

Davies, S. (1995). *The relationship between beliefs held by gifted students and the strategies they use. Unpublished Master of Educational Psychology project.* University of Melbourne, Melbourne, VIC.

de Terte, I., Becker, J., & Stephens, C. (2009). An integrated model for understanding and developing resilience in the face of adverse events. *Journal of Pacific Rim Psychology, 3*(1), 20–26. doi:10.1375/prp.3.1.20.

de Terte, I., Stephens, C., & Huddleston, L. (2014). The development of a three part model of psychological resilience. *Stress and Health: Journal of the International Society for the Investigation of Stress, 30*(5), 416–424.

Deans, J., Frydenberg, E., & Liang, R. (2012). Building a shared language of coping: Dynamics of communication between parents and preschool children. *New Zealand Research into Early Childhood Research Journal, 15,* 67–89.

Deans, J., Frydenberg, E., & Tsurutani, H. (2010). Operationalising social and emotional coping competencies in kindergarten children. *New Zealand Research in Early Childhood Education Journal, 13,* 113–124.

Deans, J., Liang, R., & Frydenberg, E. (2016). Giving voices and providing skills to families in culturally and linguistically diverse communities through a productive parenting program. *Australasian Journal of Early Childhood, 41*(1), 13–18.

Deans, J., Liang, R., Zapper, S., & Frydenberg, E. (in press). *The process of socialisation and embodiment of a social emotional learning program in an early years setting: COPE-R.* Unpublished manuscript, University of Melbourne.

DeLongis, A., & O'Brien, T. B. (1990). An interpersonal framework for stress and coping: An application to the families of Alzheimer's patients. In M. A. P. Stephens, J. H. Crowther, S. E. Hobfoll, & D. L. Tennenbaum (Eds.), *Stress and coping in later life families* (pp. 221–239). Washington, DC: Hemisphere Publishers.

Denham, S. A. (2006). Social-emotional competence as support for school readiness: What is it and how do we assess it? *Early Education and Development, Special Issue: Measurement of School Readiness, 17,* 57–89. doi:10.1207/s15566935eed1701_4.

Diener, C. I., & Dweck, C. S. (1978). *An analysis of learned helplessness: Continuous changes in performance, strategy, and achievement cognitions following failure. Journal of Personality and Social Psychology, 36,* 451–462.

Din, N. C., Bee, S. S., Subramaniam, P., & Oon, N. L. (2010). The prevalence and factors influencing posttraumatic stress disorders (PTSD) among help-seeking women experiencing domestic violence in Malaysia. *ASEAN Journal of Psychiatry, 11*(2), 158–170.

Dinkmeyer, D. C., McKay, G. D., & Dinkmeyer, J. S. (1989). *Parenting young children: Helpful strategies based on systematic training for effective parenting (STEP) for parents of children under six.* Circle Pines, MN: AGS.

Domitrovich, C., Greenberg, M., Kusche, C., & Cortes, R. (2004). *PATHS preschool program.* South Deerfield, MA: Channing Bete Company.

Dreikurs, R. (1958). *The challenge of parenthood.* New York: Duell, Soan and Pearce.

Duckworth, A., & Gross, J. J. (2014). Self-control and grit: Related but separable determinants of success. *Current Directions in Psychological Science (Sage Publications Inc.), 23*(5), 319–325. doi:10.1177/0963721414541462.

Duckworth, A. L., & Eskreis-Winkler, L. (2015). Grit. In J. D. Wright (Ed.), *International encyclopedia of the social and behavioral sciences* (2nd ed., pp. 397–401). Oxford, UK: Elsevier.

Duckworth, A. L., Peterson, C., Matthews, M. D., & Kelly, D. R. (2007). Grit: Perseverance and passion for long-term goals. *Journal of Personality and Social Psychology, 96*(6), 1087–1101.

Duckworth, A. L., & Quinn, P. D. (2009). Development and validation of the short grit scale (Grit-S). *Journal of Personality Assessment, 91*(2), 166–174. doi:10.1080/00223890802634290.

Dweck, C. (2012). *Mindset: How you can fulfil your potential.* New York: Constable & Robinson.

Dweck, C. (2015). Growth. *British Journal of Educational Psychology, 85*, 242–245. doi:10.1111/bjep.12072.

Dweck, C. S. (1990). Self-theories and goals: Their role in motivation, personality, and development. *Nebraska Symposium on Motivation. Nebraska Symposium on Motivation, 38*, 199–235.

Dweck, C. S. (2006). *Mindset: The new psychology of success* (1st ed.). Carol S. Dweck. New York: Random House, c2006.

Dweck, C. S. (2011). Book review: Mindset-the new psychology of success by Dweck, C. S. (2006): Purdue University, 2011-12-22.

Dweck, C. S., & Leggett, E. L. (1988). A social-cognitive approach to motivation and personality. *Psychological Review, 95*(2), 256–273.

Dweck, C. S., & Sorich, L. A. (1999). Mastery-oriented thinking. In C. R. Snyder (Ed.), *Coping* (pp. 232–251). New York: Oxford University Press.

Egger, H. L., & Angold, A. (2006). Common emotional and behavioral disorders in preschool children: Presentation, nosology, and epidemiology. *Journal of Child Psychology and Psychiatry, 47*(3–4), 313–337.

Eisenberg, N., Cumberland, A., Spinrad, T. L., Fabes, R. A., Shepard, S. A., Reiser, M., et al. (2001). The relations of regulation and emotionality to children's externalizing and internalizing problem behavior. *Child Development, 72*(4), 1112–1134.

Eisenberg, N., Fabes, R. A., & Guthrie, I. K. (1997). Coping with stress: The roles of regulation and development. In S. A. Wolchik & I. Sandler (Eds.), *Handbook of children's coping: Linking theory and intervention* (pp. 41–70). New York: Plenum.

Ekman, P. (1994). All emotions are basic. In P. Ekman & R. J. Davidson (Eds.), *The nature of emotion: Fundamental questions* (pp. 15–19). New York: Oxford University Press.

Elliott, E. S., & Dweck, C. S. (1988). Goals: An approach to motivation and achievement. *Journal of Personality and Social Psychology, 54*(1), 5–12.

Emery, E. E., & Pargament, K. I. (2004). The many faces of religious coping in late life: Conceptualization, measurement, and links to well-being. *Ageing International, 29*, 3–27.

Englbrecht, M., Wendler, J., & Alten, R. (2012). Depression as a systemic feature of rheumatoid arthritis. *Zeitschrift für Rheumatologie, 71*(10), 859–863. doi:10.1007/s00393-011-0926-z.

Evert, H. (1996). *Gender, culture, psychological and social resources and their influence on coping behaviour in physiotherapy students.* Unpublished Master of Educational Psychology thesis, University of Melbourne, VIC.

Fabrigar, L. R., Wegener, D. T., MacCallum, R. C., & Strahan, E. J. (1999). Evaluating the use of exploratory factor analysis in psychological research. *Psychological Methods, 4*(3), 272–299. doi:10.1037//1082-989X.4.3.272.

Fallon, B., Frydenberg, E., & Boldero, J. (1993, September–October). Perception of family functioning and coping in adolescents. Paper presented at the *28th Annual Conference of the Australian Psychological Society,* Gold Coast, QLD.

Fiske, S. T., & Taylor, S. E. (1991). *Social cognition* (2nd ed.). New York: McGraw-Hill.

Folkman, S. (1997). Positive psychological states and coping with severe stress. *Social Science & Medicine, 45*(8), 1207–1221, 1215.

Folkman, S. (2008). The case for positive emotions in the stress process. *Anxiety, Stress, and Coping, 21*(1), 3–14.

Folkman, S. (2010). Stress, coping, and hope. *Psycho-Oncology, 19*(9), 901–908. doi:10.1002/pon.1836.

Folkman, S. (2011). *The Oxford handbook of stress, health, and coping.* Oxford/New York: Oxford University Press.

Folkman, S. J. T. (2004). COPING: Pitfalls and promise. *Annual Review of Psychology, 55*(1), 745–774. doi:10.1146/annurev.psych.55.090902.141456.

Folkman, S., & Lazarus, R. S. (1980). An analysis of coping in a middle-aged community sample. *Journal of Health and Social Behavior, 21*, 219.

Folkman, S., & Lazarus, R. S. (1985). If it changes it must be a process: Study of emotion and coping during three stages of a college examination. *Journal of Personality and Social Psychology, 48*(1), 150–170.

Folkman, S., & Lazarus, R. S. (1988). The relationship between coping and emotion: Implications for theory and research. *Social Science & Medicine (1982), 26*(3), 309–317.

Folkman, S., Lazarus, R. S., Gruen, R. J., & DeLongis, A. (1986). Appraisal, coping, health status, and psychological symptoms. *Journal of Personality and Social Psychology, 50*(3), 571–579.

Folkman, S., & Moskowitz, J. T. (2000). Stress, positive emotion, and coping. *Current Directions in Psychological Science, 9*(4), 115–118. doi:10.1111/1467-8721.00073.

Folkman, S., & Moskowitz, J. T. (2003). Positive psychology from a coping perspective. *Psychological Inquiry, 14*(2), 121–125.

Folkman, S., Moskowitz, J. T., Ozer, E. M., & Park, C. L. (1997). Positive meaningful events and coping in the context of HIV/AIDS. In B. H. Gottlieb (Ed.), *Coping with chronic stress* (pp. 293–314). New York: Plenum.

Foy, D. W., Drescher, K. D., & Watson, P. J. (2011). Religious and spiritual factors in resilience. In S. M. Southwick, B. T. Litu, D. Charney, & M. J. Friedman (Eds.), *Resilience and mental health: Challenges across the lifespan* (pp. 90–101). Cambridge, UK: Cambridge University Press.

Fredrickson, B. L. (2004). The Broaden-and-Build theory of positive emotions. *Philosophical Transactions of the Royal Society of London, 359*, 1367–1377.

Fredrickson, B. L., Cohn, M. A., Coffey, K. A., Pek, J., & Finkel, S. M. (2008). Open hearts build lives: Positive emotions, induced through loving-kindness meditation, build consequential personal resources. *Journal of Personality and Social Psychology, 95*(5), 1045–1062.

Fredrickson, B. L., & Losada, M. F. (2005). Positive affect and the complex dynamics of human flourishing. *American Psychologist, 60*(7), 678–686.

Freedy, J. R., & Hobfoll, S. E. (1994). Stress inoculation for reduction of burnout: A conservation of resources approach. *Anxiety, Stress, and Coping, 6*(4), 311.

Frese, M., Kring, W., Soose, A., & Zempel, J. (1996). PI at work: Differences between East and West Germany. *Academy of Management Journal, 39*, 37–63.

Friedman, M. J., & McEwen, B. S. (2004). Posttraumatic stress disorder, allostatic load, and medical illness. In P. P. Schnurr & B. L. Green (Eds.), *Trauma and health: Physical health consequences of exposure to extreme stress* (pp. 157–188). Washington, DC: American Psychological Association.

Frydenberg, E. (1994). Adolescent concerns: The concomitants of coping. *Australian Journal of Educational and Developmental Psychology, 4*, 1–11.

Frydenberg, E. (2002). *Beyond coping : Meeting goals, visions, and challenges.* Oxford, UK: Oxford University Press.

Frydenberg, E. (2010). *Think positively!: A course for developing coping skills in adolescents.* London/New York: Continuum International Pub. Group, c2010.

Frydenberg, E. (2007). *Coping for success.* ISBN 978-0-7340-2741-2. University of Melbourne's eShowcase web site: http://eshowcase.unimelb.edu.au/eshowcase/

Frydenberg, E. (2008). *Adolescent coping: Advances in theory, research and practice.* Hoboken, NJ: Taylor and Francis.

Frydenberg, E. (2015). *Families coping: Effective strategies for you and your child.* Camberwell, VIC: ACER Press.

Frydenberg, E., & Brandon, C. (2002). *The best of coping: Developing coping skills for adolescents.* South Melbourne, VIC: Oz Child, Children Australia, c2002.

Frydenberg, E., & Brandon, C. (2007). *The best of coping: Developing coping skills for adolescents.* Camberwell, VIC: ACER Press.

Frydenberg, E., Bugalski, K., Firth, N., Kamsner, S., & Poole, C. (2007). Teaching young people to cope: Benefits and gains for at risk students. *Australian Educational and Developmental Psychologist, 23*(1), 91–110.

Frydenberg, E., Care, E., Freeman, E., & Chan, E. (2009). Interrelationships between coping, school connectedness and wellbeing. *Australian Journal of Educational Research, 53*(3), 261–276.

Frydenberg, E., & Deans, J. (2011a). Coping competencies in the early years: Identifying the strategies that preschoolers use. In P. Buchwald, K. A. Moore, & T. Ringeisen (Eds.), *Stress and anxiety: Application to education and health* (pp. 17–26). Berlin, Germany: Logos.

Frydenberg, E., & Deans, J. (2011b). *The early years coping cards.* Melbourne, VIC: Australian Council for Educational Research.

Frydenberg, E., Eacott, C., & Clark, N. (2008). From distress to success: Developing a coping language and programs for adolescents. *Prevention Researcher, 15*(4), 8–12.

Frydenberg, E., Deans, J., & Liang, R. (2014). Families can do coping: Parenting skills in the early years. *Children Australia, 39*, 99–106. doi:10.1017/cha.2014.7.

Frydenberg, E., Deans, J., & O'Brien, K. (2012). *Developing everyday coping skills in the early years.* London: Continuum.

Frydenberg, E., & Lewis, R. (1991a). Adolescent coping: The different ways in which boys and girls cope. *Journal of Adolescence, 14*(2), 119–133.

Frydenberg, E., & Lewis, R. (1991b). Adolescent coping in the Australian context. *Australian Educational Researcher, 18*(2), 65–82.

Frydenberg, E., & Lewis, R. (1991c). Adolescent coping styles and strategies: Is there functional and dysfunctional coping? *Australian Journal of Guidance and Counselling, 1*, 1–8.

Frydenberg, E., & Lewis, R. (1993a). *Manual, The adolescent coping scale*. Melbourne, VIC: Australian Council for Educational Research.

Frydenberg, E., & Lewis, R. (1993b). Boys play sport a nd girls turn to others: Age, gender and ethnicity as determinants of coping. *Journal of Adolescence, 16*(3), 253–266.

Frydenberg, E., & Lewis, R. (1996a). A replication study of the structure of the adolescent coping scale: Multiple forms and applications of a self-report inventory in a counselling and research context. *European Journal of Psychological Assessment, 12*(3), 224–235.

Frydenberg, E., & Lewis, R. (1996b). Social issues: What concerns young people and how they cope. *Peace and Conflict, 2*(3), 271–283.

Frydenberg, E., & Lewis, R. (1997). *Coping scale for adults*. Melbourne, VIC: Australian Council for Educational Research.

Frydenberg, E., & Lewis, R. (1999). Academic and general wellbeing: The relationship with coping. *Australian Journal of Guidance and Counselling, 9*(1), 19–36.

Frydenberg, E., & Lewis, R. (2000). Teaching coping to adolescents: When and to whom? *American Educational Research Journal, 37*, 727–745.

Frydenberg, E., & Lewis, R. (2002a). Do managers cope productively? A comparison between Australian middle level managers and adults in the general community. *Journal of Managerial Psychology, 17*, 640–654.

Frydenberg, E., & Lewis, R. (2002b). Adolescent wellbeing: Building young people's resources. In E. Frydenberg (Ed.), *Beyond coping: Meeting goals, vision and challenges* (pp. 175–194). Oxford, UK: Oxford University Press.

Frydenberg, E., & Lewis, R. (2009a). Relationship among wellbeing, avoidant coping and active coping in a large sample of Australian adolescents. *Psychological Reports, 104*(3), 745–758.

Frydenberg, E., & Lewis, R. (2009b). The Relationship between problem-solving efficacy and coping amongst Australian adolescents. *British Journal of Guidance and Counselling, 37*(1), 51–64.

Frydenberg, E., & Lewis, R. (2011). *Adolescent coping scale – Second Edition (ACS-2)*. Melbourne, VIC: Australian Council for Educational Research (ACER Press).

Frydenberg, E., & Lewis, R. (2014). *Coping scale for adults – Second Edition (CSA-2)*. Melbourne, VIC: Australian Council for Educational Research. (ACER Press).

Frydenberg, E., Lewis, R., Ardila, R., E., & Kennedy, G. (2000). Adolescent concern with social issues: An exploratory comparison between Australian,

Colombian, and northern Irish students. *Peace and Conflict: Journal of Peace Psychology, 7*(1), 59–76.

Frydenberg, E., Lewis, R., Kennedy, G., Ardila, R., Frindte, W., & Hannoun, R. (2003). Coping with concerns: An exploratory comparison of Australian, Colombian, German and Palestinian adolescents. *Journal of Youth and Adolescence, 32*(1), 59–66.

Fuhr, M. (2002). Coping humor in early adolescence. *Humor- International Journal of Humor Research, 15*(3), 283–304.

Furniss, T., Beyer, T., & Guggenmos, J. (2006). Prevalence of behavioural and emotional problems among six-years-old preschool children. *Social Psychiatry and Psychiatric Epidemiology, 41*(5), 394–399. doi:10.1007/s00127-006-0045-3.

Garbarino, J. (2002). Coping with resilience. *Contemporary Psychology: APA Review of Books, 47*(3), 247–248. doi:10.1037/001107.

Gilmer, D. F., & Aldwin, C. M. (2002). Trajectories of health and social support in frail young-old and old-old patients after hospitalization. *Journal of the Aging Family System, 2*, 1–14.

Goble, G. (1995). *Assessment of coping strategies.* Unpublished research report, Monash University, Melbourne, VIC.

Golant, S. M. (2015). Residential normalcy and the enriched coping repertoires of successfully aging older adults. *The Gerontologist, 55*(1), 70–82. doi:10.1093/geront/gnu036.

Goleman, D. (2005). *Emotional intelligence.* New York: Bantam Books.

Goleman, D. (2011). *The brain and emotional intelligence: New insights.* Northampton, MA: More than sound LLC.

Gordon, T. (1970). *Parent effectiveness training: The tested new way to raise responsible children.* New York: David McKay.

Gould, K., Ponsford, J., Johnston, L., & Schönberger, M. (2011). Predictive and associated factors of psychiatric disorders after traumatic brain injury: A prospective study. *Journal of Neurotrauma, 28*(7), 1155–1163.

Greenberg, L. S., & Safran, J. D. (1987). *Emotion in psychotherapy: Affect, cognition, and the process of change.* New York: Guilford.

Greenglass, E. (2002). Chapter 3. Proactive coping. In E. Frydenberg (Ed.), *Beyond coping: Meeting goals, vision, and challenges* (pp. 37–62). London: Oxford University Press.

Greenglass, E., & Schwarzer, R. (1998). The Proactive Coping Inventory (PCI). In R. Schwarzer (Ed.), *Advances in health psychology research* (CD-ROM). Berlin, Germany: Free University of Berlin. Institut for Arbeits, Organizations- und Gesundheitspsychologie. (IBN 3-00-002776-9).

Greenglass, E. R., & Fiksenbaum, L. (2009). Proactive coping, positive affect, and well-being: Testing for mediation using path analysis. *European Psychologist, 14*(1), 29–39. doi:10.1027/1016-9040.14.1.29.

Greenglass, E. R., Schwarzer, R., & Taubert, S. (1999). *The Proactive Coping Inventory (PCI): A multidimensional research instrument.* [On-line publication]. Available at: http://userpage.fu-berlin.de/~health/greenpci.htm

Gresham, F. M., MacMillan, D. L., & Bocian, K. M. (1996). Learning disabilities, low achievement, and mild mental retardation: More alike than different? *Journal of Learning Disabilities, 29*, 570–581.

Griva, F., & Anagnostopoulos, F. (2010). Positive psychological states and anxiety: The mediating effect of proactive coping. *Psychological Reports, 107*(3), 795–804.

Gulliford, H., Deans, J., Frydenberg, E., & Liang, R. (2015). Teaching coping skills in the context of positive parenting within a preschool setting. *Australian Psychologist, 50*(3), 219–231. doi:10.1111/ap.12121.

Guo, M., Gan, Y., & Tong, J. (2013). The role of meaning-focused coping in significant loss. *Anxiety, Stress, and Coping, 26*(1), 87–102.

Hadwin, J. A., Garner, M., & Perez-Olivas, G. (2006). The development of information processing biases in childhood anxiety: A review and exploration of its origins in parenting. *Clinical Psychology Review, 26*(7), 876–894.

Halpern, L. F. (2004). The relations of coping and family environment to preschoolers' problem behavior. *Journal of Applied Developmental Psychology, 25*(4), 399–421.

Henslee, A. M., Coffey, S. F., Schumacher, J. A., Tracy, M., Norris, F. H., & Galea, S. (2015). Religious coping and psychological and behavioral adjustment after hurricane katrina. *Journal of Psychology, 149*(6), 630–642.

Herbert, C., & Dweck, C. (1985). *Mediators of persistence in pre-schoolers: Implications for development.* Unpublished manuscript, Harvard University.

Herzberg, P. Y. (2013). Coping in relationships: The interplay between individual and dyadic coping and their effects on relationship satisfaction. *Anxiety, Stress, and Coping, 26*(2), 136–153.

Hewitt, P. L., & Flett, G. L. (1996). *The multidimensional perfectionism scale.* Toronto, ON: Multi-Health Systems Inc.

Heyman, G. D., Dweck, C. S., & Cain, K. M. (1992). Young children's vulnerability to self-blame and helplessness: Relationship to beliefs about goodness. *Child Development, 63*, 401–415.

Hobfoll, S. E. (1988). *The ecology of stress.* Washington, DC: Hemisphere.

Hobfoll, S. E. (1989). Conservation of resources: A new attempt at conceptualizing stress. *The American Psychologist, 44*(3), 513–524.

Hobfoll, S. E. (1998). *Stress culture and community: The psychology and philosophy of stress.* New York: Plenum Press.

Hobfoll, S. E. (2002). Social and psychological resources and adaptation. *Review of General Psychology, 6*(4), 307–324. doi:10.1037/1089-2680.6.4.307.

Hobfoll, S. E. (2010). *Conservation of resources theory: Its implication for stress, health, and resilience.* NewYork: Oxford University Press.

Hobfoll, S. E., Dunahoo, C. L., Ben-Porath, Y., & Monnier, J. (1994). Gender and coping: The dual-axis model of coping. *American Journal of Community Psychology, 22*(1), 49–82.

Hobfoll, S. E., Johnson, R. J., Ennis, N., & Jackson, A. P. (2003). Resource loss, resource gain, and emotional outcomes among inner city women. *Journal of Personality and Social Psychology, 84*(3), 632–643.

Hockenbury, D. H., & Hockenbury, S. E. (2001). *Discovering psychology.* New York: Worth Publishers.

Holahan, C. J., Moos, R. H., Holahan, C. K., & Brennan, P. L. (1995). Social support, coping, and depressive symptoms in a late-middle-aged sample of patients reporting cardiac illness. *Health Psychology, 14*, 152–163.

Holmes, T. H., & Rahe, R. H. (1967). The social readjustment rating scale. *Journal of Psychosomatic Research, 11*(2), 213–218.

Hong, P. Y. P. (2014). How children succeed: Grit, curiosity, and the hidden power of character, Paul Tough. *Qualitative Social Work, 13*(3), 438–442, 435p. doi:10.1177/1473325014530940a.

Horton, P. C. (2002). Self-comforting strategies used by adolescents. *Bulletin of the Menninger Clinic, 66*(3), 259–272.

Hsieh, M., Ponsford, J., Wong, D., Schönberger, M., Taffe, J., & Mckay, A. (2012). Motivational interviewing and cognitive behaviour therapy for anxiety following traumatic brain injury: A pilot randomised controlled trial. *Neuropsychological Rehabilitation, 22*(4), 585–608.

Hyattsville (MD): National Center for Health Statistics (US); 2006 Nov. Report No.: 2006-1232. Health, United States.

Izard, C. E. (1993). Organizational and motivational functions of discrete emotions. In M. Lewis & J. Haviland (Eds.), *Handbook of emotions* (pp. 631–641). New York: Guilford.

Jenkin, C. (1997). *The relationship between self-efficacy and coping: Changes following an Outward Bound program. Unpublished Master of Educational Psychology project.* University of Melbourne, Melbourne, VIC.

Jenkins, J. M., Smith, M. A., & Graham, P. J. (1989). Coping with parental quarrels. *Journal of the American Academy of Child and Adolescent Psychiatry, 28*(2), 182–189.

Jones, B. (1997). *The transition from secondary school to university: Who needs help coping with academic stress and when.* Unpublished Master of Educational Psychology thesis, University of Melbourne, Melbourne, VIC.

Jordan, W. (2015, February 12). A third of British adults don't believe in a higher power. Retrieved from https://yougov.co.uk/news/2015/02/12/third-british-adults-dont-believe-higher-power/

Kabat-Zinn, J. (2005). *Wherever you go, there you are: Mindfulness meditation in everyday life/Jon Kabat-Zinn.* New York: Hyperion, c2005.

Kagan, J. (1997). Temperament and the reactions to unfamiliarity. *Child Development, 68*(1), 139–143.

Kagan, J., Snidman, N., Arcus, D., & Reznick, J. S. (1994). *Galen's prophecy: Temperament in human nature.* New York: Basic Books.

Kahneman, D., & Tversky, A. (2013). Prospect theory: An analysis of decision under risk. In L. C. MacLean & W. T. Ziemba (Eds.), *Handbook of the fundamentals of financial decision making. Part I, World scientific handbook in financial economics series* (Vol. 4, pp. 99–127). Hackensack, NJ/Singapore: World Scientific.

Kerig, P. K. (2001). Children's coping with interparental conflict. In I. J. J. Grych & H. Fincham (Eds.), *Interparental conflict and child development* (pp. 213–248). New York: Cambridge University Press.

Kim, S., & Esquivel, G. B. (2011). Adolescent spirituality and resilience: Theory, research, and educational practices. *Psychology in the Schools, 48*(7), 755–765. doi:10.1002/pits.20582.

King, D. B., & DeLongis, A. (2014). When couples disconnect: Rumination and withdrawal as maladaptive responses to everyday stress. *Journal of Family Psychology, 28*(4), 460–469.

Knabb, J. J., & Grigorian-Routon, A. (2014). The role of experiential avoidance in the relationship between faith maturity, religious coping, and psychological adjustment among Christian university students. *Mental Health, Religion and Culture, 17*(5), 458–469. doi:10.1080/13674676.2013.846310.

Kobasa, S. C. (1979). Stressful life events, personality, and health: An inquiry into hardiness. *Journal of Personality and Social Psychology, 37*(1), 1–11.

Kopp, C. B. (2009). Emotion-focused coping in young children: Self and self-regulatory processes. *New Directions for Child and Adolescent Development, 2009*(124), 33–46. doi:10.1002/cd.241.

Krause, N. (2006). Twenty-two: Religion and health in late life. In *Handbook of the psychology of aging,* 499–518. doi:10.1016/B978-012101264-9/50025-2.

Labbé, E. E., & Fobes, A. (2010). Evaluating the interplay between spirituality, personality and stress. *Applied Psychophysiology and Biofeedback, 35*(2), 141–146.

Langer, E. J. (1992). Matters of mind: Mindfulness/mindlessness in perspective. *Consciousness and Cognition, 1*(3), 289–305. doi:10.1016/1053-8100(92) 90066-J.

Langer, E. J. (2009). *Counter clockwise : Mindful health and the power of possibility/Ellen J. Langer.* New York: Ballantine Books, c2009.

Lazarus, R. S. (1966). *Psychological stress and the coping process.* New York: McGraw-Hill.

Lazarus, R. S. (1991). *Emotion and adaption.* New York: Oxford University Press.

Lazarus, R. S. (1993). Coping theory and research: Past, present, and future. *Psychosomatic Medicine, 55*(3), 234–247.

Lazarus, R. S. (2000). Toward better research on stress and coping. *The American Psychologist, 55*(6), 665–673.

Lazarus, R. S., & Folkman, S. (1984). *Stress, appraisal, and coping.* New York: Springer.

Lazarus, R. S., Kanner, A., & Folkman, S. (1980). Emotions: A cognitive phenomenological analysis. In R. Plutchik & H. Kellerman (Eds.), *Emotion-Theory research and experience: Vol. I. Theories of emotion.* New York: Academic Press.

Lelorain, S., Tessier, P., Florin, A., & Bonnaud-Antignac, A. (2012). Posttraumatic growth in long term breast cancer survivors: Relation to coping, social support and cognitive processing. *Journal of Health Psychology, 17*(5), 627–639, 613p. doi:10.1177/1359105311427475.

Lemay, R. (2004). Resilience versus coping. *Child and Family, 8*(2), 11–15.

Levy, J. M., & Steele, H. (2011). Attachment and grit: Exploring possible contributions of attachment styles (from past and present life) to the adult personality construct of grit. *Journal of Social and Psychological Sciences, 16*(2), 16.

Lewis, J. S. (1997). Sense of coherence and the strengths perspective with older persons. *Journal of Gerontological Social Work, 26*(3/4), 99–112. doi:10.1300/ J083V26N03_08.

Lewis, R., & Frydenberg, E. (2004a). Students' self-evaluation of their coping: How well do they do it? In E. Frydenberg (Ed.), *Thriving, surviving, or going under: Coping with everyday lives* (pp. 23–43). Connecticut: Information Age Publishing.

Lewis, R., & Frydenberg, E. (2004b). Thriving, surviving or going under, which coping strategies relate to which outcomes? In E. Frydenberg (Ed.), *Thriving, surviving or going under: Coping with everyday lives, Series, research on stress and coping in education* (pp. 3–24). Greenwich, CT: Information Age Publishing.

Lewis, R., & Frydenberg, E. (2007). Adolescent problem-solving efficacy and coping strategy usage in a population of Australian adolescents. In G. S. Gates (Ed.), *Emerging thought and research on student, teacher and administrator stress and coping* (pp. 35–48). Greenwich, CT: Information Age Publishing.

Lewis, R., Roache, J., & Romi, S. (2011). Coping styles as mediators of teachers' classroom management techniques. *Research in Education, 85*(1), 53–68.

Licht, B. G., & Dweck, C. S. (1984). Determinants of academic achievement: The interaction of children's achievement orientations with skill area. *Developmental Psychology, 20*(4), 628–636.

Lovibond, S. H., & Lovibond, P. F. (1995). *Manual for the depression anxiety stress scales.* (2nd ed.) Sydney, NSW: Psychology Foundation. ISBN 7334-1423-0.

Lutha, S. S. (2006). Resilience in development: A synthesis of research across five decades. In D. Cicchetti & D. J. Cohen (Eds.), *Developmental psychopathology: Risk, disorder, and adaptation* (pp. 740–795). New York: Wiley.

Lutha, S. S., & Cicchetti, D. (2000). The construct of resilience: Implications for interventions and social policies. *Development and Psychopathology, 12*(4), 857–885.

Lynham, S. (1996). *Comparison between coping styles of young women with anorexia nervosa and coping styles of mothers and daughters with anorexia nervosa: An exploratory investigation.* Unpublished Master of Education thesis, La Trobe University, Melbourne, VIC.

Maddi, S. R. (2002). The story of hardiness: Twenty years of theorizing, research, and practice. *Consulting Psychology Journal: Practice and Research, 54*(3), 173–185. doi:10.1037/1061-4087.54.3.173.

Mahoney, M. J. (1991). *Human change processes: The scientific foundations of psychotherapy.* New York: Basic Books.

Mann, L., Nota, L., Soresi, S., Ferrari, L., & Frydenberg, E. (2011). The relationship between decision-making style and coping strategies in adolescence. In G. Reevy & E. Frydenberg (Eds.), *Personality and coping, Series on stress and coping in education* (pp. 25–48). Charlotte, NC: Information Age Publishing.

Manning, L. K. (2013). Navigating hardships in old age: Exploring the relationship between spirituality and resilience in later life. *Qualitative Health Research, 23*(4), 568–575. doi:10.1177/1049732312471730.

Marshall, P. (2008). *Stress and coping among professional mediators.* Melbourne, VIC: Faculty of Education, University of Melbourne.

Masten, A. S. (2001). Ordinary magic: Resilience processes in development. *American Psychologist, 56*(3), 227–238.

Masten, A. S., Hubbard, J. J., Gest, S. D., Tellegen, A., Garmezy, N., & Ramirez, M. (1999). Competence in the context of adversity: Pathways to resilience and maladaptation from childhood to late adolescence. *Development and Psychopathology, 11*(1), 143–169.

Matthews, G., Roberts, R. D., & Zeidner, M. (2004). Seven myths about emotional intelligence. *Psychological Inquiry, 15*(3), 179–196.

Mayer, J. D., Roberts, R. D., & Barsade, S. G. (2008). Human abilities: Emotional intelligence. *Annual Review of Psychology, 59,* 507–536.

Mayer, J. D., & Salovey, P. (1993). The intelligence of emotional intelligence. *Intelligence, 17,* 433–442.

Mayer, J. D., & Salovey, P. (1995). Emotional intelligence and the construction and regulation of feelings. *Applied and Preventive Psychology, 4*(3), 197–208.

Mayer, J. D., Salovey, P., & Caruso, D. R. (2012). The validity of the MSCEIT: Additional analyses and evidence. *Emotion Review, 4*(4), 403–408.

McClure, E. B., Brennan, P. A., Hammen, C., & Le Brocque, R. M. (2001). Parental anxiety disorders, child anxiety disorders, and the perceived parent–child relationship in an Australian high-risk sample. *Journal of Abnormal Child Psychology, 29*(1), 1–10.

McCullough, M. E. (2000). Forgiveness as a human strength: Theory, measurement, and links to well-being. *Journal of Social and Clinical Psychology, 19*(1), 43–55.

McDonald, A. (1996). *Approaches to learning of tertiary students: The role of coping, developmentally-related variables and study stressors.* Unpublished Master of Educational Psychology Thesis, University of Melbourne, Melbourne, VIC.

McGowan, M. (2016, January 25). Australian Open 2016: Spain's Carla Suarez Navarro beats Australia's Daria Gavrilova in fourth round. Herald Sun. Retrieved from http://www.news.com.au/

McKenzie, V., Frydenberg, E., & Poole, C. (2004). What resources matter to young people: The relationship between resources and coping style. *The Australian Educational and Developmental Psychologist, 19*(2), 78–96.

McTaggart, H. (1996). *Students at risk of school exclusion: How they cope.* Unpublished Master of Educational Psychology project. University of Melbourne, Melbourne, VIC.

Meredith, L. S., Sherbourne, C. D., Gaillot, S., Hansell, L., Ritschard, H. V., Parker, A. M., & Wrenn, G. (2011). *Promoting psychological resilience in the U.S. Military.* Santa Monica, CA: RAND Corporation.

Miller, W. R., & Seligman, M. E. P. (1975). Depression and learned helplessness in man. *Journal of Abnormal Psychology, 84,* 228–238.

Moos, R. H., & Schaefer, J. A. (1993). Coping resources and processes: Current concepts and measures. In L. Goldberger & S. Breznitz (Eds.), *Handbook of stress: Theoretical and clinical aspects* (pp. 234–257). New York: Free Press.

Moosavi, E. A., & Ahadi, H. (2011). Hardiness and attributional styles as predictors of coping strategies and mental health. *Amity Journal of Applied Psychology, 2*(1), 3–10.

Moreland, A. D., & Dumas, J. E. (2008). Evaluating child coping competence: Theory and measurement. *Journal of Child and Family Studies, 17*(3), 437–454.

Moskowitz, G. B., & Grant, H. (2009). *The psychology of goals/edited by Gordon B. Moskowitz, Heidi Grant*. New York: Guilford Press, c2009.

Moskowitz, J. T., Shmueli-Blumberg, D., Acree, M., & Folkman, S. (2012). Positive affect in the midst of distress: Implications for role functioning. *Journal of Community and Applied Social Psychology, 22*(6), 502–518. doi:10.1002/casp.1133.

Mueller, C. M., & Dweck, C. S. (1998). Praise for intelligence can undermine children's motivation and performance. *Journal of Personality and Social Psychology, 75*(1), 33–52.

National Center for Health Statistics (NCHS). (2006). *Health, United States, with chartbook on trends in the health of Americans.* Hyattsville (MD): National Center for Health Statistics (US); 2006 Nov. Report No.: 2006–1232. Health, United States.

Neff, K. D., Rude, S. S., & Kirkpatrick, K. L. (2007). An examination of self-compassion in relation to positive psychological functioning and personality traits. *Journal of Research in Personality, 41*(4), 908–916.

Neill, L. (1996). *Ethnicity, gender, self-esteem and coping styles: A comparison of Australian and South-East Asian adolescents.* Unpublished Graduate Diploma of Counselling Psychology project, Royal Melbourne Institute of Technology.

Nesbitt, B. J., & Heidrich, S. M. (2000). Sense of coherence and illness appraisal in older women's quality of life. *Research in Nursing and Health, 23*(1), 25–34, 10p.

Nicolotti, L., El-Sheikh, M., & Whitson, S. M. (2003). Children's coping with marital conflict and their adjustment and physical health: Vulnerability and protective functions. *Journal of Family Psychology, 17*(3), 315–326.

Nieder, T., & Seiffge-Krenke, I. (2001). Coping with stress in different phases of romantic development. *Journal of Adolescence, 24*(3), 297–311.

Noto, S.S. (1995). *The relationship between coping and achievement: A comparison between adolescent males and females.* Unpublished Master of Educational Psychology project, University of Melbourne, Melbourne, VIC.

Nowlan, J. S., Wuthrich, V. M., & Rapee, R. M. (2015). Positive reappraisal in older adults: A systematic literature review. *Aging & Mental Health, 19*(6), 475–484. doi:10.1080/13607863.2014.954528.

O'Brien, M., Bahadur, M. A., Gee, C., Balto, K., & Erber, S. (1997). Child exposure to marital conflict and child coping responses as predictors of child adjustment. *Cognitive Therapy and Research, 21*(1), 39–59.

O'Brien, T. B., DeLongis, A., Pomaki, G., Puterman, E., & Zwicker, A. (2009). Couples coping with stress: The role of empathic responding. *European Psychologist, 14*(1), 18–28. doi:10.1027/1016-9040.14.1.18.

Oman, D., Hedberg, J., & Thoresen, C. E. (2006). Passage meditation reduces perceived stress in health professionals: A randomized, controlled trial. *Journal of Consulting and Clinical Psychology, 74*, 714–719.

Omizo, M. M., Omizo, S. A., & Suzuki, L. A. (1988). Children and stress: An exploratory study of stressors and symptoms. *School Counselor, 35*, 267–274.

Ouwehand, C., De Ridder, D. T. D., & Bensing, J. M. (2006). Situational aspects are more important in shaping proactive coping behaviour than individual characteristics: A vignette study among adults preparing for ageing. *Psychology & Health, 21*(6), 809–825.

Pallant, J. F. (2000). Development and validation of a scale to measure perceived control of internal states. *Journal of Personality Assessment, 75*(2), 308–337.

Pang, I., Frydenberg, E., & Deans, E. (2015). The relationship between anxiety and coping in preschoolers. In P. Buchenwald & K. Moore (Eds.), *Stress anxiety* (pp. 27–36). Berlin, Germany: Verlag.

Pargament, K. I. (1997). *The psychology of religion and coping: Theory, research, practice.* New York: The Guilford Press.

Pargament, K. I., Falb, K., Ano, G., & Wachholtz, A. B. (2005). The religious dimension of coping: Advances in theory, research, and practice. In R. Paloutzian & C. Park (Eds.), *The handbook of the psychology of religion* (pp. 479–495). The Guilford Press: New York.

Pargament, K. I., Smith, B. W., Koenig, H. G., & Perez, L. (1998). Patterns of positive and negative religious coping with major life stressors. *Journal for the Scientific Study of Religion, 37*(4), 710.

Park, C. L. (2011). Implicit religion and the meaning making model. *Implicit Religion, 14*(4), 405–419. doi:10.1558/imre.v14i4.405.

Park, C. L., & Cohen, L. H. (1993). Religious and nonreligioius coping with the death of a friend. *Cognitive Therapy and Research, 17*, 561–577. doi:10.1007/BF01176079.

Park, C. L., & Fenster, J. R. (2004). Stress-related growth: Predictors of occurrence and correlates with psychological adjustment. *Journal of Social and Clinical Psychology, 23*(2), 195–215.

Park, C. L., & Folkman, S. (1997). Meaning in the context of stress and coping. *General Review of Psychology, 1,* 115–144.

Park, C. L., & Helgeson, V. S. (2006). Introduction to the special section: Growth following highly stressful life events – Current status and future directions. *Journal of Consulting and Clinical Psychology, 74*(5), 791–796.

Parsons, A., Frydenberg, E., & Poole, C. (1996). Overachievement and coping strategies in adolescent males. *British Journal of Educational Psychology, 66*(1), 109–114.

Payne, M. (2015, November 4). Michelle Payne looks to future after achieving lifelong dream of winning Melbourne Cup. *Herald Sun.* Retrieved from http://www.heraldsun.com.au/

Pearl, E. S. (2009). Parent management training for reducing oppositional and aggressive behavior in preschoolers. *Aggression and Violent Behavior, 14,* 295–305. doi:10.1016/j.avb.2009.03.007.

Pearlin, L. I., & Schooler, C. (1978). The structure of coping. *Journal of Health and Social Behavior, 19*(1), 2–21.

Perkins-Gough, D. (2013). The significance of grit: A conversation with Angela Lee Duckworth. *Educational Leadership, 71*(1), 14–20.

Pincus, D. B., & Friedman, A. G. (2004). Improving children's coping with everyday stress: Transporting treatment interventions to the school setting. *Clinical Child and Family Psychology Review, 7*(4), 223–240.

Poot, A. C. (1997). *Client factors which moderate outcome in an adolescent psychotherapy treatment program.* Unpublished Master of Counselling, School of Education, La Trobe University, Melbourne, VIC.

Poynton, E., & Frydenberg, E. (2011). Coping styles and anxiety amongst female victims of bullying. In G. Reevy & E. Frydenberg (Eds.), *Personality and coping, Series on stress and coping in education* (pp. 67–89). Greenwich, UK: Information Age Publishing.

Prince-Embury, S. (2011). Assessing personal resiliency in the context of school settings: Using the resiliency scales for children and adolescents. *Psychology in the Schools, 48*(7), 672–685.

Prince-Embury, S., & Courville, T. (2008). Measurement invariance of the resiliency scales for children and adolescents with respect to sex and age cohorts. *Canadian Journal of School Psychology, 23*(1), 26–40.

Prior, M. (1999). Resilience and coping: The role of individual temperament. In E. Frydenberg (Ed.), *Learning to cope: Developing as a person in complex societ-*

ies (pp. 33–52). Oxford, UK: Oxford University Press. vii + 360. ISBN 0-19-850318-0.

Rapee, R. M. (2002). The development and modification of temperamental risk for anxiety disorders: Prevention of a lifetime of anxiety? *Biological Psychiatry, 52*(10), 947–957.

Rapee, R. M., Schniering, C. A., & Hudson, J. L. (2009). Anxiety disorders during childhood and adolescence: Origins and treatment. *Annual Review of Clinical Psychology, 5,* 311–341.

Raver, C. C., & Knitzer, J. (2002). *Ready to enter: What research tells policy makers about strategies to promote social and emotional school readiness among three- and four- year olds.* New York: National Centre for Children in Poverty.

Resnick, B. (2014). Resilience in older adults. *Topics in Geriatric Rehabilitation, 30*(3), 155–163. doi:10.1097/TGR.0000000000000024.

Reynolds, W. M. (2001). *Reynolds adolescent adjustment screening inventory.* Odessa, FL: PAR (Psychological Assessment Resources, Inc.).

Reynolds, N., Mrug, S., Hensler, M., Guion, K., & Madan-Swain, A. (2014). Spiritual coping and adjustment in adolescents with chronic illness: A 2-year prospective study. *Journal of Pediatric Psychology, 39*(5), 542–551.

Richards, J. (2012). Teacher stress and coping strategies: A national snapshot. *The Educational Forum, 76*(3), 299–316. Retrieved from http://search.proquest.com.ezp.lib.unimelb.edu.au/docview/102 7918073?accountid=12372

Röder, I., Boekaerts, M., & Kroonenberg, P. (2002). The stress and coping questionnaire for children (school version and asthma version): Construction, factor structure, and psychometric properties. *Psychological Reports, 91*(1), 29–36.

Roeser, R. W., Pintrich, P. R., & DeGroot, E. A. M. (1994). Classroom and individual differences in early adolescents' motivation and self-regulated learning. *Journal of Early Adolescence, 14*(2), 139–161.

Romi, S., Lewis, R., & Roache, J. (2013). Classroom management and teachers' coping strategies: Inside classrooms in Australia, China and Israel. *Prospects (00331538), 43*(2), 215. doi:10.1007/ s11125-013-9271-0.

Ross, K., Handal, P. J., Clark, E. M., & Wal, J. S. V. (2009). The relationship between religion and religious coping: Religious coping as a moderator between religion and adjustment. *Journal of Religion and Health, 48,* 454–467. doi:10.1007/s10943-008- 9199-5.

Rutter, M. (1985). Resilience in the face of adversity: Protective factors and resistance to psychiatric disorder. *British Journal of Psychiatry, 147,* 598–611.

Rutter, M. (2012). Resilience as a dynamic concept. *Development and Psychopathology, 24*(2), 335–344. doi:10.1017/S0954579412000028.

Rutter, M. (2013). Annual research review: Resilience – Clinical Implications. *Journal of Child Psychology and Psychiatry, 54*(4), 474–487.

Rybak, C. (2013). Nurturing positive mental health: Mindfulness for wellbeing in counseling. *International Journal for the Advancement of Counselling, 35*(2), 110–119.

Saarni, C. (1997). Emotional competence and self-regulation in childhood. In P. Salovey & D. Sluyter (Eds.), *Emotional development and emotional intelligence: Educational implications* (pp. 35–66). New York: Basic Books.

Saklofske, D. H., Austin, E. J., Mastoras, S. M., Beaton, L., & Osborne, S. E. (2012). Relationships of personality, affect, emotional intelligence and coping with student stress and academic success: Different patterns of association for stress and success. *Learning and Individual Differences, 22*, 251–257. doi:10.1016/j.lindif.2011.02.010.

Salovey, P., & Mayer, J. D. (1990). Emotional intelligence. *Imagination, Cognition, and Personality, 9*, 185–211 .doi: 0.2190/DUGG-P24E-52WK-6CDG.

Sandage, S. J., & Morgan, J. (2014). Hope and positive religious coping as predictors of social justice commitment. *Mental Health, Religion and Culture, 17*(6), 557–567. doi:10.1080/13674676.2013.864266.

Sanders, M., Markie-Dadds, C., Tully, L., & Bor, W. (2000). The Triple P—Positive Parenting Program: A comparison of enhanced, standard, and self-directed behavioral family intervention for parents of children with early onset conduct problems. *Journal of Consulting and Clinical Psychology, 68*, 624–640. doi:10.1037//022-006X.68.4.624.

Sanson, A., Pedlow, R., Cann, W., Prior, M., & Oberklaid, F. (1996). Shyness ratings: Stability and correlates in early childhood. *International Journal of Behavioral Development, 19*(4), 705–724.

Scheier, M. F., & Carver, C. S. (1987). Dispositional optimism an physical wellbeing: The influence of generalized outcome expectancies on health. *Journal of Personality, 55*(2), 169.

Schmitt, T. A. (2011). Current methodological considerations in exploratory and confirmatory factor analysis. *Journal of Psychoeducational Assessment, 29*(4), 304–321. doi:10.1177/0734282911406653.

Schoon, I. (2006). *Risk and resilience: Adaptations in changing times.* Cambridge, MA: Cambridge University Press.

Schumm, J. A., Briggs-Phillips, M., & Hobfoll, S. E. (2006). Cumulative interpersonal traumas and social support as risk and resiliency factors in predicting PTSD and depression among inner-city women. *Journal of Traumatic Stress, 19*(6), 825–836.

Schwarzer, R. (2001). Social-cognitive factors in changing health-related behaviors. *Current Directions in Psychological Science, 10*(2), 47–51.

Schwarzer, R., & Knoll, N. (2003). Positive coping: Mastering demands and searching for meaning. In S. J. Lopez, C. R. Snyder, S. J. Lopez, & C. R. Snyder (Eds.), *Positive psychological assessment: A handbook of models and measures* (pp. 393–409). Washington, DC: American Psychological Association.

Schwarzer, R., & Taubert, S. (2002). Tenacious goal pursuits and striving toward personal growth: Proactive coping. In E. Fydenberg (Ed.), *Beyond coping: Meeting goals, visions and challenges* (pp. 19–35). London: Oxford University Press.

Seiffge-Krenke, I. (2000). Causal links between stressful events, coping style, and adolescent symptomatology. *Journal of Adolescence, 23*(6), 675–691. doi:10.1006/jado.2000.0352.

Seiffge-Krenke, I. (2006). Leaving home or still in the nest? Parent – Child relationships and psychological health as predictors of different leaving home patterns. *Developmental Psychology, 42*(5), 864–876.

Seiffge-Krenke, I. (2011). Coping with relationship stressors: A decade review. *Journal of Research on Adolescence, 21*(1), 196–210. doi:10.1111/j.1532-7795.2010.00723.x.

Seiffge-Krenke, I., & Pakalniskiene, V. (2011). Who shapes whom in the family: Reciprocal links between autonomy support in the family and parents' and adolescents' coping behaviors. *Journal of Youth and Adolescence, 40*(8), 983–995.

Seiffge-Krenke, I., & Shulman, S. (1990). Coping style in adolescence: A cross-cultural study. *Journal of Cross-Cultural Psychology, 21*(3), 351–377.

Seligman, M. E. P. (2011). *Authentic happiness. [Electronic resource]: Using the new positive psychology to realise your potential for lasting fulfilment.* London: Nicholas Brealey Publishing.

Seligman, M. E. P., & Csikszentmihalyi, M. (2000). Positive psychology: An introduction. *The American Psychologist, 5*(1), 5–14.

Seligman, M. E. P., Parks, A. C., & Steen, T. (2004). A balanced psychology and a full life. *Philosophical Transactions of the Royal Society of London. Series B, Biological Sciences, 359*(1449), 1379–1381.

Seligman, M. E. P., Peterson, C., Kaslow, N. J., Tanenbaum, R. L., Alloy, L. B., & Abramson, L. Y. (1984). Attributional style and depressive symptoms among children. *Journal of Abnormal Psychology, 93*, 235–238.

Selye, H. (1976). *Stress in health and disease.* Boston, MA: Butterworths, c1976.

Semple, R. J., Lee, J., Rosa, D., & Miller, L. F. (2010). A randomized trial of mindfulness-based cognitive therapy for children: Promoting mindful attention to enhance social-emotional resiliency in children. *Journal of Child and Family Studies, 19*(2), 218–229.

Serlachius, A. S., Scratch, S. E., Northam, E. A., Frydenberg, E., Lee, K. J., & Cameron, F. J. (2016). A randomized controlled trial of cognitive behaviour therapy to improve glycaemic control and psychosocial wellbeing in adolescents with type 1 diabetes. *Journal of Health Psychology, 21*(6), 1157–1169. doi:10.1177/1359105314547940.

Shanan, J., De-Nour, A. K., & Garty, I. (1976). Effects of prolonged stress on coping style in terminal renal failure patients. *Journal of Human Stress, 2*(4), 19.

Simpson, D. B., Newman, J. L., & Fuqua, D. R. (2007). Spirituality and personality: Accumulating evidence. *Journal of Psychology and Christianity, 26*(1), 33–44.

Sinclair, V. G., & Wallston, K. A. (2004). The development and psychometric evaluation of the brief resilient coping scale. *Assessment, 11*(1), 94–101.

Skinner, E. A., Edge, K., Altman, J., & Sherwood, H. (2003). Searching for the structure of coping: A review and critique of category systems for classifying ways of coping. *Psychological Bulletin, 129*(2), 216–269.

Skinner, E. A., & Zimmer-Gembeck, M. (2009a). Challenges to the developmental study of coping. *New Directions for Child and Adolescent Development, 2009*(124), 5–17. doi:10.1002/cd.239.

Skinner, E. A., & Zimmer-Gembeck, M. J. (Eds.) (2009b). Introduction: Challenges to the developmental study of coping,*Perspective on children's coping with stress as regulation of emotion, cognition and behavior. New directions in child and adolescent development series* (Issue 124, pp. 5–17). New York: Wiley.

Skok, M. (1996). Hearing impairment: Coping and social support. Unpublished Master thesis, University of Melbourne, Melbourne, VIC.

Smiley, P. A., & Dweck, C. S. (1994). Individual differences in achievement goals among young children. *Child Development, 65*, 1723–1743.

Smith, C. A. (1991). The self, appraisal, and coping. In C. R. Snyder & D. R. Forsyth (Eds.), *Handbook for social and clinical psychology: The health perspective* (pp. 116–137). Elmsford, NY: Pergamon.

Snyder, C. R. (1995). Conceptualising, measuring and nurturing hope. *Journal of Counseling and Development, 73*, 355–360.

Snyder, C. R. (2000). The past and possible futures of hope. *Journal of Social and Clinical Psychology, 19*(1), 11–28.

Snyder, C. R., Irving, L., & Anderson, J. R. (1991). Hope and health: Measuring the will and the ways. In C. R. Snyder & D. R. Forsyth (Eds.), *Handbook of social and clinical psychology: The health perspective* (pp. 285–305). Elmsford, NY: Pergamon Press.

Sorich, L. A., & Dweck C. (1997). *Psychological mediators of student achievement during the transition to junior high school.* Unpublished manuscript, Columbia University.

Spanjer, K. (1999). The relationship between locus of control and coping constructs as predictors of academic performance in an adult sample. Unpublished research report, Monash University, Melbourne, VIC.

Spear, L. P. (2000a). Neurobehavioral changes in adolescence. *Current Directions in Psychological Science, 9*(4), 111–114.

Spear, L. P. (2000b). The adolescent brain and age-related behavioral manifestations. *Neuroscience and Biobehavioral Reviews, 24*(4), 417–463.

Spence, S. H., Rapee, R., McDonald, C., & Ingram, M. (2001). The structure of anxiety symptoms among preschoolers. *Behaviour Research and Therapy, 39*, 1293–1316.

Spirito, A., Overholser, J., & Stark, L. J. (1989). Common problems and coping strategies II: Findings with adolescent suicide attempters. *Journal of Abnormal Child Psychology, 17*(2), 213–221.

Stark, L. J., Spirito, A., Williams, C. A., & Guevremont, D. C. (1989). Common problems and coping strategies: Findings with normal adolescents. *Journal of Abnormal Child Psychology, 17*(2), 203–212.

Stetzer, E. (2013, December 2). How Religious are Australians? Retrieved from http://www.christianitytoday.com/edstetzer/2013/december/how-religious-are-australians.html

Stevenson, R. (1996). *Academic self-concept, perceived stress and adolescents' coping styles in the VCE.* Unpublished Bachelor of Social Science (Family Studies), Australian Catholic University.

Stone, A. A., Greenberg, M. A., Kennedy-Moore, E., & Newman, M. G. (1991). Self-report, situation-specific coping questionnaires: What are they measuring? *Journal of Personality and Social Psychology, 61*, 648–658.

Suveg, C., & Zeman, J. (2004). Emotion regulation in children with anxiety disorders. *Journal of Clinical Child and Adolescent Psychology, 33*(4), 750–759.

Szczepanski, H. (1995). *A study of homesickness phenomenon among female boarding high school students.* Unpublished Master of Educational Psychology project, University of Melbourne, Melbourne, VIC.

Tabachnick, B. G., & Fidell, L. S. (2007). *Using multivariate statistics* (5th ed.). Boston, MA: Pearson Education.

Tan, K.-K., Vehviläinen-Julkunen, K., & Chan, S. W.-C. (2014). Integrative review: Salutogenesis and health in older people over 65 years old. *Journal of Advanced Nursing, 70*(3), 497–510. doi:10.1111/jan.12221.

Taylor, S. E. (2010). *Health handbook of social psychology.* Hoboken: Wiley.

Taylor, S. E., Jarcho, J., Takagi, K., Dunagan, M. S., Sherman, D. K., & Kim, H. S. (2004). Culture and social support who seeks it and why? *Journal of Personality and Social Psychology, 87*(3), 354–362. doi: 10.103710022! 3514.87.3.354.

Tedeschi, R. G., & Calhoun, L. G. (1996). The posttraumatic growth inventory: Measuring the positive legacy of trauma. *Journal of Traumatic Stress, 9*(3), 455–471.

Tedeschi, R. G., & Calhoun, L. G. (2004). Posttraumatic growth: Conceptual foundations and empirical evidence. *Psychological Inquiry, 15,* 1–18.

Terreri, C., & Glenwick, D. (2013). The relationship of religious and general coping to psychological adjustment and distress in urban adolescents. *Journal of Religion and Health, 52*(4), 1188–1202. doi:10.1007/s10943-011-9555-8.

Thoits, P. A. (1986). Social support as coping assistance. *Journal of Consulting and Clinical Psychology, 54*(4), 416–423.

Thoits, P. A. (1995). Stress, coping, and social support processes: Where are we? What next? *Journal of Health and Social Behavior, 35,* 53–79.

Thompson, R. A. (1994). Emotion regulation: A theme in search of definition. *Monographs of the Society for Research in Child Development, 59,* 25–52.

Tomás, J. M., Sancho, P., Melendez, J. C., & Mayordomo, T. (2012). Resilience and coping as predictors of general well-being in the elderly: A structural equation modeling approach. *Aging & Mental Health, 16*(3), 317–326. doi:1 0.1080/13607863.2011.615737.

Tsurutani, H. (2009). *A multi-informant approach to understanding the coping behaviours of preschool children: A comparative study of teachers' and parents' observations.* Unpublished master's thesis, University of Melbourne, Melbourne Graduate School of Education.

Valas, H. (1999). Students with learning disabilities and low achieving students: Peer acceptance, loneliness, self-esteem, and depression. *Social Psychology of Education, 3,* 173–192.

Wadey, R., Evans, L., Hanton, S., & Neil, R. (2012). An examination of hardiness throughout the sport-injury process: A qualitative follow-up study. *British Journal of Health Psychology, 17*(4), 872–893.

Wadsworth, M. E., Gudmundsen, G. R., Raviv, T., Ahlkvist, J. A., McIntosh, D. N., Kline, G. H., et al. (2004). Coping with terrorism: Age and gender differences in effortful and involuntary responses to September 11th. *Applied Developmental Science, 8*(3), 143–157.

Webster-Stratton, C. (2002). *Basic parent training program – School age.* Seattle, WA: Incredible Years.

Webster-Stratton, C., Reid, M. J., & Stoolmiller, M. (2008). Preventing conduct problems and improving school readiness: Evaluation of the incredible years teacher and child training programs in high-risk schools. *Journal of Child Psychology and Psychiatry, 49*(5), 471–488.

Weigold, I. K., & Robitschek, C. (2011). Agentic personality characteristics and coping: Their relation to trait anxiety in college students. *American Journal of Orthopsychiatry, 81*(2), 255–264.

Wells, J. D., Hobfoll, S. E., & Lavin, J. (1999). When it rains, pours: The greater impact of resource loss compared to gain on psychological distress. *Personality and Social Psychology Bulletin, 25*(9), 1172–1182.

Williams, V., Ciarrochi, J., & Patrick Deane, F. (2010). On being mindful, emotionally aware, and more resilient: Longitudinal pilot study of police recruits. *Australian Psychologist, 45*(4), 274–282. doi:10.1080/00050060903573197.

Wills, T. A., Sandy, J. M., Yaeger, A. M., Cleary, S. D., & Shinar, O. (2001). Coping dimensions, life stress, and adolescent substance use: A latent growth analysis. *Journal of Abnormal Psychology, 110*, 309–323.

Wills, T. A., Yaeger, A. M., & Sandy, J. M. (2003). Buffering effect of religiosity for adolescent substance use. *Psychology of Addictive Behaviors: Journal of the Society of Psychologists in Addictive Behaviors, 17*(1), 24–31.

Wilmshurst, L. (2008). *Abnormal child psychology: A developmental perspective.* New York: Routledge.

Wilson, G. S., Pritchard, M. E., & Revalee, B. (2005). Individual differences in adolescent health symptoms: The effects of gender and coping. *Journal of Adolescence, 23*(3), 369–379.

Wilson, H. (2012). *Teaching children with autism: The resources and coping styles of teachers.* Unpublished Master of Educational Psychology thesis. University of Melbourne, Melbourne, VIC.

Windle, G. (2011). What is resilience? A review and concept analysis. *Reviews in Clinical Gerontology, 21*(2), 152–169, 118p. doi:10.1017/S0959259810000420.

Windle, G., Bennett, K. M., & Noyes, J. (2011). A methodological review of resilience measurement scales. *Health and Quality of Life Outcomes, 9*(8), 1–18.

Wojcik, Z., McKenzie, V., Frydenberg, E., & Poole, C. (2004). Resources loss, gain, investment, and coping in adolescents. *Australian Educational and Developmental Psychologist, 19/20*(2/1), 52–77.

Yancura, L. A., & Aldwin, C. M. (2009). Stability and change in retrospective reports of childhood experiences over a 5-year period: Findings from the Davis longitudinal study. *Psychology and Aging, 24*(3), 715–721. doi:10.1037/a0016203.

Yeo, K., Frydenberg, E., Northam, E., & Deans, J. (2014a). Coping with stress among preschool children and associations with anxiety level and controllability of situations. *Australian Journal of Psychology, 66*(2), 93–101. doi:10.1111/ajpy.12047.

Youngs, B. B. (1985). *Stress in children: How to recognise, avoid, and overcome it.* New York: Arbor House.

Zamani, G. H., Gorgievski-Duijvesteijn, M. J., & Zarafshani, K. (2006). Coping with drought: Towards a multilevel understanding based on conservation of resources theory. *Human Ecology, 34,* 677.

Zambianchi, M., & Ricci Bitti, P. (2014). The role of proactive coping strategies, time perspective, perceived efficacy on affect regulation, divergent thinking and family communication in promoting social well-being in emerging adulthood. *Social Indicators Research, 116*(2), 493–507. doi:10.1007/s11205-013-0307-x.

Zautra, A. J., & Reich, J. W. (2010). *Resilience: The meanings, methods, and measures of a fundamental characteristic of human adaptation.* NewYork: Oxford University Press.

Zhao W., Dweck C., & Mueller C., (1998). *Implicit theories and depression like responses to failure.* Unpublished manuscript, New York University.

Zimmer-Gembeck, M. J., & Collins, W. A. (2003). Autonomy development during adolescence. In G. R. Adams & M. Berzonsky (Eds.), *Blackwell handbook of Adolescence* (pp. 175–204). Oxford, UK: Blackwell.

Zimmer-Gembeck, M. J., Lees, D., & Skinner, E. A. (2011). Children's emotions and coping with interpersonal stress as correlates of social competence. *Australian Journal of Psychology, 63,* 131–141. doi:10.1111/j.1742-9536.2011.00019.x.

Zimmer-Gembeck, M. J., & Skinner, E. A. (2008). Adolescents coping with stress: Development and diversity. *The Prevention Researcher, 15*(4), 3–7.

Zimmer-Gembeck, M. J., & Skinner, E. A. (2011). The development of coping across childhood and adolescence: An integrative review and critique of research. *International Journal of Behavioral Development, 35,* 1–17. Supplementary material.

Index

Note: Page numbers with "n" denote footnotes.

© The Author(s) 2017
E. Frydenberg, *Coping and the Challenge of Resilience*,
DOI 10.1057/978-1-137-56924-0

Printed by Printforce, the Netherlands